AF531705

OIL WELL TESTING

OIL WELL TESTING

Edited by
Navid Naderpour
Research and Development Center,
Bandar Imam Petrochemical Complex (BIPC)
National Petrochemical Company (NPC)
Islamic Republic Of Iran
Tarbiat Modares University of Tehran

Maryam Khoshtinat Nikoo
Research and Development Center,
Bandar Imam Petrochemical Complex (BIPC)
National Petrochemical Company (NPC)
Islamic Republic Of Iran

2009

SBS Publishers & Distributors Pvt. Ltd.
New Delhi

ISBN 13 : 9788189741648

First Published in India in 2008
Reprinted in 2009

Published by:

SBS PUBLISHERS & DISTRIBUTORS PVT. LTD.
2/9, Ground Floor, Ansari Road, Darya Ganj,
New Delhi - 110002,
INDIA
Tel: 0091.11.23289119 / 41563911 / 32945311
Email: mail@sbspublishers.com
www.sbspublishers.com

Printed in India by New Z A Printers, New Delhi.

Preface

The needs of the modern-day oil industry dictate that a professional and systematic approach is adopted when planning and carrying out well intervention operations. This requires using the latest technology combined with experienced and dedicated personnel.

Oil Well Testing is recognised by various oil and gas companies to be the most hazardous operation that they routinely undertake. There are possibilities for loss of life and assets proportionately higher than at any other time in the drilling. Therefore, it is of great importance to the industry and to the wider public that such operations are extremely well planned and executed.

Planning a well testing operation is an extremely complex task and requires a great deal of experience. This book provides an approach into the techniques and procedures that are used by the expert engineer to effectively plan and carry out a test under a various conditions.

The testing of oil and gas reservoirs is one of the few times in an operating oil company when engineers a focused objective. Therefore, well test engineering is very much a discipline that combines knowledge of all of these areas of expertise. The Test Engineer will be the focal point of this group of specialists and will obtain the views of the group before then formulating a plan to test the well to meet an agreed set of objectives.

This book covers all the major operational aspects of oil and gas well testing. It uses a structured approach to guide the reader through the various steps that are required to effectively plan and implement a well test operation under just about any circumstances world-wide onshore or offshore. This book covers the test engineers' liaison role within the various oil company departments to set realistic well test objectives. The text also covers the various types of tests that are routinely conducted. Safety procedures and recommended practices are rigorously addressed, as are the responsibilities of those persons involved in well testing operations.

Author

Contents

1 Introduction

Fossil fuels are those energy sources that formed from the remains of once-living organisms. They include oil, natural gas, coal, and fuels derived from oil shale and tar sand. The differences in the physical properties among the various fossil fuels arise due to difference in the starting materials from which the fuels are formed and changes to those materials after the organisms died and were buried within the layers of the earth. Petroleum means rock-oil, and the word "Petroleum" derived the Latin word petra, meaning rock or stone, and oleum, meaning oil. Liquid petroleum, or oil, comprises a variety of liquid hydrocarbon compounds; compounds made up of different proportions of the elements carbon and hydrogen. There are also gaseous hydrocarbons (natural gas), in which methane is the most common component. Hydrocarbon mixtures usually also contain minor amounts of nitrogen, oxygen, and sulfur as impurities.

Once the solid organic matter is converted to liquids and/or gases, the hydrocarbons need to migrate out of the source rocks in which they formed in order to form a commercial deposit. The majority of petroleum source rocks are fine grained sedimentary rocks (like shale), from which it would be difficult to extract large quantities of oil or gas quickly. However, oil and gas are able to migrate out of their source rocks into more permeable rocks over the long spans of geologic time. Most people have the incorrect notion that there are underground "lakes" of oil. The oil industry has helped feed this misconception by talking about oil "pools." The truth is that virtually all the oil is contained in tiny holes in solid rock. These holes, or pores, are filled with water, gas, or oil. But if the holes are not connected, then oil cannot flow out of the rock. The ability of liquid to flow through the pores is permeability. So, in addition to high porosity, which allows the rock to hold large amounts of oil, the rock must have good permeability, which allows oil to flow quickly out of the rock. A rock with good porosity and permeability is a reservoir rock. Most oils and all natural gases are less dense than water, so they tend to rise as well as to migrate laterally through the water-filled pores of permeable rocks.

Unless sealed by impermeable cap rocks, oil and gas may keep rising right up to the earth's surface. These substances escape into the air, the oceans, or they flow out onto the ground at oil and gas seeps. These natural seeps, which are one of nature's own pollution sources, are not very efficient sources of hydrocarbons for fuel compared with present, day extraction methods.

Commercially, the most valuable deposits are those in which a large quantity of oil and/or gas is concentrated and confined by geologic traps, such as folds and faults. If the reservoir rocks are not naturally permeable enough, it may be necessary to fracture (crack open) them artificially with explosives or with water or gas under high pressure to increase the rate at which oil or gas flows through them.

The search for oil and gas beneath the earth's surface is a risky undertaking. Indeed, it is quite a gamble to invest money in an exploration "wildcat" well, because there are so many unknowns involved in the analysis and study of the earth. A number of conditions must exist before an oil or gas accumulation can develop—hydrocarbons must have been generated and they must have migrated to a suitable location to be trapped. Geoscientists use several scientific and technical procedures to "predict" whether these conditions may have combined to create an oil or gas field, but the results are never guaranteed.

Well testing has progressed to become one of the most powerful tools for determining complex reservoir characteristics. Well tests are performed by significantly changing the flow rate of a well. Well tests give many important pieces of information which can be used to determine reservoir production ability and reservoir size.

A pressure transient test (commonly referred to as a well test) is traditionally used to determine the efficiency of a completion, check for the presence of skin damage, or to determine reservoir properties such as permeability. Many engineers perform a well test when an unexpected drop in pressure or rate occurs on a producing well. The well test is used as a diagnostic tool to determine either the cause or a possible solution. Also, well tests can be used to determine if damage is accruing or if stimulation will improve production. A build-up is the most common form of a well test because it can be done by simply shutting in a producing well and recording the pressure change and shut-in time.

The time to test depends on the permeability:

- Higher permeability, shorter test time.
- Lower permeability, longer test time.

The time required to test is also dependent on the test objectives. Without knowing the permeability, it is not possible to predict the time required to identify reservoir boundaries and/or interference.

Test duration may be minimized with real-time data acquisition. Real-time data acquisition and analysis permit the well to be restored to production as soon as sufficient data have been acquired to meet the test objectives.

Premature test termination results in lost production and wasted expense without achieving the desired objectives. Testing longer than necessary results in excess expense and lost production.

Real-time data acquisition can be accomplished with a downhole pressure recorder using surface read-out (SRO) via electric line or a surface recorder. Surface recorders are a fraction of the cost of a downhole SRO gauge but care must be taken to use a tool such as the SPIDR that has effective thermal compensation and accuracy. Once an initial well test for permeability and skin has been conducted, the results can be used to design a well test to determine the location of reservoir limits.

Running a successful well test not only provides information about the reservoir, but also makes it easier to justify future well tests. To get meaningful results from a well test, it is essential to design and execute a test plan tailored to the test objectives including the selection of equipment adequate to acquire analyzable data.

When designing a test plan, it is important to know what is/are the principle objective(s) for the test. Typical test objectives are permeability, skin, reservoir pressure, distance to limits, reserves, and deliverability. Since all of this information cannot be determined from a single well test, the engineer must select the most important objectives. Numerous other factors also play a role in designing the test, such as well deviation, liquid production, temperatures, pressures, and the phase behaviour of the well fluids. Given this information, the engineer can specify or work with the testing company to design the test.

Equipment selection plays a critical role in the test. In general, it is important to use a thermally compensated, high resolution pressure gauge for well testing. Gauges such as this are able to more accurately detect reservoir response, especially in high permeability wells. The gauges used in SCADA well monitoring systems are generally not of sufficient quality to do this. Aroper execution of the well test plan is also critical to success. If the well test is not properly performed, it increases the likelihood that no useful data will be gathered. The best test procedure minimizes the number of choke changes, thermal transients, and phase changes. Procedures with minimal rate changes have two benefits: they provide better results, and they are easier to execute in the field. One of the most effective test procedures for determining skin and near wellbore permeability is a build-up after an extended stable flowing period followed by a drawdown (DD) on a fixed choke. With this test the engineer can determine P*, look for reservoir limits and get multiple confirmations of permeability and skin.

The most commonly prescribed test for a completion/reservoir evaluation is a Pressure Build-Up (PBU) or Shut-In test.

Build-ups are done for two primary reasons:

1. The math is simple for a zero rate and data tend to be smoother than a flowing test, which makes it easier for derivative type-curve matching.
2. It is quite easy to execute the procedure: hook up a gauge; shut-in the well.

Unfortunately, build-ups are subject to more phase resegregation and cross flow problems than flowing tests. This can sometimes result in data trends that are not easy to analyze under shut-in conditions. Another problem with build-ups is that they require the well to be shut-in, which means delayed/deferred production and interrupted cash flow.

Management approval to run a build-up test is most easily obtained when the well is going to be shut-in anyway due to pipeline or facilities maintenance, slack demand, or rig moves. If the well is going to be shut in anyway, record the pressures and try to learn something about the reservoir.

Drawdown testing is the opposite of a build-up.

In a DD, the well is produced on a fixed choke setting until the test objectives have been reached. A DD is usually initiated from a "cold-start"—a shut-in well, but it may also be conducted by doubling (or more) the current rate. In order for drawdown data to be valid, there must be a critical flow across the choke (roughly a 2.2:1 ratio of upstream to downstream pressure). At these conditions, there will be an adiabatic shockwave across the choke which will isolate the well from facilities or other downstream disturbances.

The best practice for a DD is to do a constant-choke test, not necessarily a constant rate test Quite often, a well will decline in both rate and pressure on a fixed choke setting. This is a natural decay and it can be accounted for in the analysis. Therefore, there is no need to "bump" the choke to maintain a constant rate. Remember, DD analysis is based on the declining rate of pressure. If the choke is adjusted, the declining rate of pressure will be adjusted too, making the well test interpretation less reliable.

An important advantage of running a constant-choke DD test (vs a PBU) is that the well is tested and produced at the same time. This means that management sees cash flow, reservoir engineering finds the reservoir size, and production engineering evaluates the completion. Another benefit of a DD over a PBU is that in a DD, it is easier to differentiate whether a boundary/reservoir limit contacted during the test is a fault, stratout, or gas/liquid contact (edge, not bottom/ top). Also on the plus side, DD testing evaluates the well/ reservoir at production conditions. If there is multiphase flow in the reservoir or if the rock is highly compressive and/or geo-pressured, there can be significant differences between a build-up response and a DD response, in which case the DD will likely be more valid. A final advantage of DD testing is that it mitigates or eliminates the effects of phase resegregation and crossflow between layers, as long as the rate is high enough to ensure that there is no accumulation of oil and/or water in the well bore.

A possible problem with DD data is that it may be noisy and therefore take longer time to analyze than a build-up. This is especially the case of derivative-type—curve analysis. However, if MDH (Semi-log) analysis is used, accurate and timely results can be obtained. Quite often, build-ups and DD are done in succession, especially if the build-up is a "planned" shut-in. This provides two snapshots of the well/ reservoir behaviour. If the analyses of the PBU and DD are the same, then there is greater confidence in the results. If there are differences, the effect of relative permeability, moving liquid levels, crossflow, and/ or rock and fluid properties may be examined to determine the cause of the discrepancy.

Once the design well depth is reached, the formation must be tested and evaluated to determine whether the well will be completed for production, or plugged and abandoned. To complete the well production, casing is installed and cemented, and the drilling rig is dismantled and moved to the next site.

A service rig is brought in to perforate the production casing and run production tubing. If no further pre-production servicing is needed, the christmas tree is installed and production begins. To complete well it requires Conducting Drill Stem Test, 'Setting Production Casing,' Installing Production Tubing, 'Starting Production Flow,' Beam Pumping Units.

2
Fundamentals of Well Testing

Diffusivity Equation

At the start of production, pressure in the wellbore drops sharply and fluid near the well expands and moves toward the area of lower pressure. This movement is retarded by friction against the pore walls and the fluid's own inertia and viscosity. As the fluid moves, however, it in turn creates a pressure imbalance that induces neighboring fluid to move toward the well. The process continues until the drop in pressure that was created by the start of production is dissipated throughout the reservoir. The physical process occurring throughout the reservoir can be described by the diffusivity equation.

To model a well test, the diffusivity equation is expressed in radial coordinates and it is assumed that the fluid flows to a cylinder (the well) that is normal to two parallel, impermeable planar barriers. To solve diffusivity equation, it is first necessary to establish the initial and boundary conditions, such as the initial pressure distribution that existed before the onset of flow and the extent of the reservoir. Solutions for reservoirs with regular, straight boundaries, such as those that are rectangular or polygonal in shape, and that have a well location on or off center can be obtained using the same equations as for the infinite reservoir case.

This is achieved by applying the principle of superposition in space of well images. The superposition approach enables analysts to model the effects that features such as faults and changes in reservoir size could have on the pressure response.

The solution of the diffusivity equation shown in the Sidebar indicates that a plot of pressure versus the log of time is a straight line. This relation provides an easy graphical procedure for interpretation. The slope of the portion of the curve forming a straight line is used for calculating permeability. Therefore, initially well tests were interpreted by plotting the observed pressure measurements on a semi-log graph and then determining permeability estimates from the straight-line portion of the curve. Radial flow was assumed to occur in this portion of the transient.

Modeling Radial Flow to a Well

Most of the fundamental theories of well testing consider the case of a well situated in a porous medium of infinite radial extent—the so-called infinite-acting radial model. This model is based on a series of equations that compose the diffusivity equation.

$$\frac{\partial^2 p}{\partial^2 r} + \frac{1}{p}\left(\frac{\partial p}{\partial r}\right) = \frac{1}{\eta} = \left(\frac{\partial p}{\partial t}\right)$$

where,

p = formation pressure

r = radial distance to the center of the wellbore

t = time

= diffusivity constant k/fc_t (k = permeability, f = porosity, c_t = total compressibility, and m = viscosity), and equations that model the reservoir boundary conditions:

- *Initial condition*—pressure is the same all over the reservoir and is equal to the initial pressure:

$$p\ (r,\ t = 0) = p_i$$

- *Outer-boundary condition*—pressure is equal to the initial pressure at infinity.
- *Inner-boundary condition*—from time zero onward the fluid is withdrawn at a constant rate:

$$q_s = \frac{2\pi kh}{\mu}\left(r\frac{\partial p}{\partial r}\right)$$

where,

q_s = sandface flow rate
kh = permeability-thickness product (flow capacity)
r_w = wellbore radius.

The diffusivity equation solution in its approximate form is

$$p_D(r_D t_D) = 0.5\left(\ln\frac{t_D}{r_D^2} + 0.080907\right)$$

where dimensionless time is

$$t_D = \frac{0.0002637kt}{\mu\phi c_t r_w^2}$$

and dimensionless pressure is

$$p_D = 0.00708\frac{kh}{q_s\mu}(p_i - p_{wf})$$

where,

p_{wf} = wellbore flowing pressure when the dimensionless radial distance $r_D = 1$.

Figure 2.1 shows that the early-time data are distorted by wellbore storage and skin effects, concepts that are discussed in the following section. The late-time portion of the pressure transient is affected by interference from other wells or by boundary effects, such as those that occur when the pressure disturbance reaches the reservoir edges. If these disturbances overlap with the early-time effects they can completely mask the critical straight-line portion where radial flow occurs. In these cases, analysis with a straight-line fit is impossible.

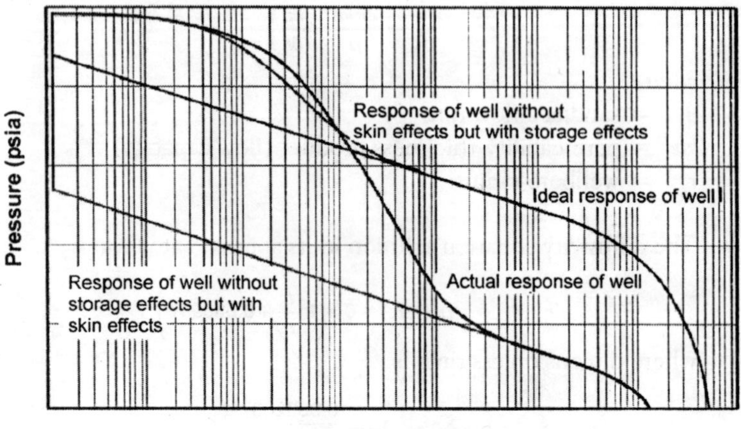

Figure 2.1 Wellbore storage and skin effects on the wellbore pressure response.

Wellbore Storage and Skin Effects

Wellbore storage effects are illustrated in Fig. 2.2. The term "skin" is brought into the computations to account for the drop in pressure that occurs across a localized zone near the well. Skin effects are caused by three main factors: flow convergence near the wellbore, visco-inertial flow velocity, and the blocking of pores and fractures that occurs during drilling and production. Well testing provides a way of estimating the resulting extra pressure drop to analyze its impact on well productivity.

Traditional well tests had to be sufficiently long to overcome both wellbore storage and skin effects so that a straight line would plot. But even this approach presents drawbacks. More than one apparently straight line can appear, and analysts found it difficult to decide which one to use. In addition, the choice of plotting scales may make some portions of the pressure response appear straight when, in reality, they are curved. To overcome these difficulties, analysts developed other methods of analysis, and the era of type curves began.

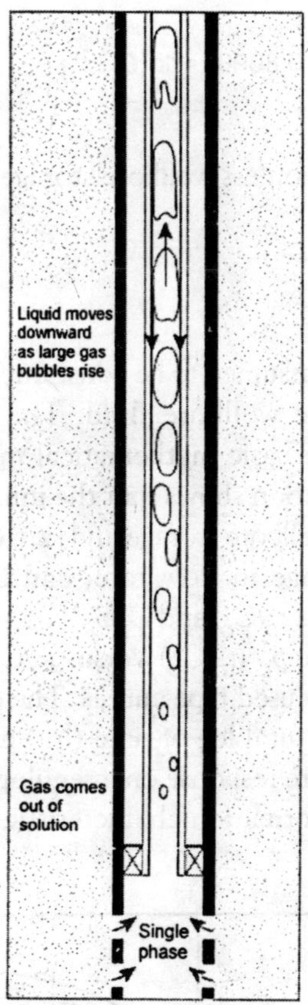

Figure 2.2 Wellbore storage effects are due to the compressibility of the fluids in the wellbore. Afterflow is induced after shutting in the well because flow from the reservoir does not stop immediately but continues at a slowly diminishing rate until the well pressure stabilizes. A further complication is the wellbore mechanics that drives fluids to segregate, which makes the wellbore storage variable with time.

Types of Curves

The infinite-acting radial flow equation derived in the Sidebar on page 4 can be written in terms of the wellbore storage coefficient C and skin factor s as follows:

$$P_D = 0.5\left[\ln\left(\frac{t_D}{C_D}\right) + 0.80907 + \ln\left(C_D e^{2s}\right)\right], \qquad \text{........... (1)}$$

where the dimensionless wellbore storage coefficient is

$$C_D = \frac{0.8937C}{\phi h c_t r_w^2} \qquad \text{........... (2)}$$

The value of C is assumed to be constant, and it accounts for the compressibility of the wellbore fluid. The radial flow equation constitutes one of the basic mathematical models for modern well test analysis. The equation shows that the infinite-acting response of a well with constant wellbore storage and skin effects, when subjected to a single-step change in flow rate, can be described by three dimensionless terms: p_D, t_D/C_D, and C_De^{2s}. The graphical representation of p_D and its derivative p_D (t_D/C_D) versus t_D/C_D on a log-log graph is one of the most widely used type curves. The derivative is computed with respect to the natural log of time (lnt) and is representative of the slope of the pressure response on a semilog graph. It amplifies the effects that different formation characteristics have on the pressure transient response.

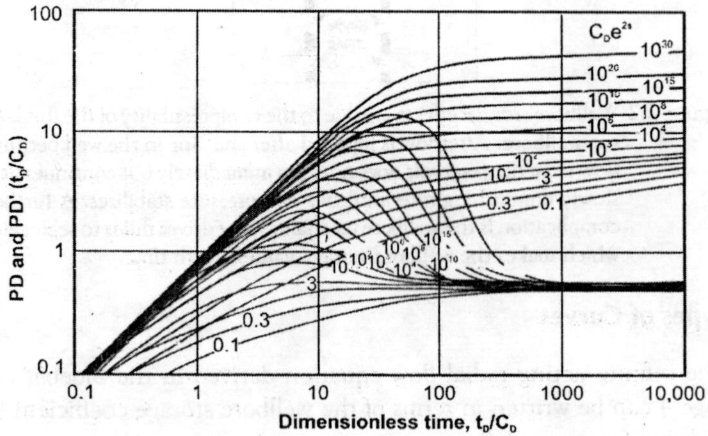

Figure 2.3 Type curves for a well with wellbore storage and skin effects in a reservoir with homogeneous behaviour.

Figure 2.3 shows a set of type curves for different values of $C_D e^{2s}$. At early time, all the curves merge into a unit-slope straight line corresponding to pure wellbore storage flow. At late time, all the derivative curves merge into a single horizontal line, representing pure radial flow. Distinctions in the shapes of the curve pairs, which are defined by the term $C_D e^{2s}$, are more noticeable in the derivative curves.

Test data are plotted in terms of the pressure change *p* and its derivative *p t* versus the elapsed time *t* and superimposed over the type curves. Once a match is found for both the pressure change and its derivative, the $C_D e^{2s}$ value of the matched curve pair, together with the translation of the axes of the data plot with respect to the type-curve axes, is used to calculate well and reservoir parameters. The permeability-thickness product is derived from the pressure match as:

$$kh = 141.2qB\mu\left(\frac{p_D}{\Delta p}\right)_M, \quad \text{..........} (3)$$

where,

q =is the flow rate,

B =is the formation volume factor and the subscript M denotes a type-curve match.

The wellbore storage coefficient is derived from the time match as:

$$C = \left(\frac{0.000295kh}{\mu}\right)\frac{\Delta t}{\left(\frac{t_D}{C_D}\right)_M},$$

and skin factor is derived from the $C_D e^{2s}$ curve as:

$$s = 0.5\ln\left[\frac{\left(C_D e^{2s}\right)_M}{C_D}\right].$$

Figure 2.4 shows how type-curve matching is used to determine *kh* and the skin effect. In this example, the test was terminated before the development of full radial flow. Application of the semilog plot technique to this dataset would have provided erroneous results. The indication of radial flow by a flat trend in the pressure derivative and the easier identification of reservoir heterogeneities make the log-log plot of the pressure derivative a powerful tool for model identification.

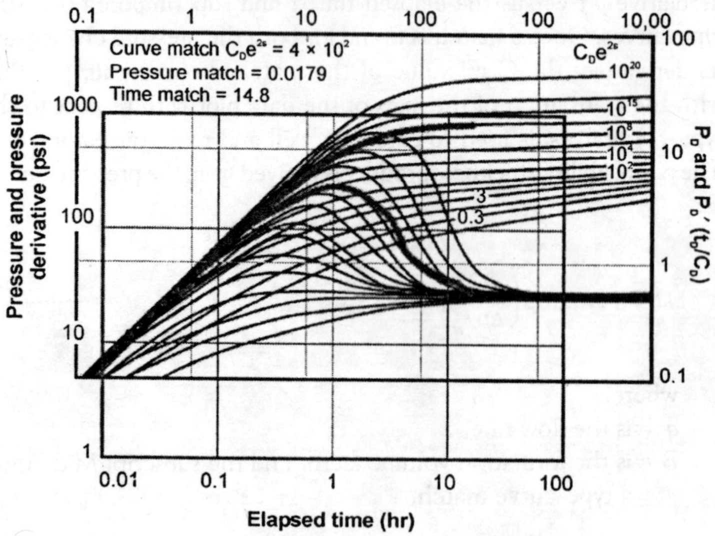

Figure 2.4 Type-curve matching of a dataset that does not exhibit radial flow. The good match between the measured and theoretical data enables the computation of *kh* and *s* even though the test was ended before radial flow appeared.

Changing Wellbore Storage

The type-curve matching techniques described so far assume constant wellbore storage. However, it is not always operationally possible to keep the wellbore storage constant. Numerous circumstances cause change in wellbore storage, such as wellbore phase redistribution and increasing or decreasing storage associated with injection well testing. Figure 5 shows typical variations in wellbore storage during a conventional pressure build-up test with surface shut-in. Downhole shut-in and combined downhole flow and pressure measurements reduce the effect of varying wellbore storage; but if the volume below the shut-in valve is compressible, downhole shut-in does not avoid the problem completely. Similarly, if the volume below the production logging tool is large or highly pressure dependent, the problem, although reduced, remains. In these situations, adding a changing wellbore storage model to the reservoir model can improve type-curve matching. This storage model can be obtained using mathematical functions that exhibit characteristics representative of field data.

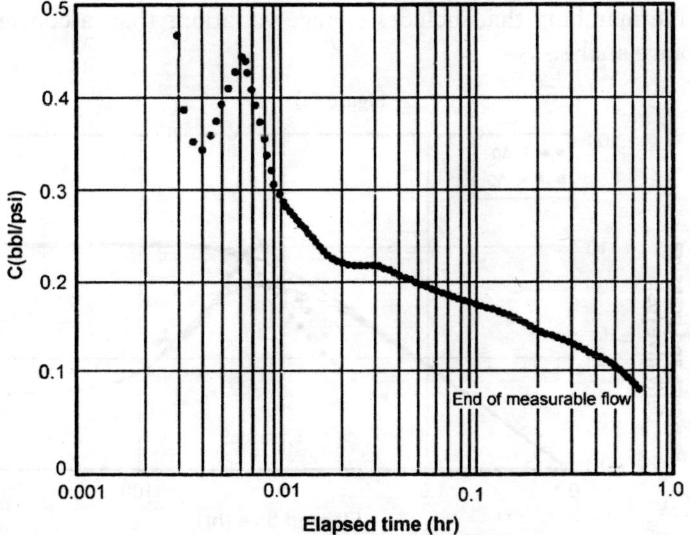

Figure 2.5 The wellbore storage coefficient can change during a build-up test that uses surface shut-in control.

Figure 2.6 shows an application of a variable wellbore storage model to a drillstem test (DST) dataset. Log-log and Horner plots are shown for the extended buildup period along with the match using a homogeneous reservoir model with constant (Fig. 6a) and decreasing (Fig. 6b) wellbore storage. The dataset is typical of the case in which the combined effects of changing wellbore storage and insufficient data complicate type-curve matching. The early-time data are severely distorted by decreasing wellbore storage effects, and the late-time data do not exhibit radial flow. Therefore, the match using a constant wellbore storage model in Fig. 6a does not convey sufficient confidence in the results. The match using a decreasing wellbore storage model in Fig. 6b shows the measured data in good agreement with the theoretical curves. This latter match resulted in a significantly lower value for C_De^{2s} with a corresponding lower value for the skin factor than the values calculated from the constant-storage match.

This example is representative of how the analysis of datasets affected by variable wellbore storage yields better results using type-curve matching that includes storage variations than a constant-storage analysis.

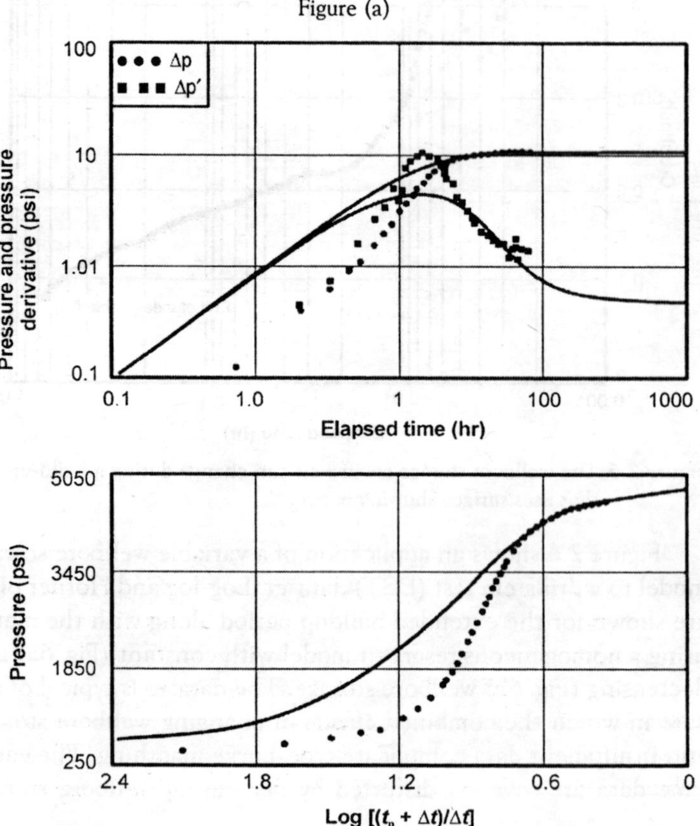

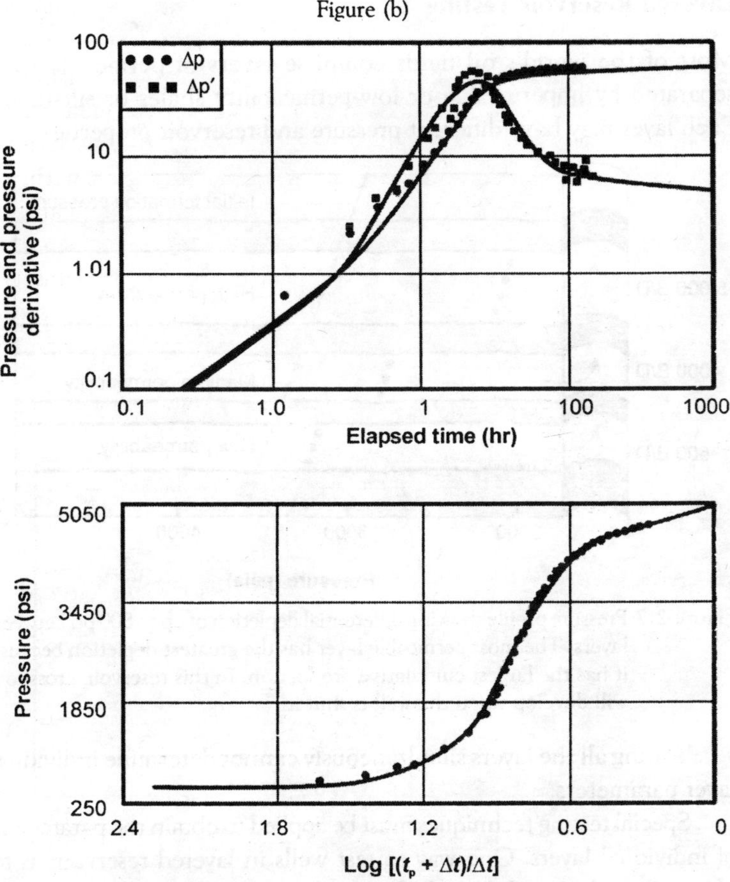

Figure 2.6 Type-curve matching of a dataset from a DST buildup period with (a) constant wellbore storage and (b) decreasing wellbore storage models. The constant wellbore storage model yielded a skin factor of 8.7. The use of the decreasing wellbore storage model resulted in a skin factor of 2.9.

Pressure Transient Test

Pressure transient tests is used for testing layered reservoirs and horizontal wells, multiple-well testing, vertical interference, and combined perforation and testing techniques.

Layered Reservoir Testing

Most of the world's oil fields comprise layers of permeable rock separated by impermeable or low-permeability shales or siltstones. Each layer may have different pressure and reservoir properties.

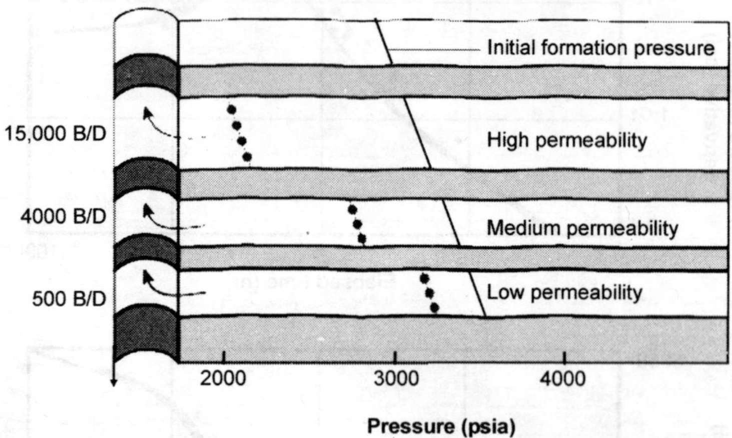

Figure 2.7 Pressure profile showing differential depletion of up to 800 psi between layers. The most permeable layer has the greatest depletion because it has the largest cumulative production. In this reservoir, crossflow will develop when the well is shut in.

Testing all the layers simultaneously cannot determine individual layer parameters.

Special testing techniques must be applied to obtain the parameters of individual layers. One way to test wells in layered reservoirs is to physically isolate each layer before performing conventional tests in it (e.g., straddle DST jobs). A rig is required, and the testing may be prohibitively expensive. A cost-effective alternative, which eliminates the need for a rig, consists of separating the layers "implicitly" using a production logging tool.

There are two rigless testing techniques for layered reservoirs. Selective inflow performance (SIP) tests are performed under stabilized conditions and are suitable for medium—to high permeability layers that do not exhibit crossflow within the reservoir. The other test is conducted under transient conditions and is known as layered reservoir testing.

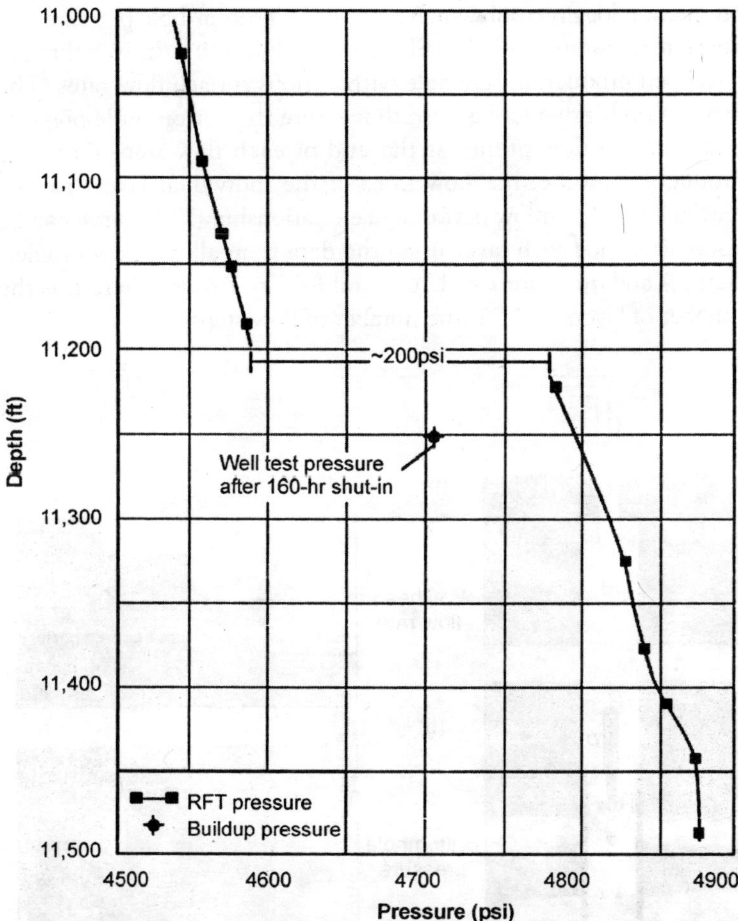

Figure 2.8 Comparison of a spot pressure profile with formation pressure obtained using a well test. The pressure values from the transient well tests do not represent those of the top or bottom layers because of crossflow. The well test pressure tends to be close to the pressure of the most permeable layer.

Selective Inflow Performance

The SIP test provides an estimate of the inflow performance relationship curve for each layer. Measurements are made with a production logging tool, which records the bottom-hole pressure and flow rate simultaneously. The SIP test is run by putting the well through a stepped production schedule with various surface flow rates. The production logging tool is used to measure the bottom-hole pressure and obtain a flow profile at the end of each flow step. From the production profile, the flow rates of the individual layers can be determined. An inflow performance relationship (IPR) curve can be constructed for each layer using the data from all the flow profiles: $pwf(i, j)$ and $q(i, j)$ for $i = 1$ to L and for $j = 1$ to F, where L is the number of layers and F is the number of flow steps.

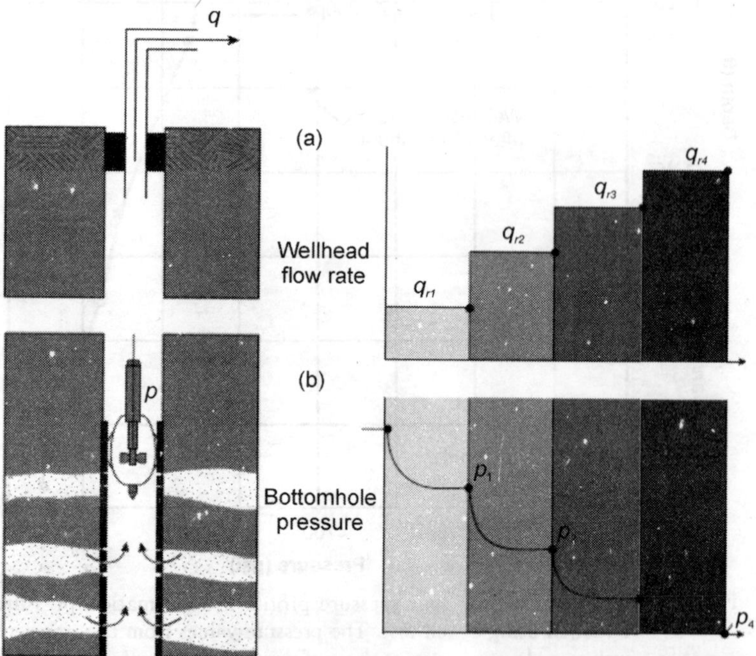

Figure 2.9 Surface flow rate history (a) and associated changes in bottom-hole pressure (b) During an SIP test. q_t = total flow rate.

Figure 2.9 is an SIP plot from a well that produces from a four-layer reservoir. The SIP survey was conducted using six flow steps. The shape of the IPR curves is characteristic of oil wells that flow below bubble point pressure or, alternatively, that have rate-dependent pressure drops.

The static pressure of each layer can be estimated from the point at which the IPR curve of the layer intersects the vertical axis. This estimate is valid provided that the flow steps during the SIP survey are sufficiently long to ensure that at the end of each step the pressure drop stabilizes both in the layer and within the well drainage area. SIP tests provide the formation pressure and IPR for each layer but do not give unique values of k and s for an individual layer. A transient test is required to determine those parameters.

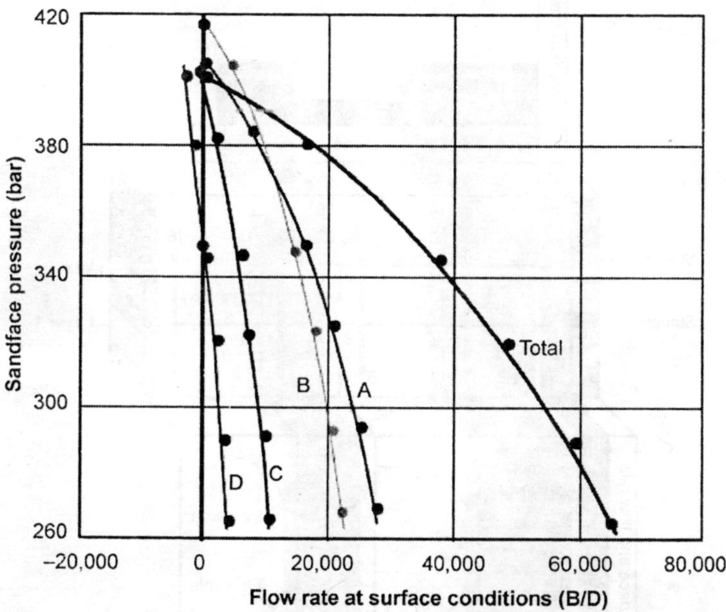

Figure 2.10 IPR curves of a multilayered reservoir showing uneven depletion between layers. The pressure is highest in layer B and lowest in layer D.

Transient Layered Testing

Layered reservoir tests differ from SIP tests in that, in addition to the acquisition of a flow profile, the downhole pressure and flow rate are simultaneously recorded versus time during each flow period. These measurements are obtained with the tool stationed at selected locations— between layers and above the topmost layer—which implicitly separates the layers.

The LRT procedure uses a continuous recording of the bottom-hole pressure, whereas the rate per layer is measured only at discrete time intervals. During the first transient, only the bottom-layer flow rate is measured. Flow rate changes in all layers above the bottom one cannot be measured directly because the flowmeter sensor measures the combined flow from all the layers below the tool.

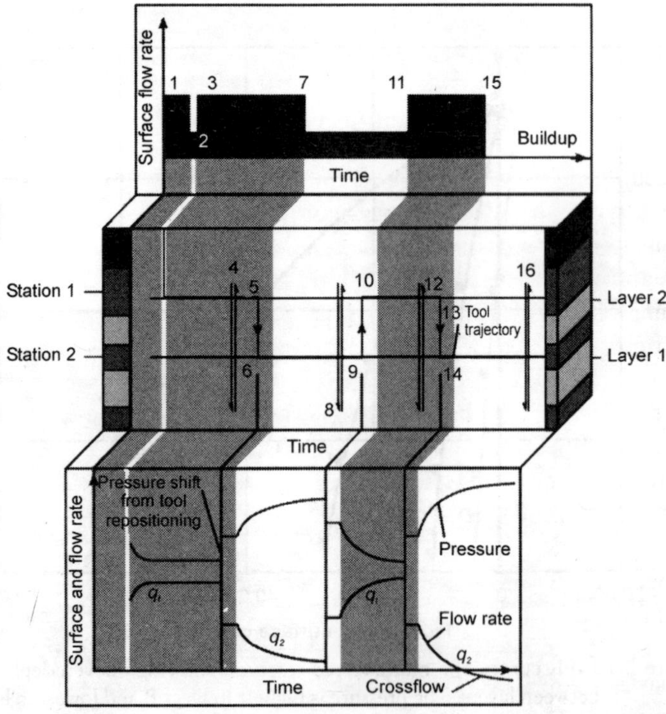

Figure 2.11 Simplified layered reservoir test sequence.

The LRT test requires careful planning and rigorous wellsite logging procedures because of the numerous events that occur during the test. The tool must be equipped with sensors that can monitor flow rate, pressure, density, and temperature. In addition, changes in flow rates are critical and must be controlled precisely using fixed choke sizes. Low flow rates generally occur during the survey of the bottom layers, while recording the afterflow during a buildup and when investigating crossflow during the final buildup. The survey must be conducted using surface recording equipment that enables real-time test follow-up and data quality control. This procedure is particularly critical in LRT operations because it is often necessary to adjust the original test programme according to the well's behaviour.

For a two-layer test, the flowmeter is stationed at only two locations: station 1, above the topmost layer, and station 2, between the two layers. The green line is the trajectory of the production logging tool. The top and bottom graphs show the behaviour of the wellhead flow rate and bottom hole pressure and flow rate, respectively.

Interpretation of Layered Reservoir Testing

Interpreting layered reservoirs is complex because it not only involves the identification of the reservoir model but also requires the estimation of a large number of unknown parameters such as the values of *k* and s and the reservoir geometry and pressure for each layer. For example, a simple three-layer reservoir has at least nine unknowns (permeability, skin effect, and pressure for each layer) in addition to the task of model identification. For these reasons, LRT interpretation relies heavily on techniques that indicate the reservoir model and initial parameter values, which are necessary input for the history-matching process used for interpretation. The first step is preparation of the data to a suitable form for interpretation. Pressure values are referred to the same datum to remove gravity effects. Once this is done, the pressure potential plot becomes a continuous curve—a useful feature for subsequent history matching.

LRT interpretation is conducted by seeking a match between the behaviour of the reservoir and the modeled response. The model has as many individual layers as tool stations used during the test, and each layer model can be different. The total reservoir response is calculated by stacking the single-layer models. The three stages for analyzing a single-layer test—model identification, parameter estimation, and model and parameter verification—are also followed during LRT interpretation.

Sequential Analysis

The simplest approach to identify reservoir geometry is to start by examining the response of the bottom layer. When the production logging tool is stationed at the top of the bottom layer, it measures only the flow rate changes induced in the bottom layer. Thus, interpreting the response of the bottom layer is a single-layer interpretation problem. As with single-layer DD tests, the reservoir model and the dominant flow regimes must first be identified. The first step is to calculate the pressure and flow rate changes that occur after the stabilized trend is established and to generate an approximate flow history of the layer. The pressure values are then normalized using the corresponding flow rate changes. A log-log plot of the rate-normalized pressure change and its derivative with respect to the SFRCT function is used to identify the model and flow regime. The relevant reservoir parameters are then calculated using specialized interpretation plots.

Initial Parameter Estimation for the Remaining Layers

Once a satisfactory model of the lowest layer is established, the interpretation proceeds with the next layer above it. During this transient, the measured flow rate is the cumulative total of the two layers.

Under these circumstances, analysis of the cumulative flow rate and wellbore pressure provides a close estimate of the "average" values of *k* and *s* for the two-layer system. The sequential analysis continues until all the layers are included in the interpretation process. In a three-layer reservoir, this method uses a three-layer model to estimate the parameters of the newly added top layer. The analyst assumes that the parameters for the two lower layers are known and searches for the parameters of only the new layer, and so on. The disadvantage of this method is that errors are propagated as the bottom-up analysis progresses, but these errors may be corrected during the simultaneous history matching performed in the final stage of LRT interpretation.

Verification of the Model and its Parameters

Once the model is identified and an initial estimate of the parameters is available, the next stage is the simultaneous history-matching process. In this procedure, the pressure history is used as the boundary condition and history matching is conducted by reproducing the observed flow rates.

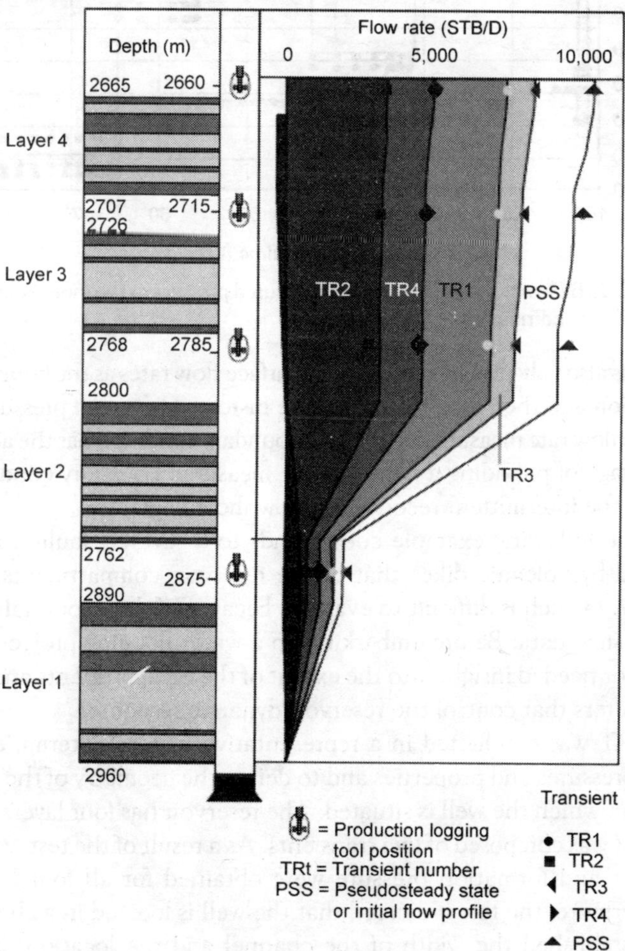

Figure 2.12A Fluid flow distribution at the end of each transient in a four-layer reservoir.

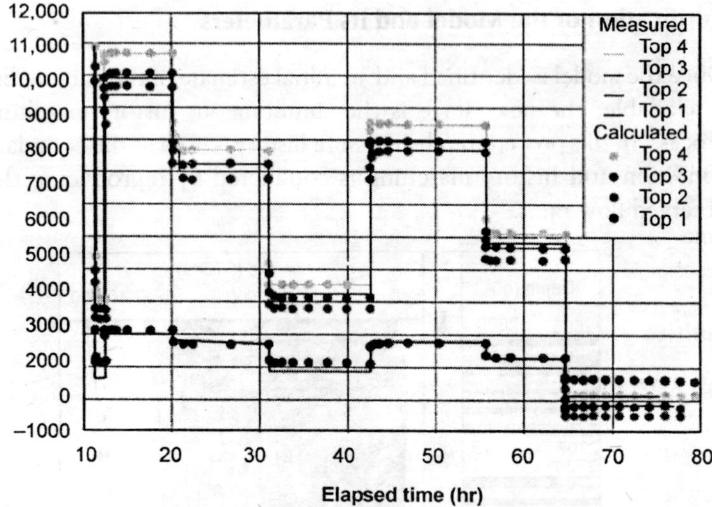

Figure 2.12B Flow rate match using the measured pressure as the inner boundary condition.

It is also valid to use downhole or surface flow rates as the boundary condition and then match the pressure history. The use of pressure or surface flow rate measurements as the boundary condition has the added advantage of providing a continuously measured boundary condition during the intermittent recording of downhole flow rates.

The following example corresponds to a severely faulted field, crossed by volcanic dikes that create reservoir compartments, the extent of which is difficult to evaluate because of the poor quality of the seismic data. Before embarking on a water flooding project, the operator needed insight into the extent of the compartments and the parameters that control the reservoir dynamic response.

LRT was conducted in a representative well to determine the layer pressures and properties and to define the geometry of the fault block in which the well is situated. The reservoir has four layers, and the test was composed of five transients. As a result of the test, values of kh, s and formation pressure were obtained for all four layers. Furthermore, the test indicated that the well is located in a channel and established the width of the channel and the location of the nearest boundary to the well.

Flow rate history matching was performed using the measured pressure as the boundary condition.

Figure 2.12A is a comparison of the simulated flow profiles and the vertical fluid flow distribution observed with the production logging flowmeter at the end of each transient. Figure B shows the flow rate versus time match. The quality of both matches—against depth and time—indicates that the selected model and its parameters properly describe the dynamic behaviour of the tested reservoir compartment.

Multiple-Well Testing

In single-well testing, the primary target is the nearby well region. However, to investigate the interwell region, more than one well must be directly involved in the test. In multiple-well testing, the flow rate is changed in one well and the pressure response is monitored in another. These tests are conducted to investigate the presence or lack of hydraulic communication within a reservoir region. They are also used to estimate interwell reservoir transmissivity and storativity. The two main types of multiple-well testing are interference tests and pulse tests. Some vertical interference tests are classified as multiple-well tests. As subsequently discussed, they are performed between two sets of perforations or test intervals in a well to investigate vertical communication and estimate vertical permeability. Multiple-well tests are more sensitive to reservoir horizontal anisotropy than single-well tests. Therefore, multiple-well tests are typically conducted to describe the reservoir anisotropy based on the directional permeabilities.

Interference Testing

Interference tests require long-duration production or injection rate changes in the active well. The associated pressure disturbance recorded in the observation well yields valuable information regarding the degree of hydraulic communication within the interwell region. Figure shows a plan view of two wells used in an interference test, the rate history of the active well, and the pressure response in the observation well.

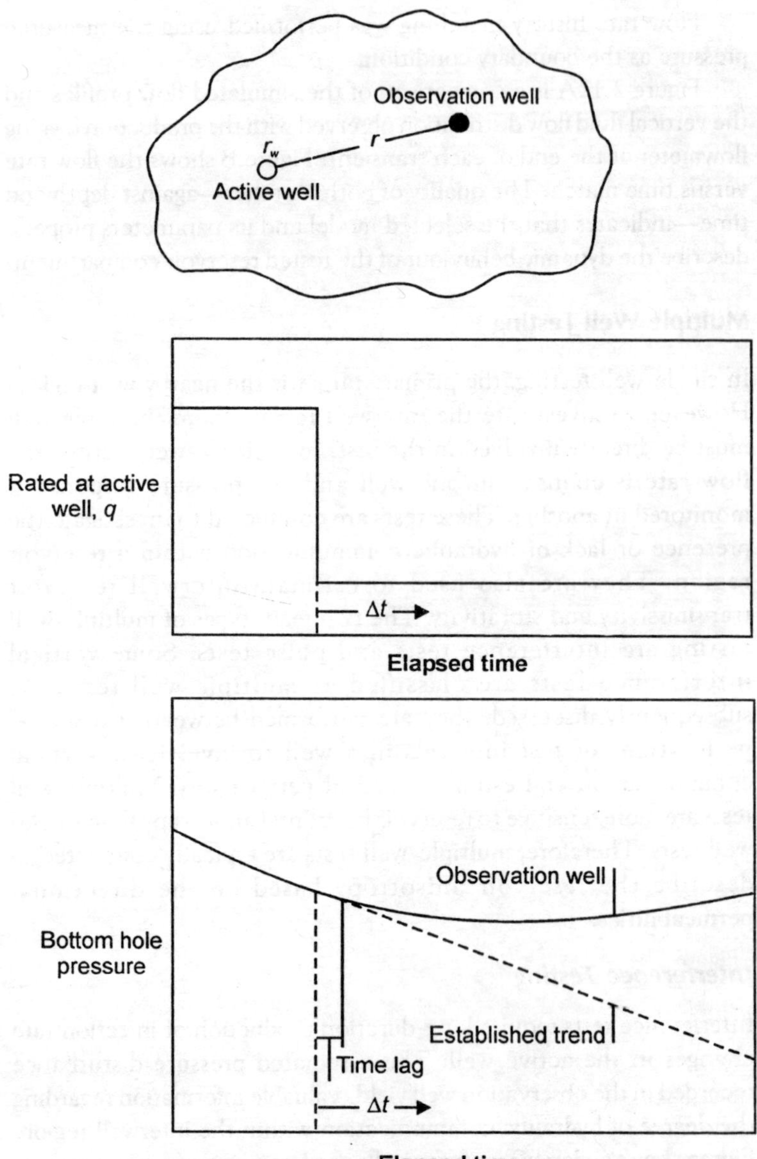

Figure 2.13 Active and observation wells and their respective rate and pressure changes during an interference test.

If single-phase conditions prevail within the investigated region of the reservoir, the pressure response can be analyzed to estimate interwell reservoir properties. The analysis technique uses the same type-curve matching approach as for DD tests, but with a different type curve because, unlike for single-well tests, the pressure response is observed at some distance from the location where the perturbation was originally created. Figure shows a type-curve match for an interference test using the homogeneous line-source solution (also known as the exponential integral solution) as the referenced theoretical model.

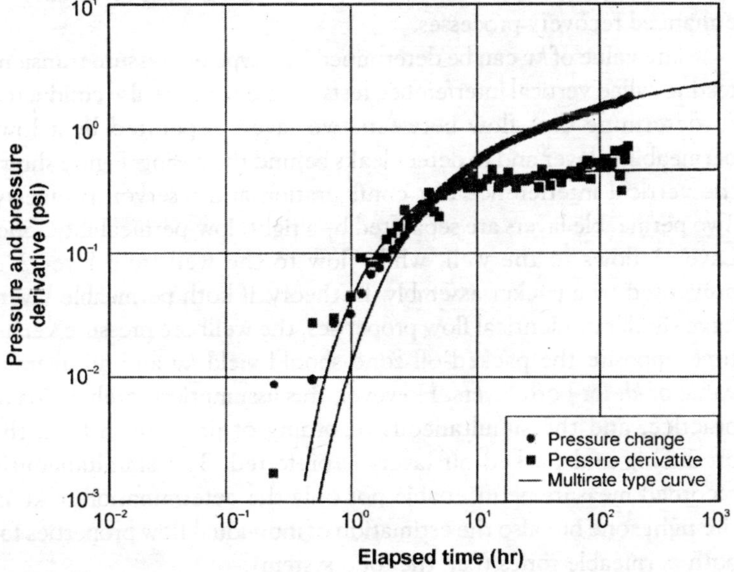

Figure 2.14 Type-curve match of an interference test.

Pulse Testing

Pulse testing is a special form of the multiple-well testing that may last from a few hours to a few days. This technique uses a series of short rate perturbations at the active well. Pulses are created by alternating periods of production or injection and shut-in. The pressure response to the pulses is measured at one or more observation wells. Since the pulses are of short duration, the pressure responses are small.

Therefore, high-resolution gauges are usually required to measure the small variations in pressure. The advantages of pulse testing compared with the interference testing derive from the relatively short pulse length; reservoir pressure trends and noise are removed with appropriate analysis techniques.

Vertical Interference Testing

Understanding the vertical flow behaviour is essential for effective reservoir management. Vertical permeability is an important parameter, particularly for completion decisions in thick or layered reservoirs. It is even more critical for working with secondary or enhanced recovery processes.

The value of *kv* can be determined by a type of pressure transient testing called vertical interference tests. These tests are also conducted to determine crossflow between two layers separated by a low-permeability layer and to detect leaks behind the casing. Figure shows the vertical interference test configuration and reservoir geometry. Two permeable layers are separated by a tight, low-permeability zone. Layer 1 flows to the well, while flow to the well from layer 2 is prevented by a packer assembly. In theory, if both permeable layers have similar or identical flow properties, the wellbore pressure versus time opposite the packed-off zone should yield *kv* and an average value of *kh* for both layers. However, this assumption rarely holds in practice, and the simultaneous recording of pressure in both the producing and packed-off layers is preferred. The simultaneously recorded measurements enable not only the determination of *kv* in the tight zone but also the estimation of individual flow properties for both permeable zones (i.e., the total system).

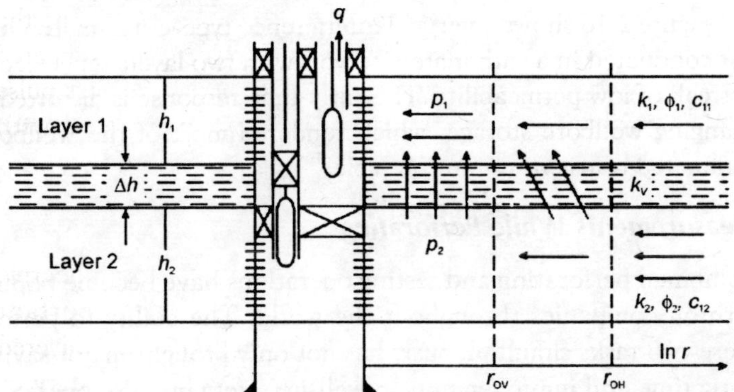

Figure 2.15 Test and reservoir configuration for a vertical interference test across a tight zone. r_{eH} = inner radius of the horizontal flow region, r_{eV} = outer radius of the vertical flow region.

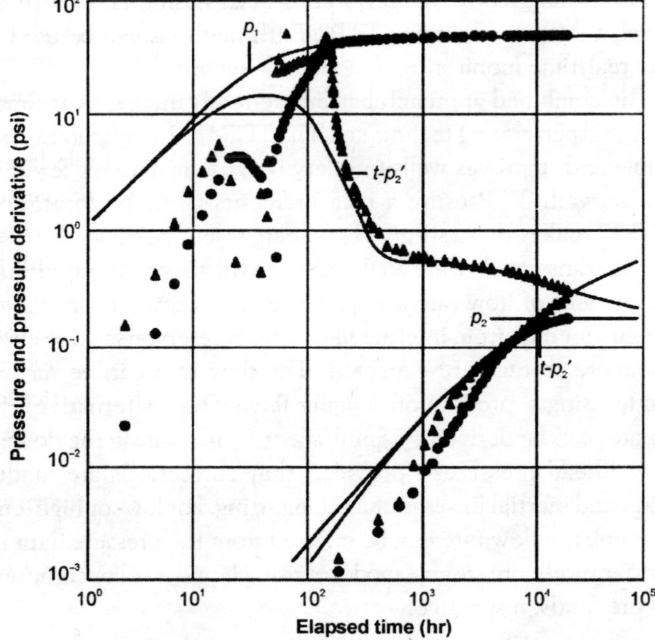

Figure 2.16 Vertical interference type-curve match for a two-layer carbonate reservoir divided by a tight streak, with k_1 = 806 mD, s_1 = 36, k_2 = 2120 mD, k_v = 3.7 mD, permeability ratio k = 0.33, and storativity ratio w = 0.56

Figure 2.16 shows a vertical interference type-curve match for a test conducted in a carbonate reservoir with two layers separated by a streak of low permeability. The early-time response is distorted by changing wellbore storage, which rendered most of the wellbore-dominated transient uninterpretable.

Measurements While Perforating

Combined perforating and testing operations have become popular with oil companies throughout the world. The ability to perform these two tasks simultaneously has not only brought major savings in rig time and improvements in wellsite safety but also opened up new possibilities in well testing.

Although the range of tool configurations for measurements-while-perforating jobs is wide, there are two types of combined systems—tubing-conveyed perforating (TCP) using a DST string and through-tubing perforation (TTP). Both methods can be used with either real-time monitoring or downhole recording.

The combined approach has inherent advantages over separate testing and perforating techniques. The TCP-DST configuration saves rig time and improves wellsite safety because it requires fewer trips into the well. TTP using a measurements-while-perforating tool (MWPT) makes the testing of low-energy wells possible.

The transient data are analyzed using the theory for simultaneous measurement of flow rate and pressure. This method is particularly necessary for data from intermediate-energy reservoirs where changes in wellbore storage are expected. The flow rate can be measured directly using a production logging flowmeter. Alternatively, flow estimates can be derived by simultaneously measuring the downhole and wellhead pressures—provided that corrections are made for friction and inertial losses in the tubing string. For low- or high-energy reservoirs, the flow rate can be inferred from the pressure data using a constant wellbore storage model of rising liquid level or compressing wellbore fluids, respectively.

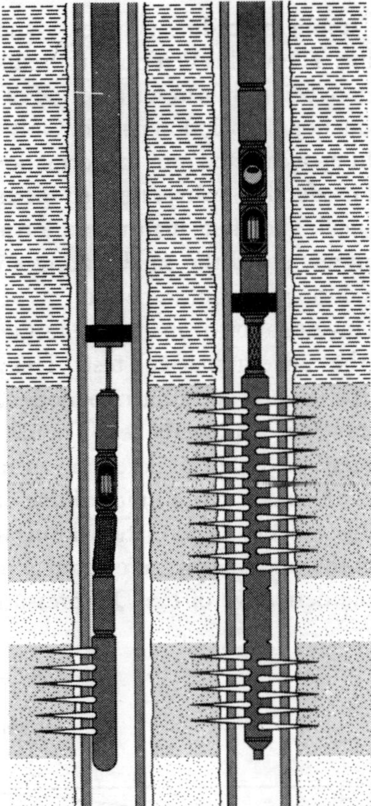

Figure 2.17 TCP (right) is preferred in exploration or new wells where a large interval will be perforated. TTP (left) is usually more economical for small jobs and is commonly used to perforate producing wells.

Impulse Testing

Auick and simple, impulse testing is particularly useful for wells that do not flow to the surface, wells in which extended flow may not be desirable (e.g., because of sanding problems), and extremely tight or vuggy formations where wireline formation testers fail to perform. The technique requires knowledge of the initial reservoir pressure, and the resulting estimated parameters include *kh* and *s*. An Impulse testing can also be used to detect and evaluate near wellbore heterogeneity in the reservoir.

The impulse testing procedure is an easy and extremely quick form of well testing. The well is first put on production or injection for 3 to 4 min before being shut-in for a period of 6 to 20 times the length of the production or injection period. Only a small amount of fluid is removed from or injected into the formation during the short impulse period of production or injection, so the associated pressure disturbances are small. Therefore, high-resolution pressure gauges are required to accurately study the small changes in the reservoir's pressure response during the shut-in period.

The depth of investigation of an impulse test is relatively small in comparison with the conventional well tests. This is due to the short duration of both the impulse and shut-in periods as well as the small pressure changes developed during the test. Therefore, impulse testing is most appropriately used for the detection of near-well features. Impulse test theory assumes that a unit volume of fluid is instantly removed from or injected into the formation during the impulse period. Theory shows that the resulting pressure changes in the reservoir are proportional to the derivative of the DD pressure response of the reservoir.

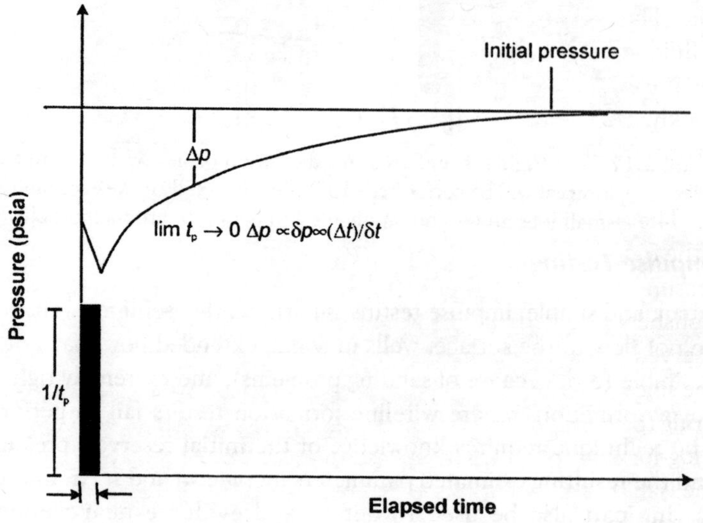

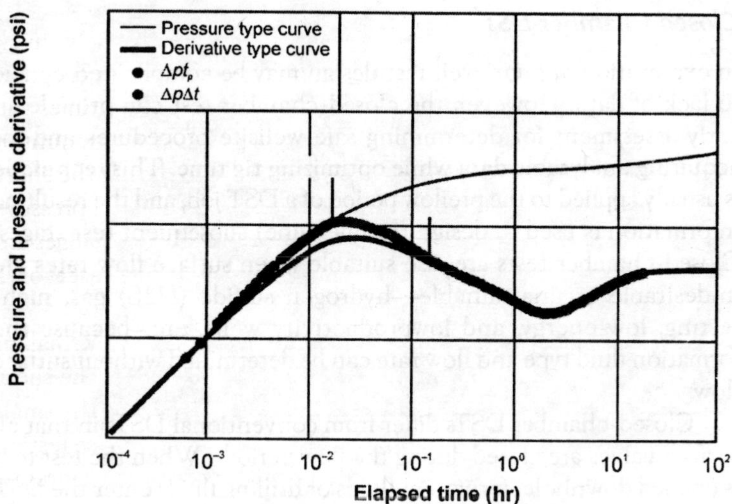

Figure 2.18 Pressure response plot (a) and impulse plot (b) of a simulated test in a double-porosity reservoir p_{DD} is the drawdown pressure in the same well.

In practice, the impulse period is not instantaneous because the removal or injection of a unit volume of fluid takes a finite period of time. The pressure changes in the reservoir produced by this change in fluid volume initially do not follow the theory and do not match the pressure derivative curve. Fortunately, these effects dissipate quickly, and generally the pressure response matches the pressure derivative curve once the shut-in time exceeds three times the impulse time.

The analysis of impulse test data requires accurate measurement of the quantity of fluid removed or injected and modification of the measured pressure response so it can be matched directly with the published type curves. The data are modified by multiplying the observed pressure change during the shut-in period by the elapsed time since the end of the impulse period. In addition, pressure changes during the impulse period are multiplied by the duration of this period. A log-log plot of the transformed pressure data versus the shut-in time is matched with selected DD type curves to obtain the reservoir parameters.

Closed-Chamber DST

In exploration, *a priori* well test design may be complicated by due to lack of data. However, the closed-chamber test can provide an early assessment for determining safe wellsite procedures and for acquiring analyzable data while optimizing rig time. This technique is usually applied to the preflow period of a DST job, and the resulting information is used to design (or fine-tune) subsequent test stages. Closed-chamber tests are also suitable when surface flow rates are undesirable or unattainable—hydrogen sulfide (H2S) gas, night testing, low-energy, and lowproductivity wells, etc.–because the formation fluid type and flow rate can be determined without surface flow.

Closed-chamber DSTs differ from conventional DSTs in that all surface valves are closed during the flow periods. When the test tool is opened downhole, formation fluids or drilling fluids enter the DST string, displacing the fluids that initially occupied the internal drill stem volume. Since the surface valves are closed, the pressure rises in the closed chamber. The pressure rise continues until the formation fluids cease to flow (shut-in period commences), at which point the pressure begins to stabilize. Once stabilization has been reached, the drill stem pressure is released following a controlled bleedoff period. The recording of the pressure increase during the closed-chamber flow period and the pressure decrease together with the gas rate during the bleedoff period are used to identify the type of produced fluids and to estimate the fluid entry rate and liquid recovery.

The increase in surface pressure during a closed-chamber DST flow period is caused by:

- increase in the mass of gas contained in the chamber (pure gas entry),
- decrease in the gas-filled portion of the string (pure liquid entry),
- combined gas and liquid entry.

The pressure increase can be translated into approximate flow rates using the principle of conservation of mass and the real gas law.

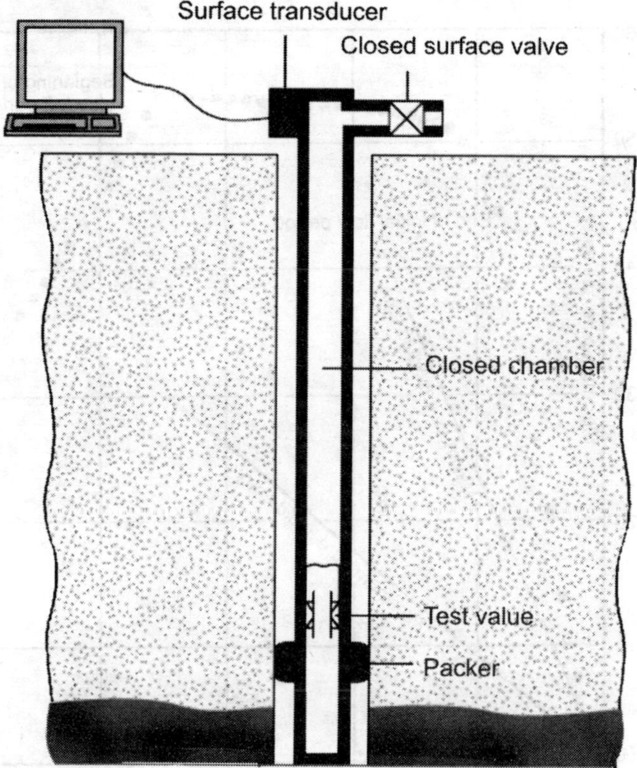

Figure 2.19 Equipment schematic for closed-chamber testing.

The rate of increase of the surface pressure indicates gas entry because pure liquid entry at the maximum possible rate could not produce such a rapid increase. The continuous increase in surface pressure during shut-in is an indication of phase segregation, suggesting the entry of gas and liquid during the flow period. The subsequent bleedoff test confirmed this interpretation.

Knowledge of the formation fluid type and flow rate prior to the initiation of subsequent flow periods enables optimizing the remainder of the test. Considerable rig time was saved during the test plotted in Figure as a result of the early determination of the average produced gas/oil ratio, which indicated that surface flow was improbable.

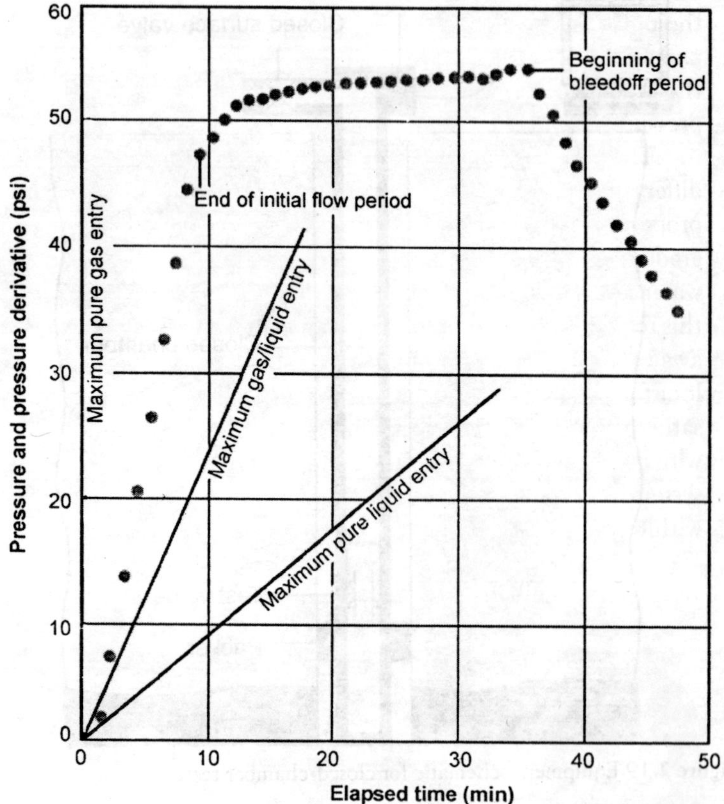

Figure 2.20 Surface pressure versus time for a closed-chamber DST operation. The slopes of the lines represent the maximum rates of change in pressure that would occur if pure gas, pure liquid or gas-saturated water entered the DST string at the maximum possible rates allowed by the test tool.

Water Injection Wells

Waterflooding is used throughout the world to increase the oil recovery. The success of waterflooding projects depends largely on adequate prediction of the reservoir response. Pressure transient testing—usually in the form of falloff or injectivity tests—is conducted to obtain parameters for modeling injection schemes. In addition to these same parameters as obtained with the conventional well testing, the pressure transient tests also provide information for monitoring parameters that change with time in a waterflood (i.e., location of the water front, well injectivity, and average interwell reservoir pressure).

The pressure transient response in a reservoir under waterflooding differs from single-phase flow behaviour because of differences in the properties of oil and water. Soon after injection begins, a saturation gradient is established in the reservoir. This forms a region of high water saturation around the wellbore, termed the water bank. Outside this region is the transition bank, in which water saturation decreases away from the wellbore until the flood front is reached. The region located ahead of the injection front—with the initial water saturation—is called the oil bank. A system that consists of regions with different properties is called a composite reservoir The composite system is modeled assuming that the fluid properties are constant within each bank but change sharply at an interface.

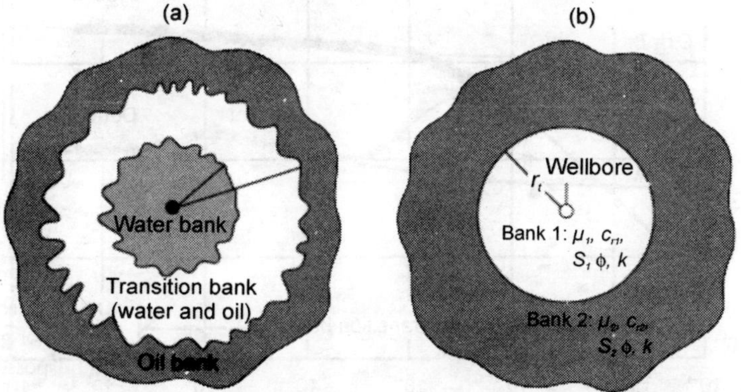

Figure 2.21 Composite system of a waterflooded reservoir: (a) multibank and (b) two-bank models. S = saturation, rf = radial distance to the fluid front.

In a water injection well test, three main features can be identified after the wellbore storage effects have disappeared. Initially, the pressure response is identical to single-phase flow, and is governed by the rock and fluid properties of the water bank.

For a pressure transient test to contain all features of waterflood and therefore provide a unique solution, the test should be conducted during the early stage of injection. It should also be sufficiently long to detect the reservoir response in the oil zone, but interference from nearby wells can hamper the capture of all three features. Consequently, the performance of tests early in the life of the injector well is recommended.

The interpretation of pressure transient tests in water injection wells can be refined through use of the multibank model. This model incorporates the saturation distribution within the transition bank, which makes it particularly useful when the various banks exhibit substantial storativity contrasts. These customized type curves are constructed on computers and require the relative permeability and individual rock and fluid compressibility values. Therefore, the type curves are field dependent.

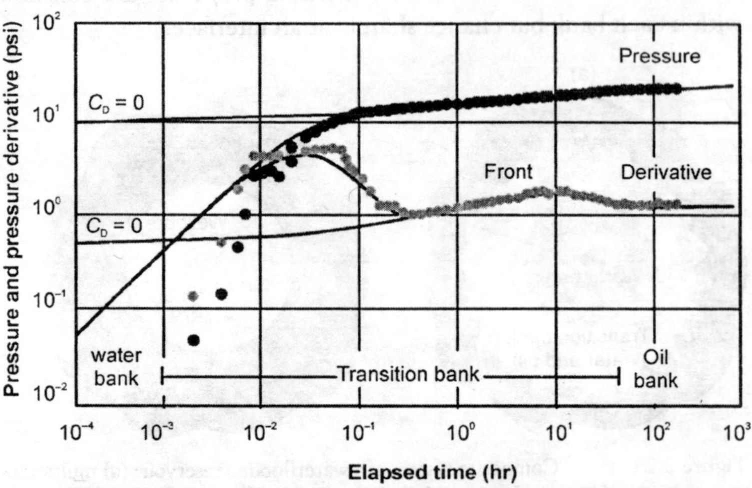

Figure 2.22 Type-curve match for a falloff test conducted two months after injection began.

Figure shows the comparison between a falloff dataset and the theoretical response of the multibank model. The data are from a 24-hour falloff test conducted two months after injection began. The type curve that assumes no wellbore storage is also shown. Although wellbore storage masks the response from the water bank and part of the transition zone in the data, analysis was possible because the test was sufficiently long to detect the total reservoir response. The pressure match yielded the permeability to water at residual oil saturation. The time match provided the location of the water front. A second test performed four months later found that the water front had moved 300 ft farther away. This example clearly shows how using falloff tests as monitoring tools assists operators in the management of waterflooding projects.

Pumping Wells

Sucker-rod pumping wells present special well testing problems. The first difficulty relates to the mechanical constraints resulting from the presence of the rods inside the tubing string (Figure). This configuration precludes the running in hole of pressure gauges—unless the rods and pump are pulled out of the hole or there is enough room in the annular space for a gauge. The second problem is associated with the long duration of the wellbore storage period during shut-in. The low reservoir energy and low productivity associated with pumping wells, compounded by high fluid compressibility in the wellbore, cause these long periods. Both problems, however, can be overcome.

Testing pumping wells by removing the pump from the hole is quite expensive. Workover or pulling rigs are needed twice—to extract the pump and rods and then to rerun them after the test is completed. Furthermore, the bottomhole flowing pressure before shut-in and the early-time data cannot be recorded in these tests because of the nature of the operation, which leaves the values of *s* and the productivity index undetermined.

A cost-effective alternative is to compute the bottomhole pressure and flow rate from indirect measurements: casing head pressure *pc* and the height of the gas/liquid interface *hL* of the rising liquid column in the annulus. The first measurement is acquired with the conventional pressure transducers, and the second is determined by the acoustic well-sounding techniques. The conversion of these indirect measurements to downhole pressure and rate requires an accurate determination of the changing liquid gradient in the well annulus. The controlling parameter is the gas void fraction *fg* of the annular liquid column, which can be derived using a hydrodynamic model or from empirical correlation.

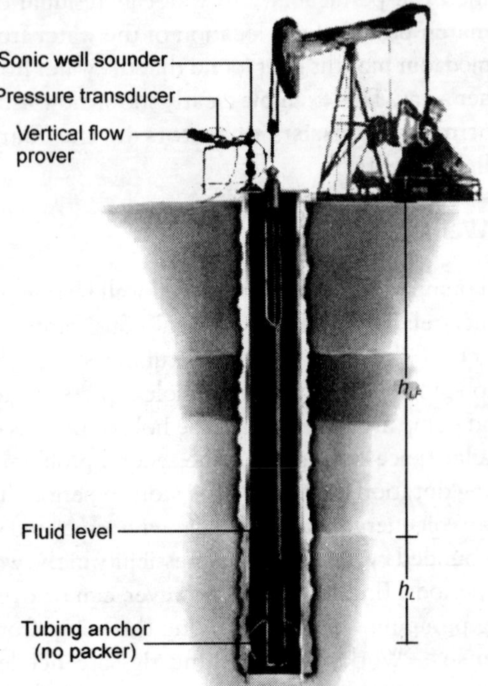

Figure 2.23 Sucker-rod pumping well configuration.

The use of a hydrodynamic model—which requires the values of *dc* (diameter of the casing) and *dt* (diameter of the tubing), gas and liquid densities, and surface tension—is preferred to empirical correlation. This is because the prediction of *fg* (pressure gradient of the gas) is crucial for the afterflow period, during which gas continues to bubble through the liquid column. Afterflow normally dominates buildup tests in pumping wells, and in most cases radial flow is seldom reached. Moreover, this period exhibits a variable value of C, which complicates type-curve matching that uses pressure only. In such cases, reliable interpretation of afterflowdominated tests uses both downhole pressure and rate transient data.

System Analysis

In general, system analysis helps determine the cost effectiveness of treatments under consideration and assists in completion decisions, such as a hydraulically fractured vertical well versus a horizontal well. The critical parameters for system analysis can be determined from transient tests.

NODAL system analysis is a methodical approach to optimizing oil and gas well deliverability. This thorough evaluation of the complete producing system establishes the flow rate versus pressure drop relation for each component of the producing system—reservoir, near-wellbore completion configuration, wellbore strings, and surface facilities. The major source of restriction for flow in the system is then identified. If the major pressure drop is associated with a component that can be modified, a sensitive study is performed to determine options for removing the flow restriction; this assessment provides reliable guidelines for optimizing the well performance.

The following example shows the application of NODAL analysis to an offshore oil well that had a level of performance far below that of the neighboring wells. Production was about 25 per cent of the average production for other wells in the reservoir. Formation damage was the suspected cause of the low productivity, and the well was tested. Interpretation of the pressure transient data identified a severely damaged well with s = 210. NODAL analysis was used to study the effect of damage removal on IPR.

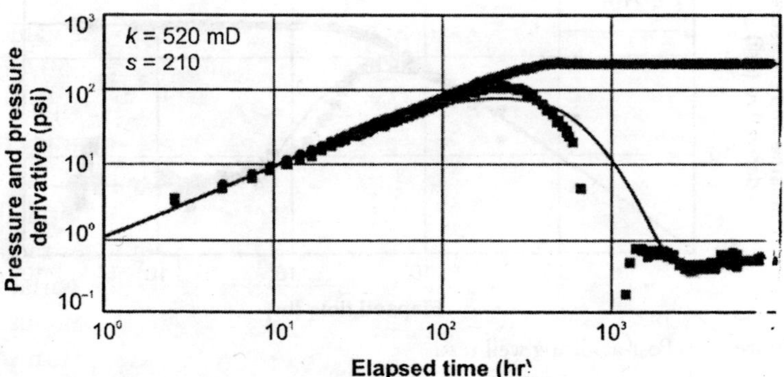

Figure 2.24 Pressure trans ient analysis using type-curve matching.

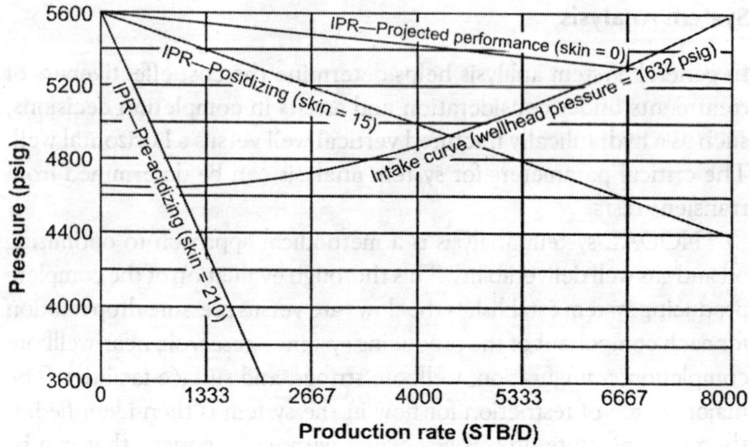

Figure 2.25 NODAL analysis of pressure transient data.

The plot shows that the flow rate could be increased by a factor of about 5 at the same wellhead pressure if the impeding damage around the wellbore was removed. This could be achieved by an acid treatment without jeopardizing the integrity of the gravel pack. The well was treated with a specially designed acid injection program, and a post-acidizing well test was conducted to evaluate the effectiveness of the acid job. The interpretation results of the post-acidizing well test show that *s* was reduced to 15 from its preacidizing value of 210.

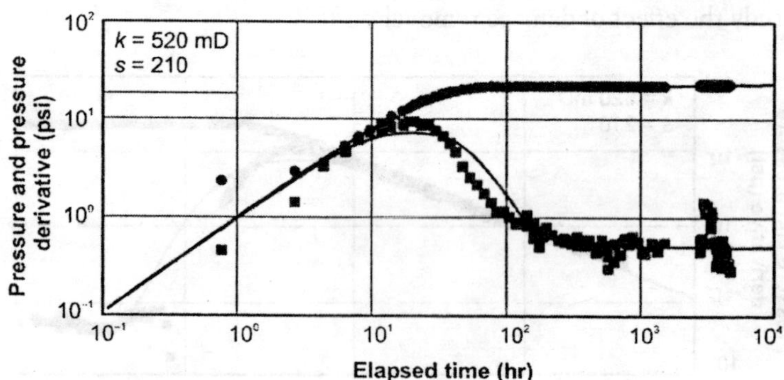

Figure 2.26 Post-acidizing well test.

The final stabilizedate of the well agreed with the post-acidizing predictions made by NODAL analysis (4300 STB/D, as indicated by the intersection of the tubing intake curve and the reservoir performance curve for s = 15).

3
Technology Overview

Well testing is the science of measuring pressure changes in wells and interpreting those pressure changes. The analysis of test data provides estimates of flowing properties and reservoir geometry.

The commonly performed tests include the following:

- Pressure drawdown,
- Pressure build-up,
- Step rate,
- Drill stem,
- Productivity,
- Injectivity,
- Multi-rate,
- Interference,
- Pulse.

The applications of these tests include the following:

- Degree of reservoir damage,
- Area of drainage,
- Potential well productivity,
- Injectivity,
- Permeability of different intervals,
- Transmissibility (kh/μ),
- Capacity (kh),
- Productivity Index,
- Length of fracture system,

- Radius of drainage,
- Distance to fault or barrier,
- Open flow potential,
- Oil and/or gas in place.

All of these tests, regardless of the end purpose, are based on the principle that the flow rate is proportional to the driving forces (static or capillary pressure) over resisting forces (matrix geometry and fluid properties). The input to the test is a measured period of shut-in and flowing rates. The output is the reservoir response (pressure). A computational model that describes the relationship between the pressure, flow rate and reservoir rock and fluids properties is required. In its simplest form, the relationship of input to output is a form of the diffusivity equation for a well in the center of a circular, homogeneous, horizontal reservoir of uniform thickness and a one-phase fluid that obeys Darcy's law. While this equation cannot be solved directly, indirect techniques provide a satisfactory estimate.

The three areas addressed by well testing are as follows:

1. *Reservoir evaluation*—To determine if the well has sufficient flow capacity to complete and to obtain reservoir information for predicting and analyzing reservoir behaviour;
(2) *Reservoir management*—To diagnose the condition of production and injection wells to optimize performance, identify candidates for workover, and track the movement of fluid fronts in the reservoir; and
(3) *Reservoir description*—To identify heterogeneities such as different rock types, stratigraphic interfaces, and faults and barriers.

The actual reservoir model is constructed from the basic equation described above. It must take into account the geometry of the reservoir, the number and types of fluids, and the flow regime. The flow geometry for that area affected by the test can be radial linear, elliptical, or spherical. The most common model used to represent the pressure behaviour of the reservoir is radial flow, where all flow occurs radially toward the well between impermeable upper and lower boundaries at a constant surface flow rate. The interpretation of test data will yield average reservoir properties even when reservoir heterogeneities exist.

Determination of the relationship between wellbore pressure and the wellbore flow rate is a basic test of the reservoir. These tests allow the engineer to determine the average wellbore pressure for use in volumetric and material balance calculations as well as forming the foundation to estimate the physical characteristics of the reservoir. The type of information obtained by well testing includes estimates of permeability, formation damage or stimulation, pressure, length and conductivity of fractures, flow barriers, and communication between wells and drainage volume.

The presence of a single barrier or a finite reservoir is evident when comparing actual well build-up data to the theoretical build-up curve with no after production and no completion damage in an infinite reservoir. This is evident in the Horner plot with pressure as the vertical axis, and the log of $(t + ?t)/ ?t$ on the horizontal are is. The degree of skin damage is evident in the plot in the early time as a deviation from the theoretical plot. Skin factor is a function of skin due to damage, restricted entry, perforations, turbulence, and slanted wells.

The reservoir behaviour can be categorized as homogeneous, dual porosity, or dual permeability. The dual porosity systems consist of two porous media regions, primary and secondary porosity. Most of the fluid is contained within the primary porosity, which has very low permeability. Fluid flow to wells only occurs through the secondary porosity system because it has much greater permeability than the primary porosity system. The flow periods are modeled in three phases:

1. The high permeability (fissure) phase in which only the secondary porosity is contributing;
2. the transition phase characterized by transient interporosity and pseudosteady state interporosity flow; and
3. total system flow, which is controlled by flow from the lower permeability primary porosity.

Well Test Data Interpretation

There are three major steps to a unified approach to well test data interpretation: Identification of the proper model for the classification of the reservoir (finite, infinite, homogeneous, dual porosity, dual permeability, skin, fractures); specific analysis and calculations to estimate well and reservoir characteristics; and verification of results to ensure that the process resulted in the best answer.

By plotting the *?p* vs *?t*, the proper model can be selected based on the nature of the curve. In addition, plotting the pressure and pressure derivative versus time provides a powerful tool in distinguishing between different behaviours and in finding a unique solution. For instance, the difference between plots of single and dual porosity reservoirs can be seen clearly, and the proper model selected. However, accurate pressure measurements are required for the evaluation of the pressure derivative.

Well test interpretation is based on patterns of pressure change and the derivative of pressure change to identify the type of reservoir behaviour. An effective way to interpret pressure data is by using a diagnostic graph. A diagnostic graph is a plot of the pressure change and the derivative of the pressure change versus time on a log-log paper. It can be used to identify each flow period. Behaviour specific plots can be useful to identify heterogeneous behaviour, effects of wellbore storage, and high and low conductivity fractures.

The second step in the unified approach to interpretation methodology is the calculations of the basic reservoir parameters, such as the *kh*, skin, and wellbore storage capacity. This can be done conventionally, through the use of specific plots, or with type curves.

Using the conventional method, the engineer identifies the various flow periods from the diagnostic shape of each of the flow periods and determines the stabilized derivative value, if present. *Kh* and skin can then be calculated directly. The wellbore storage coefficient can be estimated if the unit slope line appears in both the derivative and the pressure change data.

It may not be possible to recognize the diagnostic shape of the derivative, if the derivative values are erratic. If the infinite-acting period can be identified from the diagnostic pressure plot, semi-log analysis can be used to analyze the pressure data during infinite-acting period.

The type-cure matching technique is used when it is not possible to accurately identify the location of the flow periods from the diagnostic plot. The curves are dimensionless well model solutions that are plotted on log-log paper. The shapes apparent in the diagnostic log-log plat are matched to the type curves. The best way to analyze the post-stimulation well tests is by type-curve matching. The procedure is similar to that used for the radial flow model.

The final step in the interpretation methodology is the verification of the validity of the model and calculations. The engineer can compare the result from well to well and from time to time with the same well for matching. Another method is to prepare and analyze a dimensionless semi-log plot. Finally, the calculated parameters can be used as input to a reservoir simulation model and run to see if it matches the input data.

Horizontal Well Technology

Horizontal well technology and application has grown dramatically over the last 10 to 15 years, and in some settings it is now seen as the first choice.

The deeper the target reservoir, the less incrementally expensive a horizontal well is relative to a vertical well. The incremental cost of additional horizontal length within the reservoir is minimal to irrelevant.

When considering horizontal development, operators are encouraged to ask "why not?" versus "why?" Candidates for horizontal wells are formations that have coning tendencies, unconsolidated zones or sand-producing tendencies, low pressure, low permeability, natural fractures, thin production intervals, compartments, viscous oil, or any combination of the above. The key strategy and "why" of a horizontal well are directly related to its profile. This profile will control all capabilities of well construction, completion, and workover options. Profile can be utilized with completion refinement to control the production mechanism and maximize recovery.

The "Three W" Design Criteria

The drilling function, or the "how" to drill the well, is typically the least problematic and should be the last element to be defined. First, the team must define:

- Where (geology, structure);
- Why (reservoir, drive mechanism, profile);
- What (production engineering, reservoir management, EOR, completion).

Having defined the above, then the team can develop the "how" (drilling, detailed well design, well construction contingencies, Go/No-Go decision points).

Geology and Reservoir Engineering

Developing a 3-D picture/model is essential for planning horizontal applications. As more horizontals have been drilled, industry has been surprised the degree of lateral variation that is evident. Fortunately new technical options are available to control the cost and time of developing a 3-D image. For the more basic settings, analytical models are often adequate for screening purposes. For more complex situations, numerical simulation is required. Given the geological setting and production mechanism, modeling points toward what would be the optimum horizontal plan.

One key aspect of the geological model is the vertical permeability relative to the horizontal permeability. Sometimes one wants a flat, straight hole; in others such as reservoirs having flat impermeable shale barriers, a flat, straight hole would not be desirable.

With vertical wells a geologist's role has been primarily to evaluate "what has been drilled." With horizontals geologists become involved in actively steering the well to its desired profile, responding to data as drilling occurs. This requires an openness to rethink the geological model as data continually arrive.

Managing undulations (ups and downs in profiles) is part of the challenge. Excessive undulation causes excess friction, which may limit lateral length, and, since horizontals are extremely efficient horizontal separators, can cause pressure drop or multiple phase flow complications.

Directional Drilling, Guidance, and Geo-Steering

Horizontals are based primarily on modern steerable motor capability. Drilling can occur in either the rotary or slide mode. When the bottom-hole assembly (BHA) is rotated by the drill string, the assembly will tend to drill in a straight line. Thus, corrections are made in the slide mode and straight-ahead drilling is conducted in the rotary mode. Three measurements (inclination, azimuth, and tool face orientation) are key to knowing where the well is (and where it is going). Dogleg severity is a key constraint of the profile. All potential downhole components must be checked for the maximum allowable dogleg severity. One should avoid the tendency to oversteer—the more corrections made, the more difficult it becomes to make corrections.

Measurement while drilling (MWD) systems include mud pulse telemetry. An alternative when multiphase fluids are used, which is often the case with underbalanced drilling, is electromagnetic pulse telemetry. With coil tubing drilling wireline telemetry is an option made viable by improvements in hardware/systems. Advancements are continuously being made to allow placing sensors closer to the bit, which is good but can be costly. Over-utilization of highly instrumented assemblies, which can be more prone to failure and are more costly (especially if lost downhole), is a common error in horizontals.

Geo-steering is much more than measuring a log response along the horizontal well length. It is a choice of numerous real-time observations made while drilling, starting at the kickoff point. The curve shape, use of tangents, and pilot holes are examples of geo-steering to help find the target. Observations can include mud logging, drilling parameters, inflow observations, etc. Since mud-logging operations are not dramatically altered in horizontal applications, mud logging is very cost effective with the basic mud-gas monitoring being a direct indicator of drilled rock porosity and hydrocarbon saturation. Advanced gas traps and customized interpretive software have been developed. Sophisticated logging while drilling capabilities exist, but operators must beware considering them the answer. Critically evaluate whether they are needed, keeping in mind the "keep it simple" principle.

Evaluation And Production Logging

After drilling, conventional wire line-logging assemblies can be pushed (tools won't fall with the hole angles above 60°) into the lateral with pipe or tubing. Data are transmitted by conventional wire line. Wellbore imaging tools have become very popular, particularly in fracture identification, bedding orientation, etc. Note that it has been observed that both drilling induced and natural fractures are much more common than was thought based on vertical well evaluation.

Production logging tools are most often conveyed by coil tubing. Technology has advanced rapidly with larger tubes, improved modeling, quality assurance, etc. Fluid phase segregation, wellbore undulation, relatively low in-flow velocities, tool centralization, inflow fluxing, and cross flow all dramatically complicate data interpretation. A common misinterpretation is that the majority of inflow is coming from the heel. Spinner and density logs that work well in vertical applications are only marginal in horizontals. Vendors are developing new "vane-type" tools designed to identify the degree of phase segregation, occurrence of phase override, and other dynamics with multiphase fluids. For many reasons, segment testing, for which new tools are being introduced, is becoming accepted as the most reliable production logging method.

Completion Design

Completion design starts in the curved section of the well with respect to the hole size and procedures employed to construct and case or isolate the non-productive curve. In general, it is recommended that the curve be drilled into the target and immediately cased in the first horizontal well in a field. Completion designs can range from open hole through conventionally cased, cemented, perforated and gravel-packed. Outside North America slotted-liner completions have been common, but they are losing favour because of inherent difficulty in defining the condition of free space behind the liner or the inability to impact this free space (i.e., water shutoff, stimulation). Globally, industry is becoming more comfortable with the integrity and flexibility of open-hole completions.

Damage is a major failure mechanism in horizontals. Effective cutting removal is critical, particularly in finer/tighter applications. Pipe/fluid surging and ECD effects are amplified in horizontals. Drilling fluid damage is an obvious focus. There is no substitute for core tests to evaluate damage mechanisms and optimize drill-in and clean-up/ stimulation fluids. Special steps and contingencies can be employed to minimize the perceived risk of coring in horizontal wells. Stiff coring assemblies must be short enough to make the curve.

CDX'S "Pinnate" Drilling Process

"Pinnate" drilling technique is best applied in thick, low permeable coals that have good lateral continuity. It's so-named because the final drilling pattern resembles the veins of a leaf and the system begins with two closely-spaced (within 20 ft) vertical wells: one well serves as an air injection well early in the project and then as a producing well; and the second well serves as the horizontal and service wellbore.

Air injected into the cavity through the first well forces fluid and sediment up the second well to the surface. Once this is done, the first well becomes a producing well. The horizontal leg continues to be drilled from the second well, usually reaching a length of 4,800 feet before the drilling stops and the drill bit begins to be retracted. As the drill bit is retracted along this main lateral, side laterals are drilled at 45° angles to the main and 90° to each other. This drilling of side laterals continues as the drill bit is retracted all the way to the vertical producing well. Each successive side lateral is longer than the previous hole, resulting in an essentially square drainage area.

After the first quad is drilled, second, third, and fourth mains can be drilled from the horizontal service well, and side laterals can be drilled along each as the drill bit is retracted toward the dual well system. Early in the development stage of this technique, three additional vertical production wells were drilled, with each being intersected by a horizontal main. Now a 360°-pattern can be drilled using only three vertical wells, not five or even eight as before. The final 360°-pattern drains 1,280 acres and replaces 16 vertical wells, while providing uniform drainage and pressure depletion. The environmental impact is significantly reduced as well. These patterns can be expanded to drain more than 2,000 acres, and can be developed in more than one coal seam in the same area, using the same producing and service wells.

Coiled Tubing Technology

Coiled tubing has been well accepted as a cost-effective alternative for performing a number of downhole operations. It can also perform a variety of tasks on live wells without creating overbalanced conditions that risk formation damage, which is a significant advantage over conventional technologies. Several following advancements in coiled tubing design have made it a more attractive option

- Better metallurgy has resulted in higher tensile strengths and resistance to buckling, better properties for welding, and stronger resistance to corrosion (coatings also are available).
- Improved manufacturing methods and quality control have led to better products at a lower price.
- The availability of more size options (¾ in to 4½ in) and lengths (up to 3,500 ft) have opened up a wider variety of applications.
- Coiled-tubing drilling can be done safely and effectively with conventional rigs in vertical, deviated, and horizontal wells. The development of large diameter (larger than 2 inches) tubing provides strength to resist buckling and higher capacity to transport the mud volume required for drilling motors. Tubing with installed electric lines is used for steering downhole drilling.

As compared to the conventional drilling, the advantages of coiled tubing include: a greatly reduced risk of formation damage by fluid leakoff and fines migration by allowing underbalanced drilling. Coiled tubing also reduces time tripping in and out of the hole. Also, real-time, full-time readout of subsurface conditions allows better well control.

Coiled tubing production strings can be installed under pressure (*i.e.*, without killing the well), thus minimizing opportunities for formation damage. Other advantages include quicker installation and retrieval of strings (no connections to make or break) and easier downhole service access.

Coiled-tubing completions, stimulations, and workovers also have distinct advantages over conventional methods. Small- and intermediate-diameter coiled tubing in multifunction strings with electric lines have applications in well logging, well testing, and other tool conveyance, especially in horizontal wells. Stimulation with coiled tubing can be performed underbalanced (e.g., removing scale mechanically followed by solvent cleanup) or under highly overbalanced conditions for perforating existing skin damage.

Workovers and repairs performed with coiled tubing on both vertical and non-vertical wells are feasible under no-kill conditions when operating underbalanced. Further advantages include the ability to easily and accurately place well treatments, to set hydraulic packers, and to perform straddle-packer treatments. It is easier to perform well-head replacements, set/retrieve plugs, test casing pressure, address vertical extensions, and do cleanouts.

Coiled tubing usage in pipelines, flowlines, and highpressure injection lines also can be economic. Design life and flow characteristics are good. Long lengths with fewer welds mean fewer X-ray inspection steps and faster installation. With less equipment, the overall environmental impact is reduced. Coiled tubing is pre-hydro-tested and inspected for corrosion.

Windows-based software is available to help design successful applications of coiled tubing. This software addresses:

The prediction of flow characteristics in wells and tubing, including flow rates and pressure losses; tubing force and stress analysis for run-in and runout and for a number of in-situ operations; and cleanout analysis for predicting circulation of particulate matter to the surface.

New Logging Tools and Techniques Key to Enhanced Recovery

Even for operators with substantial expertise in traditional wireline logging technologies, it is difficult to monitor advances and stay abreast of the new tools and methods that could substantially affect the bottom line. Logging technology has advanced rapidly. New specialized tools can measure previously unobtainable reservoir rock and reservoir/

borehole fluid properties. Also, the capability to accurately and efficiently collect, analyze, and interpret the tool response data has greatly increased.

Wireline logging is the major technology available to quantitatively and qualitatively describe the architectural, rock, and fluid properties of the subsurface reservoir. The same logs, interpreted by different professionals, provide a range of information. Geophysicists determine depths, boundaries, and rock/ fluid properties. Geologists study formation tops, environments of deposition, the types and amounts of hydrocarbons present, and potential production and reserves. Engineers examine wellbore irregularities, pay thickness/ uniformity, the best depths to set packers for testing, ideal completion intervals to maximize hydrocarbon and minimize water production, recommended completion techniques, and volume of cement needed.

Among the more important new technologies are the formation microimaging tools (for identifying the presence of fractures and sedimentary structures) and the nuclear magnetic resonance tools (for identifying the type and movability of reservoir fluids).

With the advent of highly deviated and horizontal wellbores, operators can more efficiently contact and produce hydrocarbons. However, technologies that work for measuring multiphase flow behaviour and determining flow profiles in vertical wells do not yield good results in highly deviated wellbores. The gravitational segregation of phases (oil, water, and natural gas) in horizontal and undulating wellbores is responsible for the problem. New flowmeter instrumentation and interpretation techniques relying on arrays of capacitors now allow the measurement of flow regime, holdups (i.e., phase thicknesses/proportions in the volume of the borehole), and phase velocities across the wellbore. Data from the new tools are combined with data from spinner, pressure, temperature, and nuclear measurement to determine the optimal levels.

For many operators, getting the log data in digital or raster format is the first step. New options for handling data have become available. NeuraLog's digitizing system—a neural network-based software that transforms scanned paper images into usable digital data—is one solution. An essential quality control feature is the onscreen comparison of scanned data with the original scanned image.

The enhanced processing of wireline log data enables more accurate interpretations of reservoir conditions, but additional insights are gained through digital processing and data handling capabilities. For example, a combination of new induction tools with the multiple depths of investigation and advanced data processing is enabling more accurate location of thin pays in interbedded sections. During logging runs, new digital communication capabilities allow critical decision-making based on real-time analysis of logging data. This is done using surface processing facilities, which broadcast encrypted, real-time data to the home office.

In mature reservoirs, the importance of a reservoir-wide approach to log analysis, rather than on a well-by-well basis, cannot be overemphasized. This is required to gauge overall reservoir productivity, determine communicating volumes within the reservoir, target new opportunities, and tailor specific recovery strategies.

New features of the PfEFFER spreadsheet multiwell log analysis software include movable oil plots and forward modeling capabilities for petrophysical properties.

DeepWave (Fluid Pulsation) Technology

The proven DeepWave (fluid pulsation) technology uses pulsed fluids to enhance both production and injection. It has shown to be effective in all types of geological formations, including consolidated and unconsolidated sediment, sedimentary soils, and fractured rock. It can enhance production from waterfloods, light and heavy oils, and is applicable in wells of any depth and angle from vertical to horizontal.

Production response to earthquakes has been well documented. In 1999, Lost Hills, California, responded with a 16 per cent production over several months following an earthquake. Similar responses have been seen in Kern and Northridge fields. The DeepWave technology is a large energy controllable pulse placed in the reservoir through either jointed pipe or coiled tubing. The applications include an add-on to waterflood injectors to improve sweep efficiency, well intervention, improved water disposal rates, and ground water remediation. The theory dates back 20 years and the initial field demonstration took place in 1998. To date, 150 single well and 5 field-wide applications have taken place.

The Double Displacement Process (DDP) Using Air Injection

In a water-drive oil reservoir, the oil-water contact (OWC) moves upstructure as depletion occurs. Near depletion there is a large water-swept oil zone with oil saturation near residual oil saturation. In a dipping light oil reservoir, upstructure air injection can improve oil recovery in two ways: (1) air injection can raise reservoir pressure increasing production rates and (2) gas displacement of water from a water-invaded oil column can mobilize a fraction of residual oil. Laboratory corefloods indicate that more than 50 per cent of residual oil to water can be mobilized. This mobilized oil moves downstructure via gravity drainage to down structure producers.

The DDP was demonstrated in the West Hackberry Field (Cam C-1 sand, Reservoir A) in Louisiana in the mid 1990s in a DOE-supported Class I field demonstration project. Goal was to inject 4 MMSCFD of air at 4,300 psig maximum surface pressure. High-pressure air injection requires special design and operation practices to deal with the ignition/combustion hazards. It is critical that air and hydrocarbons should not mix in the surface equipment and in the injection wells. In the reservoir, ignition with low-temperature oxidation actually occurs.

In West Hackberry in July-1996 when air injection began, production from four producers had declined to about 225 bopd with a 50 per cent water cut. Response to air injection occurred quickly with production rising to 250 bopd over normal decline. By December 1997, more than 70,000 bbls of incremental oil was produced.

The physics of the technology lies in the dynamic excitation device that creates a fluid displacement wave that is propagated down the arteries into the capillaries. The rise time of the pulse is short with a longer fall time. This results in an elastic response that expands the aperture, which leads to accelerated flow and greater overall distribution of injected liquids. Unlike pressure injection, it is not affected by high permeability channels. Laboratory injectivity tests show it to be effective in water-wet reservoirs, and particularly effective in oil-wet reservoirs. It can be applied to the reservoir with pinpoint accuracy to maximize the results. A typical stimulation would be applied through coiled tubing at a rate of 1 barrel/min, generating 1,000 to 1,200 psi amplitude waves at 17 pulses per minute.

A case study was presented of a naturally fractured shale in California with 600 feet of net pay. Other stimulation techniques had been tried in the area with poor results. A DeepWave service tool was used to apply 12,000 gallons of FE acid and 25,000 gallons of 12 per cent HCL/3 per cent HF acid. Daily production before treatment was 7 barrels of oil and 144 barrels of water. After treatment, production was 22 barrels of oil and 117 barrels of water.

A second case study was presented of a well in Oklahoma. Initial production was 1.7 MMCF/Day and 50 barrels of water. Within three weeks, production had fallen to 0 MCF/Day and 225 barrels of water, and was constrained by sand. The DeepWave tool was used in conjunction with temperature-activated chemicals for sand consolidation and water shut off. Five months following the treatment, the well was still economical.

Single-Well Cyclic CO_2 (Huff & Puff) Injection

Cyclic CO_2 injection consists of injecting a slug of CO_2, allowing it to soak for a period of time, and then placing the well back on production. Production interruption during the soak period is more than made up for with stimulated production when the well is brought back on line following the soak period. Production may decline rapidly, approaching the preslug after a period of time. At this point (or sooner), the process is repeated—thus termed cyclic. There are three major recovery mechanisms: oil swelling, viscosity reductions and decreasing water saturation near the wellbore. There may be additional benefits from injection increasing the bottom hole pressure, which increases the rate when the well is brought back on production. Compared to the full scale CO_2 flooding, much smaller amounts of CO_2 are involved and project life, even with multiple cycles, is shorter. If there is poor inter-well communication, huff & puff is still feasible whereas actual field-scale flooding would be difficult.

In 1989, Louisiana State University compiled a database of field results with CO_2 huff & puff treatments. Data from 106 projects in 12 fields were collected. Oil gravities ranged from 23° to 38° API; pressures ranged from 100 to 4,450 psia; and depths ranged from 1,200 to 13,000 ft. The entire spectrum of primary reservoir drive mechanisms was represented in the database.

82 per cent of the projects were deemed successful. Not surprisingly, the more CO_2 that was injected, the higher the incremental oil production with a fairly good correlation evident. Slug volumes are designed to limit undesirable interference with other wells. The higher the swelling factor, the higher the incremental oil production. The swelling depends upon oil composition with heavier oils swelling less. All other conditions being equal, higher production is seen as pay thickness increases. The longer the soak period, up to a point, the higher the incremental recovery.

Reservoir simulation can be used to predict performance. Since success is not that sensitive to reservoir heterogeneity, reservoir description need not be extensive. This is attractive considering that data may not be available or the time and effort for detailed description would not be warranted for economically marginal reservoirs.

Mapping, Locating, and Recovering By-Passed Hydrocarbons

Fluid distribution and saturation are largely a function of petrophysical properties. Their understanding is fundamental to the predicting location of by-passed hydrocarbons through reservoir simulation. Single-phase petrophysical properties include porosity, permeability, permeability-porosity relationships, and the tensorial character of permeability. These are all engineering properties, as opposed to geologic or geophysical, because they are needed for flow calculations. Single-phase porosity is an important predictor of hydrocarbon in place. Permeability is an indicator of production rate. They form a central part of the input to numerical simulators. Single-phase properties and their distributions allow geology and geophysics to be inserted into such models.

Two-phase flow properties include capillary pressure, relative permeability, and trapped phase saturation. Local heterogeneity (sorting), ratio of pore throats to pore bodies, and wetting state play large roles in quantifying two-phase flow properties. Some two-phase properties have analogs in single-phase flow. Saturation is an analog to porosity and phase permeability is an analog to permeability. Two-phase properties are more complex than in single-phase flow because saturation is introduced and surface or interfacial forces play a central role.

Interfacial forces, as manifest in capillary pressures, are the strongest local forces in multiphase flow. Capillary pressure is the most basic rock-fluid characteristic in multiphase flow. It is a function of interfacial tension (a fluid property), the pore radius (a medium property), and contact angle (a property of both). Because of this mixing and because it is a static property, capillary pressure provides a unique insight into the interrelationships between fluid and rock properties. An Insightful interpretation of capillary pressures can greatly aid in understanding the fluid distribution within a reservoir. Capillary pressure curves give us important information about heterogeneity through the distinction between pore throats and bodies and through the variable pore throat size. The curves can give us information about oil in place, local rock properties, and imbibition into fractures.

Relative permeability curves and their associated parameters are the most relevant petrophysical relations for oil displacement. Relative permeability in a two-phase system is the permeability of one of the phases compared to the total permeability. The values can range from 0 to 1.0. Relative permeabilities largely depend upon fluid saturations and the wetting state of the medium.

Moving Domain

Thomas Hampton from Holditch - Reservoir Technologies introduced "*Moving Domain*," a method that uses a mosaic of computer-automated and linked production studies, and derives empirical and statistical conclusions about individual wells and field performance. The purpose of Moving Domain is to rapidly process field-wide production datasets in order to make profit-enhancing recommendations about current wells and about infill drilling options. Areas for application of this method include infill and stepout well potential, scoping studies, production projections, stimulation evaluation, completion optimization, and others.

Moving Domain analysis workflow includes calculation of "Production Indicators" for each well. Production indicators are statistically analyzed as a function of time and then are used to compare wells. An Evidence of depletion is found by comparing new and old wells. Using this methodology, infill wells can be spotted and their recovery potential can be quantified because undrained areas can be identified.

Moving Domain is useful for large datasets from complex reservoirs and when rapid analysis is required. It can rely solely on public data, if necessary. Required data include at least latitude/longitude and monthly production for each well. More advanced analysis requires petrophysical data, such as porosity, permeability, and initial pressure. The software used in Moving Domain is all PC - based: Visual Basicä programming, Accessä database, Excelä, PROMATä, and Geographixä for mapping results.

Accurate 3-D Geologic Modeling

An important aspect of locating bypassed hydrocarbons is accurate 3-D geologic modeling. Jeffrey Schwalm and John Penny of Dynamic Graphics, Inc. discussed some of the latest techniques for 3-D geologic modeling using software called "EARTH VISION." The methodology uses a natural order of modeling to yield a plausible 3-D geological model that honors geologic and geophysical interpretations. The 3-D geologic model can then be used as a common earth model from which numeric and visual outputs can be generated.

Using input from geology, geophysics, petrophysics, maps, cross sections, etc., the workflow is accomplished in five steps: (1) determining data range and projection of the model area, (2) modeling faults in 2-D or 3-D grids, (3) modeling horizons as a stratigraphic sequence, (4) modeling rock properties, and (5) generating output. Output consists of contour maps, cross sections, and volumetric computations that can be sent directly to the reservoir simulator.

Nonparametric Statistics

The Spearman rank correlation coefficient has been investigated as a reservoir characterization tool. The technique is a nonparametric statistics, used to determine lateral autocorrelation and permeability trends. It provides an alternative to interference tests. The method can indicate the presence of transmissibility barriers, permeability anisotropy, and, in some instances, range anisotropy. The method appears to be successful as measured by consistency with tracer breakthrough. However, additional research comparing this technique with accurate field results still seems necessary to provide more confidence on Spearman rank correlation coefficient applicability.

4

Wellsite Validation

Whether acquired through surface readout in real-time or by downhole recorders, data must be validated at the wellsite. Validation ensures that the acquired data are of adequate quality to satisfy the test objectives. On-site validation also serves as a yardstick for measuring job success. When used with surface readout in real time, wellsite validation reveals when sufficient data have been acquired to terminate the test, thereby optimizing rig time.

Examining the acquired transient data in a log-log plot of the pressure change and its derivative versus elapsed time is the focus of wellsite validation. If the downhole flow rate and pressure are measured at the same time as the bottomhole pressure, the convolution derivative is also plotted.

On-site validation can be complemented by a preliminary estimation of the formation parameters accomplished using specialized plots such as a generalized superposition or Horner plot (pressure data alone) or a sandface rate-convolution plot (downhole rate and pressure data). These plots are used for computing formation parameters such as kh, the near-wellbore value of s and the extrapolated pressure at infinite shut-in time p^*.

Figure shows the validation of a test conducted using a surface pressure readout configuration, followed by an early estimation of formation parameters. The validation plot at the top of the figure shows that infinite-acting radial flow was reached during the test. The superposition (or generalized Horner) plot shown on the bottom has the pressure plotted on the y-axis and the multirate (or superposition) time function on the x-axis. The selected straight-line portion (highlighted) corresponds to where the derivative is flat. Its intersection with the y-axis defines p^*, and kh and s can be calculated from the slope.

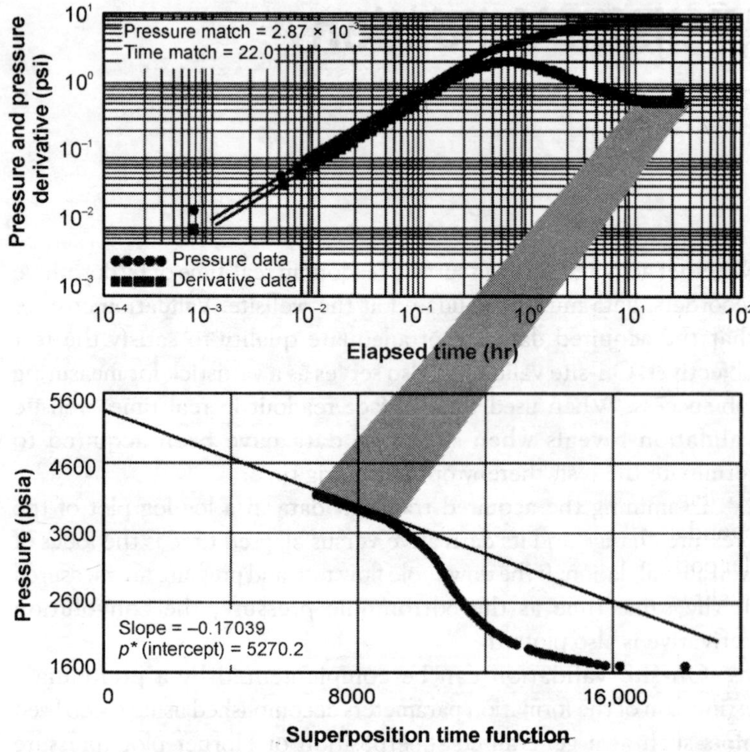

Figure shows the log-log plot of a DD test with transient downhole flow rate and pressure data. The plot also shows the convolution derivative curve. This curve accounts for flow rate variations during the transient, which cannot be interpreted using pressure data alone. It is particularly useful in this example because the changes in flow rate during the test resulted in a pressure derivative curve with a complete lack of character, precluding any estimation of the reservoir parameters. However, the convolution derivative contains enough information to enable parameter estimation. It also suggests that part of the tested interval was not open to flow. A flow profile run at the end of the test confirmed this hypothesis.

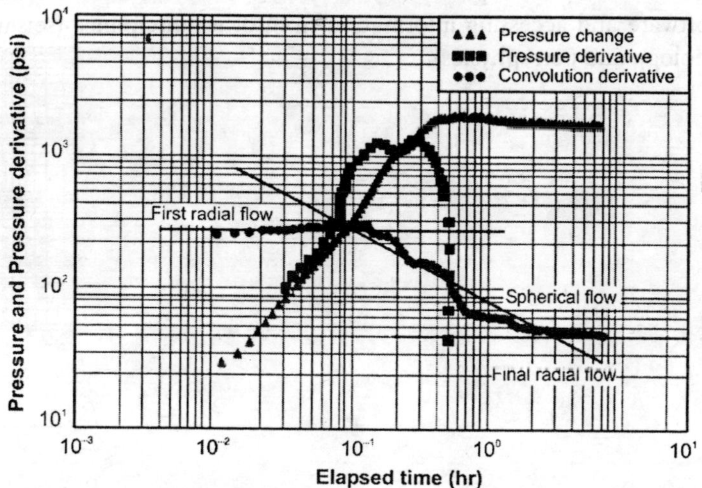

Figure shows a validation plot for a test dominated by outer-boundary effects. Like previous Figure, this dataset does not exhibit a flat portion in the derivative curve. However, the data are of excellent quality and can be interpreted by type-curve matching.

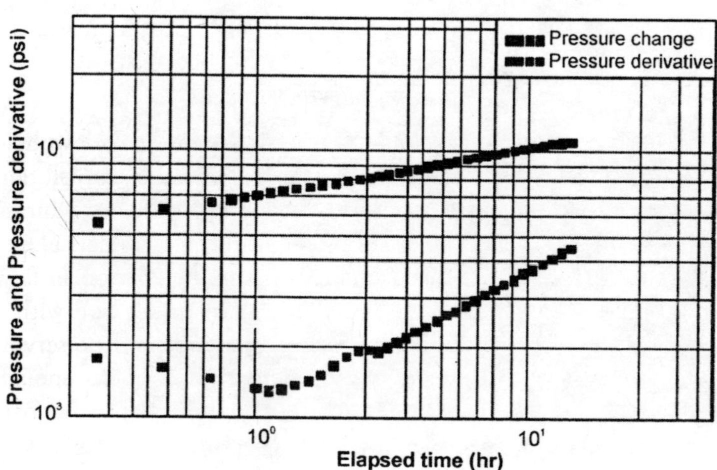

A complete analysis of these data types requires detailed modeling techniques. The best results are realized when the interpretation is conducted by an expert analyst, using sophisticated well testing software and accessing information from other disciplines (seismic, geology, and petrophysics).

5

Cross Well with Core Study

One of the most promising oil recovery technologies to emerge in recent years is carbon dioxide (CO_2) injection with intermittent water injection, called WAG (water-alternating-gas). The downside of CO_2 injection is the high cost of obtaining CO_2, building infrastructure, and separating t he CO_2 from produced oil for reinjection. For the process to be economical, a reservoir must contain substantial reserves, the geology must be well understood, and the mobilized oil must be tracked and produced to recover the CO_2.

A second important development is the emergence of crosswell geophysical technologies for inter-well reservoir characterization and recovery monitoring. These techniques have proven invaluable for tracking subsurface fluid movements from injection and production. The crosswell technologies provide physical property images at a scale similar to that of reservoir simulation models, which is crucial for having a direct impact on production.

The crosswell electromagnetic (EM) method is interesting because of its high sensitivity to reservoir fluids.

The biggest challenge to the widespread use of this technology is its ability to propagate and measure EM signals through steel well casing.

Case Study 1

First step in designing a crosswell system for the Permian Basin conditions was to make preliminary field tests in Texaco's Vacuum Oil Field with the existing prototype field system, the XBH2000.

The Vacuum Oil Field lies in the western part of the 200,000 square mile Permian Basin oil province located in west Texas and New Mexico. The Permian contains many oil and gas fields, and it has produced more than 30 billion barrels of oil since its discovery, during water well drilling, in the early 1920s. At its peak, the basin produced more than 2 million barrels of oil and 5 billion cubic feet of gas per day, from more than 100 individual fields.

Oil and gas production in the Permian Basin has been declining since the early 1970s.

Although most fields are on water flood to maintain pressure, a few of the larger fields are also injecting CO_2 gas to boost production. Miscible CO_2 injection has been shown to be effective in a number of fields due to the nature of the CO_2 interaction with oil. CO_2 naturally forms a continuous phase with oil that lowers the viscosity and eases flow to producers. The gas also penetrates in many areas where water cannot access the oil, thereby accessing bypassed pockets. In many fields, the CO_2 injection is alternated with water injection, a process known as Water Alternating Gas or WAG, to "push" the CO_2 toward the producing well.

The flow of the injected CO_2 is unpredictable, because its flow properties depend on whether there is oil, water, or gas in its flow path as on well as the location and orientation of fractures in the reservoir.

EM Field Test at Vacuum

For the test, analyst selected a triangular grouping of three vertical wells. Two of the wells are steel-cased and separated about 1,200 ft. The third well, which is uncased below 4,100 ft, is about 850 ft from the other two wells. These tests would allow them to collect crosswell EM data between two open-steel well pairs and one steel-steel. Although analysts were incapable of interpreting these data from the latter well pairs, the data were useful for establishing signal and noise levels. In addition, the well pairs would provide different angles to the theoretical flow stream directions of the previous waterflood pattern.

They first pulled production tubing from production well VGSA57 and packers from injection wells VGSA150 and VGSA157. They then swabbed all wells to remove obstructions. The wells were then fitted with blowout preventers to eliminate the flow of fluids or gasses to the surface. All geophysical deployments were made using isolation lubricators and well packoffs. During the survey, however, the wells did not re-pressurize and analysts were able to log during relatively benign conditions.

Measurements were made between production well VGSA57, which is an uncased producer in the main reservoir (4000-4700 ft), and steel-cased injection wells 150 and 157. The well separations were approximately 220 m (~700 ft) for both well pairs.

The logged section (4000-4600 ft) has an average resistivity of more than 50 ohm-m and several intervals that exceed 1000 ohm-m. The higher resistivities usually indicate impermeable limestone and dolomite sections, or regions of high oil saturation.

The wells show a fair-to-poor degree of continuity and the resistivity values can change by more than 50 per cent for correlatable intervals. This suggests substantial variation in formation properties, fracture density, or fluid saturation. The challenge for the crosswell EM data is to interpret data in an area where the formation resistivity is very high. The inductive formation signal is directly proportional to the frequency and inversely proportional to its resistivity. The steel well casing forces anlyst to use lower frequency transmission thereby reducing formation response and the high resistivity reduces the response even further. Analysts estimate that the formation response for these conditions is only about 5 per cent of the total measured field. This compares to a response of more than 50 per cent for many open hole surveys and it constitutes a significant obstacle for the generation of high-resolution images. After some initial start-up problems, the surveys proceeded smoothly. Data quality for the survey was, in general, good. Considering that injection and production wells can often induce substantial tool noise as a result of fluid-induced motion, the data collected in these wells were surprisingly quiet. Analyst did full tomography for both well pairs in the interval from 3950 to 4600 ft. The data also suggested a noise level for the system of about 10 microvolts for the vertical sensors and about 30 microvolts for the horizontal sensor. With these conditions, it should be possible to acquire useful crosswell data with the new system to well separations of 2,000 ft or more.

Crosswell EM data were collected using analyst three-component sensor package. This tool measures the vertical and two horizontal components of the field originating at the transmitter. It is a high-resolution measurement of the field that can produce better quality images than the single component (vertical) receiver but it is much slower to deploy. Analysts chose to deploy it in these wells because analyst objective is to measure downhole conditions and attempt to produce one or two high-quality images. The plots indicate a good quality dataset for the vertical sensor and noisier profiles from the horizontal sensors. This profile is typical of the data quality during the survey at 24 Hz. Notice that when the transmitter enters the base of the casing string, above a depth of 4050ft, the fields dramatically decrease but the system is still able to recover them. This bodes well for future surveys to be made with the newer more powerful system.

Data Interpretation

The data processing consisted of first editing the files to remove spikes and outliers, then adjusting the data for the casing effect using the borehole logs and a single point in the profiles to make the adjustment. The data are then combined into a single file for the data inversion. These data are interpreted by fitting the observed data to model derived data for a 2D model. In this process, cover case analysts first derive a starting model from the logs and/or geology and adjust this model until the misfit is within a given tolerance, usually 2-3 per cent. Analyst note that in this case, well VGSA57 did not have a resistivity log available; so the interwell section was constructed assuming that an interwell extrapolation of the resistivity log from well VGSA150 was a good first guess at the interwell resistivity. After 15 iteration of the inverse code, the misfit was reduced from about 8 per cent to about 3 per cent. Analysts notice that most of the formation information, at these low frequencies, reside in the imaginary field component so the 10 per cent data fit means that the image resolution is low to moderate. The section indicates that the formation resistivity ranges between 50 and 500 ohm-m which is very high for a typical oil field, but perhaps typical of a Permian Basin field. Analysts notice that at the right margin, the section agrees with the one log that analysts have available in well 150. This indicates that the oil-bearing zone has a relatively high resistivity, dips from well VGSA57 toward well VGSA150, which is in accord with the geological models.

Analysts find that the resistivity and porosity sections agree in the dip and overall structure in this part of the field, and the zones of highest porosity (red on plots) match with the higher resistivity (red-yellow) horizons in the resistivity section. The lower resistivity interval is typically 80-150 ohm-m sandy intervals that correspond to lower porosity formation. These depths are typically at the base of the section, within the producing upper San Andreas section. Although the attached model is reasonable and fairly consistent with the geology, the resolution is fairly low and the match of calculated to the observed secondary field data is worse than 10 per cent in several intervals. Analysts feel that the residual noise in the secondary field component is prohibiting a closer data fit and therefore limiting the confidence of this final model. Unfortunately, analyst feels that this is the limit of this technology with the older field system. One important result from this test was to establish the noise level of the system in this environment and, to analyst surprise and delight, it is quite low. Analysts were able to collect and fit field data at signal levels that approached the predicted sensor noise, about 50 picoteslas. Analysts feel that the results of this survey is a very encouraging sign for the future deployment if X2C. If the noise level of future surveys is similar to the present survey then the new instrumentation will allow us to collect better quality data at a higher frequency. In addition, it appears that analyst ambitious goal of crosswell EM in two steel cased wells separated by 500m is now possible.

Notes from the Tests at Vacuum Field from these tests, the following information became clear:

- The transmitter power and/or receiver sensitivity of the XBH2000 system was inadequate. Data collection was made at low frequency (24 Hz), and this made high-resolution imaging impossible due to the high background resistivity. A frequency of 100 Hz is the minimum acceptable which would require a signal to noise increase of approximately a factor of 5.

- The noise level of the deep measurements was surprisingly small, about 10 microvolts (or 50 picoteslas).
- Tool reliability was a major issue in this field, as the client often must remove the production tubing. The breakdown frequency of the XBH2000 system was unacceptably high.

Development of an Advanced Crosswell EM System

A primary goal of this case study is to develop a new high-power high-sensitivity crosswell EM system designed for oil field conditions, where well spacings are moderate to large and most wells are steel-cased. More specifically, the system would be designed for CO_2 injection well field patterns in the Permian Basin. Design objectives for the system are 2,000 ft.

Crosswell EM

The crosswell EM method is designed to map the interwell resistivity distribution in a 2-D (or 3-D) sense. These data can be used to characterize reservoirs structurally and stratigraphically as well as to track ongoing processes where pore fluid is replaced or moved. A crosswell EM field system consists of a transmitter tool deployed in one well and a receiver tool deployed in a second well located up to 3,000 ft from the source well. The tools are connected with surface wire telemetry and deployed with standard wireline equipment. By positioning both the transmitter and the receiver tools over a vertical interval roughly equal to the well spacing analyst can achieve adequate coverage for tomographic imaging. The depths must include positions above, below, and within the zone of interest for an effective tomographic interpretation of the resistivity distribution between the wells. The tools are typically deployed at depth intervals of 2 to 5 per cent of the well spacing, which is also roughly equal to the image resolution.

Analyst field instrumentation uses downhole electronics and computers for signal generation and data acquisition. The recent placement of source and receiver electronics downhole, instead of at the surface, has resulted in very accurate and efficient data collection using standard wireline equipment. Analysts use small surface stations, at both the tranmsitter and the receiver sites, for communication and power supply and a laptop computer to control the acquisition and log the data.

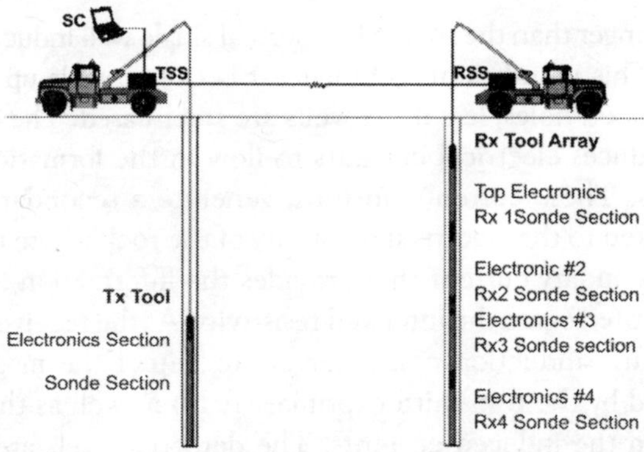

Figure 5.1: Schematics of crosswell EM.

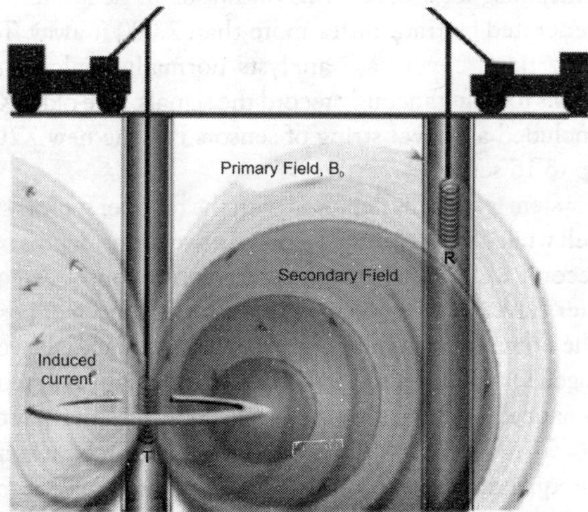

Figure 5.2: Interwell tomography, showing secondary field generation.

The transmitter antenna is a vertical-axis magnetically permeable core wrapped with several hundred turns of wire and driven to broadcast a continuous monochromatic sinusoidal signal at frequencies from 10 Hz to 2 kHz. The frequency selection depends upon the borehole environment (steel-casing or open hole), the well separation, and the formation resistivity. Steel well-casing, larger well separation, and low formation resistivity necessitate the use of lower frequencies. The transmitter generates a magnetic field that is more than 100,000 times stronger than the source in a normal single well induction logging system. This is sufficient to broadcast between wells up to 2,000 ft apart in open holes, less if the wells are steel-cased. The transmitter signal induces electrical currents to flow in the formation between the wells. These currents, in-turn, generate a secondary magnetic field related to the electrical resistivity of the rock where they flow. It is this secondary current that provides the information that analyst seeks to interrogate the interwell resistivity. At the receiver borehole, analysts use induction coil receivers to detect the magnetic field generated by the transmitter (primary field) as well as the magnetic field from the induced currents. The detection coils are extremely sensitive devices consisting of many thousands of turns around high permeability magnetic cores; this allows us to accurately measure signals generated by transmitter more than 2,000 ft away. To reduce the logging time, cover case analysts normally deploy a string of receiver coils to simultaneously record the signals. The older XBH2000 system included a 4-level string of sensors but the new X2C system allows up to 16 sensors.

The system is typically deployed with the receiver sensors stationary in one well while the transmitter moves between the depths of interest in the second well, broadcasting signal continuously. A completed transmitter traverse, or profile, is made for each receiver position. To reduce the noise, the incoming signals, which are normally very weak, are averaged several hundred times before sampling. This reduces the noise dramatically and also slows data collection. The transmitter moves at a rate of 5 to 30 ft per minute depending on the amount of averaging and the frequency of operation. After a complete profile is measured, the receivers are then repositioned and the process is repeated until all desired receiver positions are occupied. A typical crosswell deployment requires roughly 12-30 of field recording for a vertical section of 1000 ft. Data are typically averaged until they can be repeated to within 1 per cent or 2 per cent. The transmitter and receiver tools are linked together with a surface cable, which is used for phase synchronization, sending of commands, and collection of digital data streams. The logging is done at the transmitter location because at this site, the tool is moving during the logging, as opposed to the receiver side where it is stationary. The logging operation is controlled through the logging surface station and the laptop computer. Analysts notice that the operation requires two wireline units and a mast or crane at each well. All crosswell data are processed in the same manner. Analysts first edit the profiles to remove any spurious points, apply calibration corrections, and, if required, adjustments for steel casing and then resample the profiles using spline interpolation. The final edited dataset is then displayed in contour form to examine for tears or misties. This difference section is crucial for data quality control as well as to accurately position the tools in 3-D space. Errors in tool position are probably the largest single source of error in crosswell data. The crosswell EM data are interpreted by computer inversion. The interwell formation is divided into two-dimensional square blocks whose sides are 2—5 per cent of the well spacing. Analyst applies a two-dimensional inversion based on a finite difference forward code. Each block is assigned an electrical resistivity value, estimated from the borehole resistivity logs or known geology. The inversion code then modifies the resistivity of these blocks until the calculated and measured EM data agree to within a specified tolerance level. This is often related to measurement error, which is typically 1—3 per cent. This process usually requires 12—30 per dataset on a fast computer workstation to produce a detailed image of the underground strata. The resolution of the images is roughly 2—5 per cent of the well spacing. Analysts notice that the images produced by this process are not unique. That is, analyst could define a different resistivity distribution that might fit the data as well. By constraining the inversions with the borehole logs and a good knowledge of the geology, analyst can reduce this uncertainty dramatically.

Design of the X2C Field System, the X2C field system was designed to provide maximum power and sensitivity in a steel well-casing environment. X2C is an acronym for crosswell (X) EM through 2 steel casings (2C). The system was also designed for high reliability and straightforward deployment and make up, with full compatibility with other standard wireline tools. Analyst philosophy was to use the existing XBH2000 technology as a base and strive to make improvements in every aspect of tool performance and reliability. In particular, analyst made major efforts to maximize the source power in a steel-cased well, improve the receiver sensitivity in a steel-casing, and to improve system dynamic range and data collection software.

In addition, analyst has also incorporated technology to compensate collected data for steel well-casing thereby allowing data collection and interpretation in steel-cased wells. The system described below is a pre-commercial prototype that has been used in more than 30 surveys since its initial testing in 2002. At the present time, five field systems of the X2C are being read out for commercial operations in the US and worldwide market.

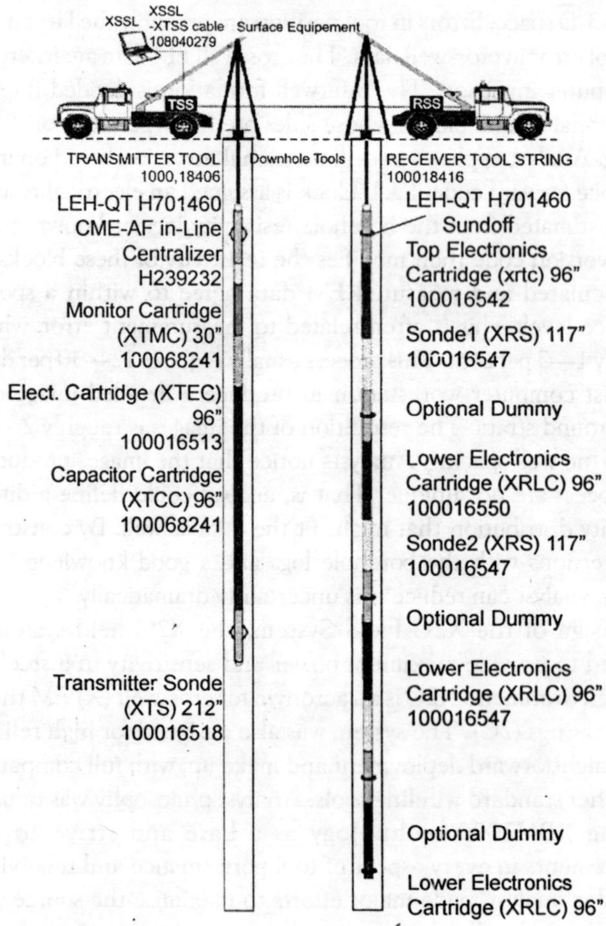

Figure 5.3: Schematic diagram of the X2C system.

Key components of this design are:

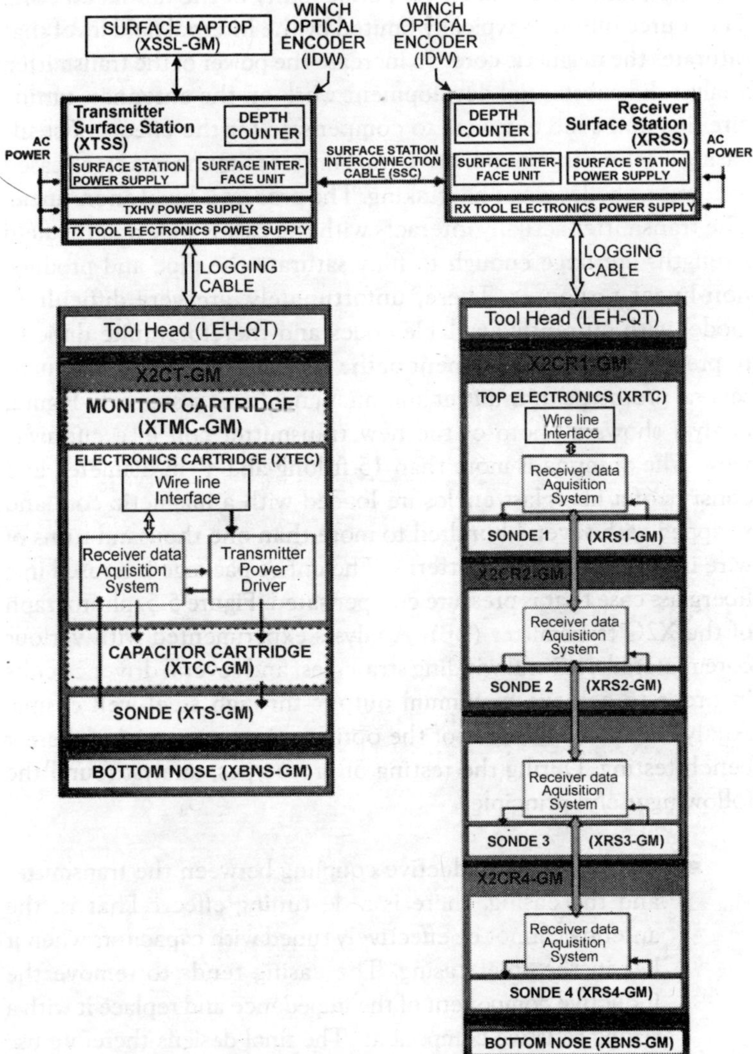

Figure 5.4: Block diagram of the X2C.

Transmitter Antenna and Driver The transmitter output is the product of the cross-sectional area of the inductive source, the number of windings on the core, the current flowing through the windings, and the 28 magnetic permeability of the mu-metal core. The source output is typically limited by the internal field level that saturates the magnetic core. To increase the power of the transmitter, analyst did substantial development work on the antennas, tuning circuits, and source drivers to compensate for the effects of steel-casing. Optimizing an inductive transmitter antenna in a steel-cased well was a challenging undertaking. The process is highly non-linear. The transmitter actually interacts with the casing pipe and the field strengths are large enough to fully saturate the pipe and produce non-linear responses. These, unfortunately, are very difficult to model with currently available codes and therefore quite difficult to predict. In the development of the system, analyst manufactured several prototype transmitter antennas and driver systems. In Figure, analyst shows a photo of the new transmitter coil in a cut-away view. The antenna is more than 15 ft long and 4" in diameter, and consists of a fiberglass enclosure loaded with a magnetic core and wrapped with several hundred to more than one thousand turns of wire in specific winding patterns. The entire package is housed in a fiberglass case that is pressure compensated. Figure 5.5. photograph of the X2C transmitter (BB). Analysts experimented with various core materials, several winding strategies, and several driver circuits in order to achieve maximum output through steel-well casing. Analyst actually did most of the optimization using trial and error bench testing. During the testing of prototypes, analyst found the following useful principles.

- Because of the inductive coupling between the transmitter and the casing, there is a de-tuning effect. That is, the antenna cannot be effectively tuned with capacitors when it lies in the steel-casing. The casing tends to remove the inductive component of the impedance and replace it with a strong resistive component. The final designs therefore use bare or untuned source coils.

  The EM source field is attenuated logarithmically with frequency in steel-casing. Analyst goal is to optimize the performance in the frequency range of 1-100 Hz, which provides an acceptable balance between casing attenuation and geologic resolution.

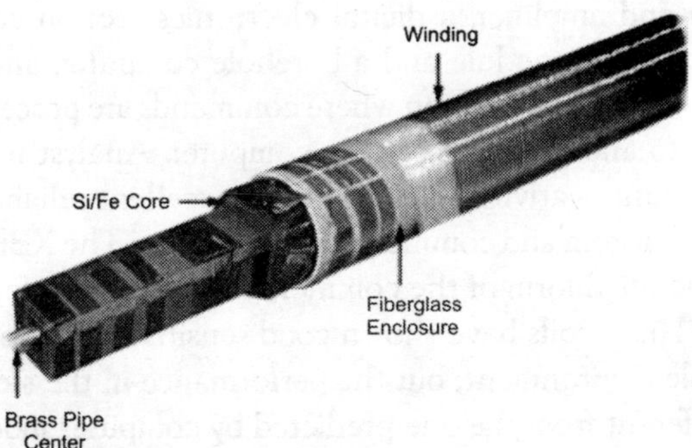

Figure 5.5: Photograph of the X2C transmitter (BB).

- After a series of tests, analysts found that the transmitter optimum core material has a large saturation limit but only a moderate magnetic permeability. The optimum moment is a unique combination of the core volume, the driver current, and the number of turns.

In an open hole, the X2C system is 20-40 times stronger than the XBH2000. This marked improvement was made by increasing the transmitter volume, increasing the voltage limit on the power supply and optimizing the number of turns to ensure that the casing core was fully saturated.

The power improvement supplied by the new transmitter in the open hole did not completely pass through into a cased hole environment. In steel-casing, the X2C system is approximately three times stronger than the XBH2000. Although smaller than anticipated, it will still provide a major improvement over the old system. The reasons for the much smaller improvement relates to the interaction between the transmitter windings and core and the steel-casing. Transmitter actually induces currents to flow in the casing pipe that cancel its own field. This effect varies with the casing properties, tool diameter, the current in the windings, and the properties of the core. The final design for the X2C transmitter was optimized from a series of tests through steel-casing.

Receiver Antenna and Amplifier

The receiver system consists of a sonde section, which contains the antenna and amplifier, a digital electronics section consisting of a data acquisition module and a borehole computer, and a telemetry and communication section where commands are processed and data are sent to and from the surface computer. Analyst induction coils have used innovative design and have excellent reliability in a wide variety of custom and commercial applications. The XBH2000 system uses a modified form of the commercial BF6 sensors for the receiver sondes. These coils have shown good sensitivity and reliability in an open hole environment, but the performance in the steel-casing has been different from the one predicted by computer models.

Figure 5.6: Photo of X2C receivers.

The goal of this project is to improve the sensitivity of the coils, to fully understand the effect of the casing and downhole noise, and to achieve a robust mechanical design that will survive hostile downhole conditions. Analysts designed three coils for operation in casing and four separate field amplifiers. The sensors featured two different cores and three different core windings. In a quiet environment, the new coils have up to a factor of 10 improvement in sensitivity over the receiver coils in XBH2000 system. After testing, these coils on the bench and in open and steel-cased wells during field tests, analyst found several surprising things.

- The coil sensitivity function depends somewhat on the casing. That is, the casing becomes part of the electronic circuit and the sensitivity is a function of the casing magnetic and electrical properties.
- At depths above 4,000 ft, the signal-to-noise ratio of the sensors mostly depends on the background noise. The coil sensitivity is a much less important function. Below these depths, the boreholes are normally quieter and the coil sensitivity is more important.
- The background noise in the borehole primarily consists of mechanical or vibration noise, and electrical noise from sources propagating down the casing or through the formation. In Figure, analysts show a noise spectrum for three prototype sensors measured at an operating southern California oil field. In the same plot, analysts show the theoretical BF6 magnetic sensor noise and the expected system noise. The plot shows a significant variation of sensor noise with the coil design although in all cases the measured noise was much in excess of the sensitivity of the BF6 coil. Analysts also note that the noise in a cased hole is considerably higher than in an open or in a fiberglass-cased well in the field at the same depth.

After considerable research in this area, analyst discovered that in applications shallower than 5,000 ft, the sensor used in the XBH2000 system was adequate; design improvements made with the X2C were mainly to improve thermal characteristics, manufacturing simplicity, and tool reliability. For deeper applications, the sensitivity achieved with the new system is worthwhile. These findings have changed the data acquisition strategy. It seems that the main constraint on the receiver side is the level of background noise. Analyst will therefore design the system to mitigate this noise. For this, analysts are testing three strategies.

- Smart-stacking software: If the time series data had impulse noise spikes related to shock or EM pulses, then the data will be contaminated. These spikes can often be recognized by software and deleted from the time series prior to data averaging and this will greatly reduce the error.
- Sensor string: If the noise distribution is random (Gaussian), then the only noise reduction possible is by averaging. Analyst can optimize data collection by simply adding more receivers to the string, improving electronic filters, and optimizing tool operation.
- Auxiliary sensors: It is also possible that much of the noise is acoustic and may be removed with an acoustic sensor. Here, analysts are testing the coherence of the EM noise to the signal from an acoustic sensor (accelerometer).

Data Acquisition System and Software in addition to the redesign of antenna and tool hardware, analyst also did an extensive redesign of the data acquisition system and the software. Chief goal here is to employ a 24-bit acquisition technology to improve system dynamic range to take full advantage of the sensor range. Analysts also wish to improve the signal averaging routines and reduce data overhead, so that more time is spent collecting data and less time in sending commands and data transmission. A second goal is to improve the reliability of electronic components, especially under conditions of high heat and vibration. Operating software for this system is a critical component not only for smooth data collection but also for optimizing the system performance. The software component consists of a firmware, or software resident in the tool, and a surface software that communicates to the borehole tool and to the other surface systems.

Final design configuration: The above provides an overview to the present working experimental prototype tool. This system has been used in more than 30 surveys worldwide, and has been effective in collecting data in a variety of field conditions and well casings. Analysts have, in fact, collected and interpreted data in dual steel-cased wells spaced up to 1,000 ft apart. Analysts expect that the optimization process to continue for several more years by which time analyst hope to expand the well spacing range to 2000 ft and improve the image resolution.

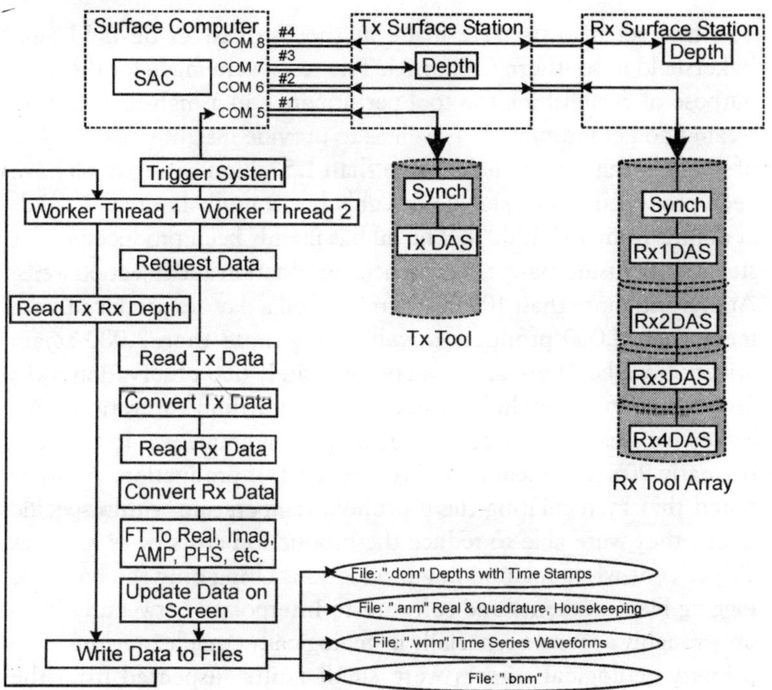

Figure 5.7: Block diagram of the X2C software.

Table 5.1:

	4" (Cased-Cased)	*3 3/8" (Open-Cased)*
Transmitter Moment (Air) A-m2	12,000	8,000
Transmitter Moment (Casing)	50-500	50-300
Receiver sensitivity (microG)	0.1	0.3
Effective sensitivity (micro G)	5-50	5-50
Effective Range (Open)	1 km	800 m
(Open-Steel)	700 m	500 m
(Dual Steel)	200 m	200 m
Frequency Range	1-200 Hz	1-1000 Hz
Pressure Rating	10,000 ft	10,000 ft
Temperature Rating	125 °C (250 C ft)	125 °C 250 C ft)

Steam Flood Monitoring at the Kern River Oil Field, Southern California

The first set of tests were made at the Kern River oil field near Bakersfield in southern California. The tests were made for the joint purpose of establishing the tool performance in a high-temperature steam flood environment, as well as to provide insight in to the flow of steam in this mature field. More than 1.5 billion barrels of oil have been produced from a stack of roughly horizontally layered oil sands at depths from 500-1500 ft. The oil has mainly been produced under steam drive, using many closely spaced production and injection wells. At present, more than 100,000 barrels of oil a day are produced from more than 4,000 production wells using more than 2,000 steam injection wells. There are also approximately 600 observation wells for monitoring downhole temperatures and fluid saturations. An aggressive steam and heat management programme was initiated in the early 90's as a means to lower the cost of production. Analysts found that by regulating the downhole temperature within specific limits, they were able to reduce the production costs by as much as 50 per cent while maintaining production. Using only the borehole logging measurements and software to interpolate between holes is only roughly accurate especially in geologically complex regions. The primary geological targets were small faults suspected from the borehole logs and geologic cross sections that may be redirecting the steam flow. A secondary goal was to use inferred resistivity variations to map zones where the temperature and fluid saturation levels are changing due to the steam flooding and fluid production. The EM tests were run episodically over a one-year period, in 2002 to 2003, using several of the temperature observation wells for tool deployment.

All data were collected in steel-cased observation wells. The wells used in the tomography were separated from 350 ft to more than 800 ft. Analysts typically logged the interval from 400 ft to 1200 ft, which covers the five primary pay zones in this part of the reservoir. Borehole temperatures ranged from ambient to more than 260 F in the steam-flooded zones. Crosswell logging proceeded slowly due to the noisy downhole conditions and the frequent tool breakdowns in this stage of tool development in these hot holes. With no breakdowns, a typical crosswell survey would require more than 30 for the logging because of the high background noise. At the shallow 400-1200 ft reservoir depths, the ambient noise in the boreholes was very high. This is likely due to the high level of surface activity in this very busy oilfield.

For two of the well pairs measured (RCA1-RCA2 and RCA1-RCA5), analysts obtain the data of very good quality.

Analysts obtain different images by keeping track of resistivity model adjustments made by the inverse code as it strives to match the observed data. If the initial model is a good representation of the interwell resistivity at the time that the wells were first logged, the model changes should reflect resistivity changes over time. For this case, analysts base the initial model on an interpolation of the borehole logs in the wells used in the tomography. In an area of fairly simple geology, such as Kern River, this interpolation is a reasonable estimate of the interwell resistivity.

At Kern River, where there has been significant local heating and large areas of desaturation, this difference display is invaluable as a guide to reservoir changes. Since there have been no baseline surveys made, it is only means of measuring changing reservoir conditions. In fact, analysts expect that much of the ongoing reservoir processes at Kern River to be visible with crosswell EM. From laboratory measurements, resistivity decreases of 40—60 per cent due to local heating are expected as the temperature changes from 80 F to more than 260 F in steam-flooded regions. Similarly, production-induced saturation effects will likely increase the resistivity, as fluid withdrawn is not completely replaced by injected fluid. A 40—80 per cent increase was expected for this latter process.

The arcuate shape of the low-resistivity zone that stretches from deep to shallow in the interwell space suggests that faulting may influence the steam flow. Analysts guess that a fault cross somewhere near 400 ft from well RCA2 may be helping to channel steam upward into the shallow section near well RCA1.

The difference image indicates several interwell areas where changes are occurring. For example, the image indicates a broad arcuate area, shallow near well RCA1, and deeper near well RCA2, where the resistivity has decreased by up to 50 per cent from the starting model. This level of change is consistent with a temperature increase caused by steam injection, and it suggests that a recent steam flooding is progressing to shallow depths near well RCA1.

The temperature log (well RCA1) indicates that the well has been heating up at depths from 400-600 ft in recent years. The position of the low-resistivity anomaly almost exactly matches the zone of increasing temperature measured at the observation well. The 50 per cent decrease is somewhat smaller that what analysts would expect from a temperature effect alone. Analysts suspect that oil and water are also being withdrawn from these depths, which would tend to change the resistivity in the other direction and therefore dampen the resistivity decrease. The repeated temperature log indicates that the temperature at these depths is stable, so analysts suspect that the resistivity increase is a saturation effect. The resistivity versus saturation function suggests that the observed resistivity increase of 30—50 per cent could be explained by a decrease in water saturation of 6—10 per cent. This suggests that the deeper portions of the section are desaturating due to production. That is, there is a net withdrawal of fluid (both water and oil) from these depths that is resulting in a higher formation resistivity. Analysts notice, however, that if the temperature falls, the resistivity will also increase, so it is difficult to distinguish between these alternatives without the temperature data.

In general, the resistivity section derived from the crosswell EM data replicates the log-based resistivity but at a lower resolution. Analysts notice significant differences between the section in the overlay cross-section. Some of the difference may be due to dropped detail, but most of difference between these sections is due to the formation resistivity changes that have occurred after the wells were drilled. That is, this part of the field is being actively produced and steamed so the resistivity is constantly changing, and these changes will not be reflected in the older logs.

The crosswell system ultimately performed well at Kern River. The crosswell EM data could be accurately collected between two steel-cased wells spaced more than 800 ft part. The inversion provided interwell images consistent with the logs and the field data. These images could be used to identify interwell structure and also to determine interwell temporal resistivity changes associated with the steam injection. The data are particularly useful for identifying intervals that are heating, or desaturating and for identifying faults that serve as active transporters or blockers of subsurface steam flow.

The resistivity interpretation is clearly enhanced by the good working knowledge of the geology and steam flow characteristics in the field.

Case Study 2

The crosswell survey was made in 2004 at the Gudao oil field in the Shandong province in China. Gudao is an anticlinal trap located along the Yellow River delta along the eastern coast in central China. The field consists of channel and deltaic sands deposited in an ancient flood plain. Large parts of the field are characterized by continuous deltaic sands and other parts by distinct channels but generally both channel and flood sands are present in each area. The configuration of the sands and the controlling structure is crucial in understanding the ongoing water flood and in optimizing the oil production strategy. At present, it is estimated that 25 per cent of the reserves in this field have been recovered but also that another 15 per cent are recoverable with improved reservoir knowledge.

Gudao is a large mature field with many production and injection wells; the production is roughly 50,000 barrels of oil per day. A typical well in this field produces 20-30 barrels of oil per day and more than 500 barrels of water. With the water cut rising each year, it is critical to find the bypassed reserves and locate and shut off the fast-path water channels.

The project consisted of four separate surveys using three well pairs. The goals of the project were: 1) to test and establish performance data for the new system in the Chinese environment; 2) to provide interwell resistivity data within this chosen well pattern to help better understand the waterflood dynamics and locate bypassed reserves. These wells are located in a mature part of this waterflood. Flooding started in this part of the field in 1985 and has progressed continually since then.. Wells 29-412 and 30-26 are producers, well 29-413 is a water injector, and well 31-523 is a newly drilled producer that was used in the tomography.

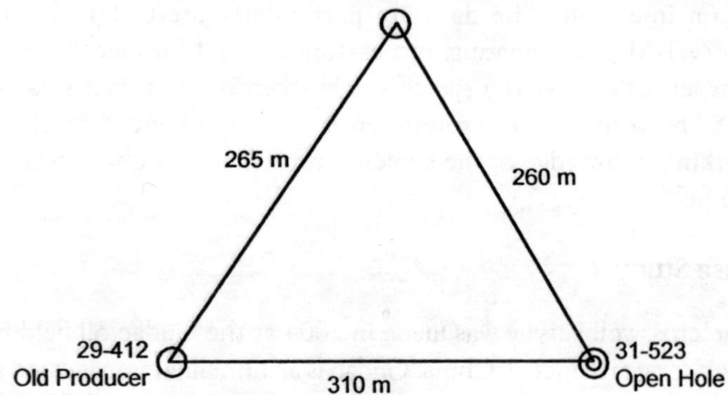

Figure 5.8: Crosswell EM sections.

Several resistivity logs from wells were obtain The earlier log (1984) indicates that the oil sands have an initial resistivity of 15-25 ohm-m, and the background silts and clay have a resistivity of 2-4 ohm-m. The flooding and production are centered in three principal zones. Zones 3 and 4 are well-defined continuous deltaic sands that range in thickness from 4 to 12 m; these have been continually flooded since 1985. Zone 5 is a less continuous zone with heavier oil that has had less success in water flooding operations. After years of water flooding, the resistivity of the oil sands in zones 3 and 4 has decreased to 8-10 ohm-m from 15-25 ohm-m. This is mainly the result of saturation changes as the injected water replaces the oil. Obtaining the present saturation level is difficult because it is necessary to know the salinity of the formation water. In this field, this quantity is poorly known because the source of the injected fluid has changed a number of times during the waterflooding.

The crosswell measurements were made with the X2C-GM system. Crosswell EM is used to provide formation resistivity between wells. This interwell resistivity is used for reservoir characterization, structural mapping, and most importantly for tracking processes such as water and steam floods where the formation fluid (oil, gas, and water) is exchanged with injected fluid (water). This fluid exchange typically results in a large resistivity change due to the saturation change, and thus the process is traceable via the interwell resistivity and resistivity variation.

The data collection plan called for the use of open hole 31-523 (523) to collect open-steel datasets using wells 30-413 (413) and 29-412 (412) for the receiver tools. The final survey was made between steel-cased wells 413 and 412. The tomography covered the depth interval between 1150 m and 1350 m. The system operates with a stationary four level receiver string and a moving transmitter. The transmitter moves from the bottom to the top of the interval at a rate of 3-6 m/min; data are collected every 1-2 m depending on the amount of signal averaging and the logging rate. After each transmitter profile, the receivers are repositioned and the process is repeated until the entire depth interval was covered. For these surveys, receivers were spaced 5 m apart and the transmitters covered the same interval at 1 m measurement spacing. The tomography required 20-35 h for completion for each crosswell survey. The longer time periods were for the dual-casing surveys.

Analysts initially deployed the transmitter in well 523 and the receiver in well 413 and collected complete open-to-casing data at two frequencies, 32 Hz and 104 Hz. These data were used to compare the image resolution with frequency. Next, data were collected in well pair 523-412, and steel-cased well pair 413-412 was measured.

The variation in maximum field levels for each profile mainly reflects the different properties of the steel casing pipes in the receiver well.

The dual-steel data are far more jittery in nature, and the curves are less bell-like. This is due primarily to the steel-casing that imparts a different attenuation as the transmitter moves through each pipe. However, the excellent correlation of the high-frequency jitter in the receiver profiles. This coherency is what allows analysts to separate the formation and casing signal from these data. Note that the field level of these data are more than 20 times smaller than the open-steel data eventhough the well separation is roughly the same. This suggests that the attenuation due to the steel-casing on the transmitter is a factor of 20.

Repeated data profiles in the open-steel surveys suggest a system noise level of approximately 2-4 microvolts, or about 6-12 microgammas. This is slightly better than posted specifications and suggests that at these depths in this oilfield, the background is electromagnetically quiet, and at least from a data collection viewpoint, a very good spot for crosswell EM. This is a very positive result as it established that system bias is below the measured noise level of roughly 6-12 microgammas. Analysts notice that for each doubling of the well spacing, the field level drops by a factor of 8.

Analysts first reduced the data for the open-steel surveys, applied calibration corrections and interpreted the results using a 2-D computer-based inverse code. The code fits the collected data to a 2-D model with an initial or starting model based on available geology and logs. The code essentially takes the best guess and the collected data, and adjusts the model until the data are fit within the data measurement error, 1—3 per cent in this case. For the dual-casing data, the casing correction is more complex and requires longer to implement.

One of the chief indications that the inversion process is successful is to examine the misfit section, or the difference between the observed and the calculated data, after the data have been fit by the inversion. This misfit section should fit within the error tolerance, and have a roughly random structure. A high degree of structure in the misfit section suggests error due to calibration, well separation, and tool position or initial formation model. The misfit for well pair 523 to 413 displays and average fit within 1—2 per cent. The dual casing data (412-413) show an average misfit of roughly 2—3 per cent.

Interpretation

The interwell resistivity image between well pair 523 and 413 is a smooth section consistent with a flatlying multilayered section and concordant the well logs at the margins. The low-resistivity upper section represents clays and silts; within this section there are thin discontinuous higher-resistivity sands note, for example, the layer at a depth of 1150 ft. The oil-bearing zones 3, 4, and 5 are associated with continuous high- resistivity layers. Layer 3 is higher in resistivity near well 523 and grades gradually lower towards well 413. The layer thickness stays relatively constant. Layer 4 stays roughly constant in resistivity but seems to thicken gradually from well 523 to well 413. The most interesting part of the image is near location 80 m where the 4-layer basal unit 5 grades at well 523 into a 2-3 layer section.

The section also indicates slight stratigraphic thinning in layers 3 and 4 and some variation in the overburden silts and muds at this same lateral position. Variations in layer resistivity may be associated with the saturation and/or water salinity. Clearly, the resistivity has fallen from the initial 20-25 ohm-m to the present day 8-10 ohm-m due to replacement of oil by injected water. As the oil desaturation continues, this trend will continue but it can be offset by variations in injected water salinity. Analysts know that the injected water supply for this field has changed a number of times in this field, but analysts were uncertain as to the salinity. This therefore adds an uncertainty on ability to associate higher oil saturated intervals with a higher resistivity.

The nature of the injected water will have an impact on the crosswell EM section. Fortunately, a borehole tool is available to measure the resistivity at the well bore through the steel-casing.

Model Adjustments Using the New Logs

CHFR logs were measured in wells 413 and 412 wells. In well 413, the cased hole logs follow the original open hole logs very well except for the shallowest depths in the interval. These data suggest that in the reservoir layers, the resistivity has increased during the past several years, presumably due to the introduction of polymers and fresher injection water. In the deeper low-resistivity silts, no resistivity change was observed but in the shallower silty layers, an increase was also measured. Analysts did not expect a change in these shallow silty layers and experienced CHFR interpreters suggest that this change may be due to near well effects, (i.e., due to injected water leaking up the annulus) but probably does not indicate a true formation change and analysts did not include it in starting model.

The change from 8 ohm-m to more than 15 ohm-m in reservoir layers 3 and 4 is substantial, and was included in the crosswell EM interpretation.

The log data were then used to adjust the starting models for the crosswell EM, and the inversion was repeated. The main adjustment was to increase the resistivity in layers 3 and 4 from 8 to 18 ohm-m, but analysts made no adjustment on any other part of the starting model. Analysts then repeated inversion from well pairs 523-413 and 413-412.

The interwell EM would have difficulty resolving the type of formation resistivity change observed in CHFR independently because it involves a resistivity increase that may be localized. This type of structure is difficult to map with an inductive system as it has a relatively small influence on the data. Knowing such information independently (from CHFR for example) allows the inversion code to begin at a more accurate starting model and thereby provides a better resolution of this subtle feature.

The main difference is observed in reservoir layers 3 and 4 where we observe the higher resistivity which was inserted at well 413 in the starting model, and has extended to approximately 2/3 of the way across the section.

6

Interpretation

A comprehensive interpretation of acquired data is critical for efficient reservoir development and management because it quantifies the parameters that characterize the dynamic response of the reservoir.

Interpretation Methodology

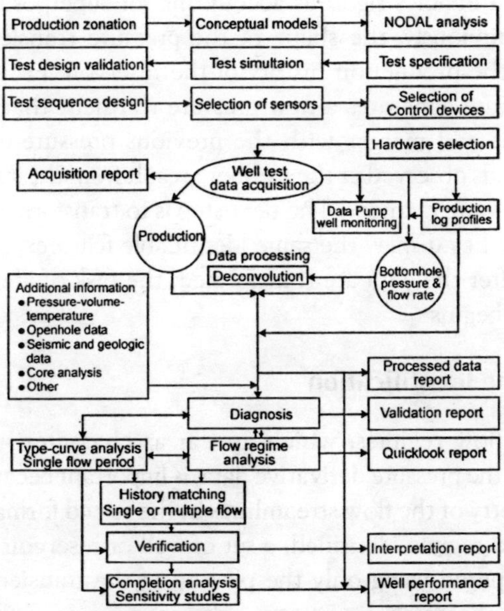

Figure 6.1: Flowchart describing all stages of a testing job, encompassing test design, hardware selection, data acquisition, data validation, interpretation, and reporting of the results.

The objective of well test interpretation is to obtain the most self-consistent and correct results. This can be achieved by following a systematic approach. Figure 6.1 shows a logical task sequence that spans the entire spectrum of a well testing job.

Data Processing

The first step in data processing is to split the entire dataset into individual flow periods. The exact start and end of each flow period are specified. Because the sampling rate is usually high, each transient typically includes many more data points than are actually required. A high density of data is needed only for early-time transients. Therefore, special algorithms are usually employed to reduce the dataset to a manageable size. Because of the nature of the pressure disturbance propagation, a logarithmic sampling rate is preferred.

The sequence of events should incorporate the recent flow rate history of the well with the surface flow rate changes observed during the test. This enables rigorous accounting for superposition effects. As stated previously, the shape of the pressure transient curve is affected by the production history of the reservoir. Each change in production rate generates a new pressure transient that passes into the reservoir and merges with the previous pressure effects. The pressure trends observed at the wellbore result from the superposition of all the pressure changes. The next step is to transform the reduced data so that they display the same identifiable features, regardless of test type. After the data are transformed, the task of identifying the flow regime begins.

Flow Regime Identification

Identifying flow regimes, which appear as characteristic patterns displayed by the pressure derivative data, is important because a regime is the geometry of the flow streamlines in the tested formation. Thus, for each flow regime identified, a set of well or reservoir parameters can be computed using only the portion of the transient data that exhibits the characteristic pattern behaviour.

The eight flow regime patterns commonly observed in well test data are radial, spherical, linear, bilinear, compression/expansion, steady-state, dual-porosity or -permeability, and slopedoubling.

(*a*) *Flow Regime Identification Tool*

The popular Flow Regime Identification tool is used to differentiate the eight common subsurface flow regimes on log-log plots for their application in determining and understanding downhole and reservoir conditions.

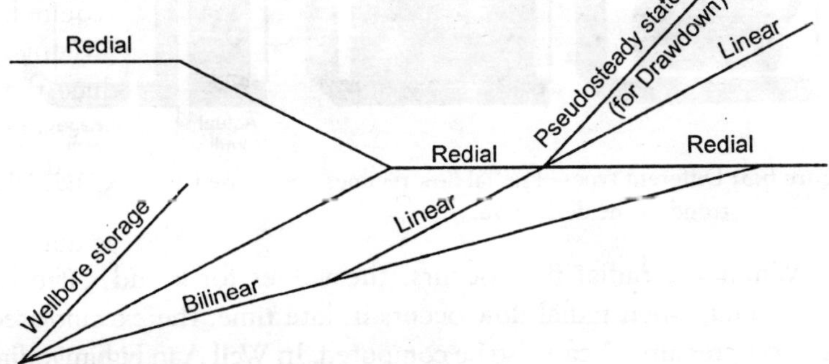

Figure 6.2: Flow Regime Identification tool.

(*b*) *Radial Flow*

The most important flow regime for well test interpretation is radial flow, which is recognized as an extended constant or flat trend in the derivative. Radial flow geometry is described as flow streamlines converging to a circular cylinder (Fig. 6.3). In fully completed wells, the cylinder may represent the portion of the wellbore intersecting the entire formation. In partially penetrated formations or partially completed wells, the radial flow may be restricted in early time to only the section of the formation thickness where flow is directly into the wellbore. When a well is stimulated or horizontally completed, the effective radius for the radial flow may be enlarged. Horizontal wells may also exhibit earlytime radial flow in the vertical plane normal to the well. If the well is located near a barrier to flow, such as a fault, the pressure transient response may exhibit radial flow to the well, followed by radial flow to the well plus its image across the boundary.

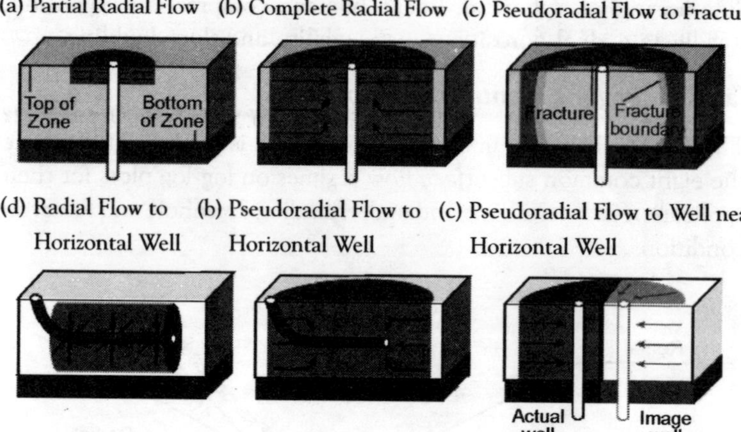

Figure 6.3: Different types of radial flow regimes, recognized as an extended flat trend in the derivative.

Whenever radial flow occurs, the values for k and s can be determined; when radial flow occurs in late time, the extrapolated reservoir pressure p^* can also be computed. In Well A in Figure radial flow occurs in late time, so k, s, and p^* can be quantified.

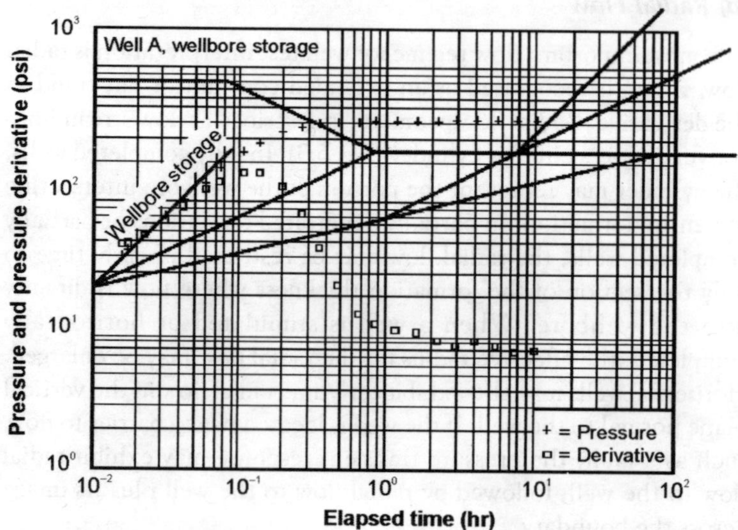

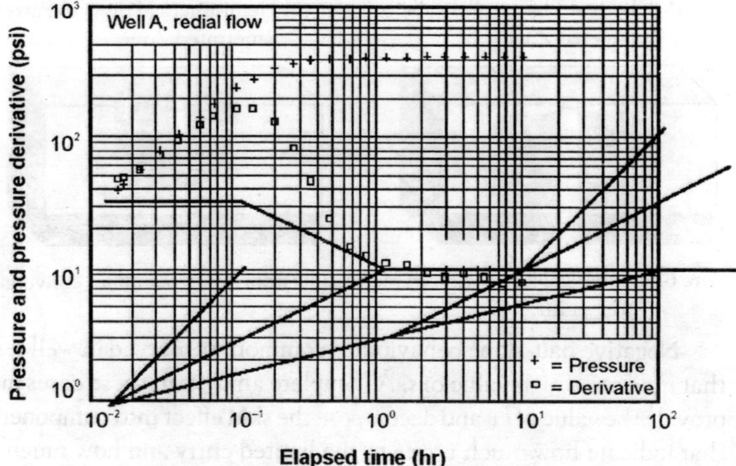

Figure 6.4: Radial flow occurring at late time. Values for the permeability, skin effect, and extrapolated pressure to infinite shut-in can be computed.

(c) *Spherical Flow*

Spherical flow occurs when the flow streamlines converge to a point (Fig.). This flow regime occurs in partially completed wells (Fig. a) and partially penetrated formations (Fig. b). For the case of partial completion or partial penetration near the upper or lower bed boundary, the nearest impermeable bed imposes a hemispherical flow regime. Both spherical and hemispherical flows are seen on the derivative as a negative half-slope trend. Once the spherical permeability is determined from this pattern, it can be used with the horizontal permeability *kh* quantified from a radial flow regime occurring in another portion of the data to determine the vertical permeability *kv*. The importance of *kv* in predicting gas or water coning or horizontal well performance emphasizes the practical need for quantifying this parameter. A DST can be conducted when only a small portion of the formation has been drilled (or perforated) to potentially yield values for both *kv* and *kh*, which could be used to optimize the completion engineering or provide a rationale to drill a horizontal well.

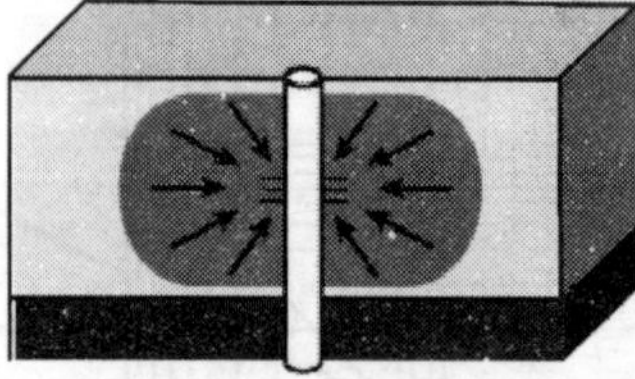

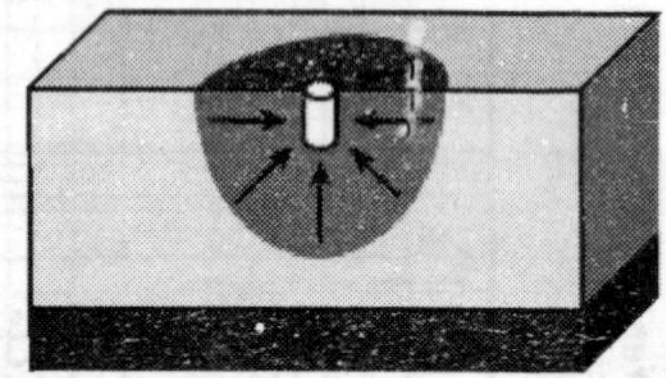

Figure 6.5: Spherical flow regime, which results from flow streamlines converging to a point.

Negative half-slope behaviour is commonly observed in well tests that indicate a high value of *s*. A complete analysis in these cases may provide the value of *kv* and decompose the skin effect into components that indicate how much is due to the limited entry and how much to damage along the actively flowing interval. The treatable portion of the damage can then be determined and the cost effectiveness of damage removal and reperforating to improve the well productivity can be evaluated.

(*d*) *Linear flow*

The geometry of linear flow streamlines consists of strictly parallel flow vectors. Linear flow is exhibited in the derivative as a positive half-slope trend. Figure shows why this flow regime develops in vertically fractured and horizontal wells. It is also found in wells producing from an elongated reservoir. Since the streamlines converge to a plane, the parameters associated with the linear flow regime are the permeability of the formation in the direction of the streamlines and the flow area normal to the streamlines. The *kh* value of the formation determined from another flow regime can be used to calculate the width of the flow area. This provides the fracture half-length of a vertically fractured well, the effective production length of a horizontal well, or the width of an elongated reservoir. The combination of linear flow data with radial flow data (in any order) can provide the principle values of *kx* and *kv* for the directional permeabilities in the bedding plane. In an anisotropic formation, the productivity of a horizontal well is enhanced by drilling the well in the direction normal to the maximum horizontal permeability.

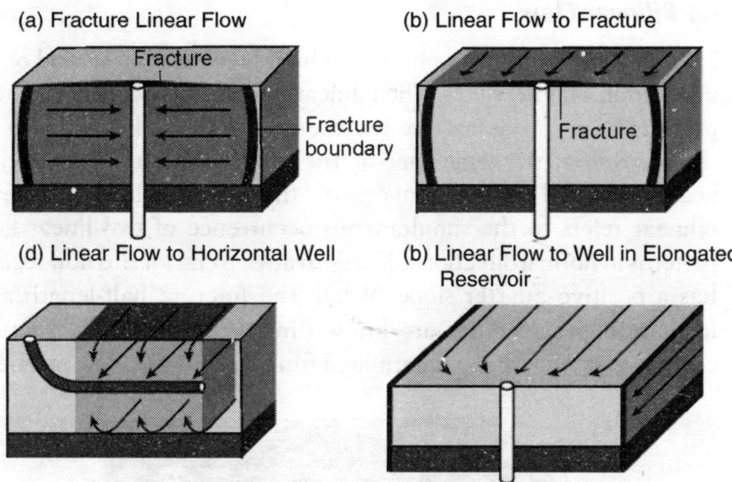

Figure 6.6:

Well C is a water injection well that exhibits linear flow (Fig.). Although no radial flow is evident, the time of departure from linear flow coupled with an analysis of the data that follow the half-slope derivative trend provides two independent indicators of the formation permeability and fracture half-length, enabling the quantification of both. The subtle rise in the derivative after the end of linear flow suggests a boundary, which was interpreted as a fault.

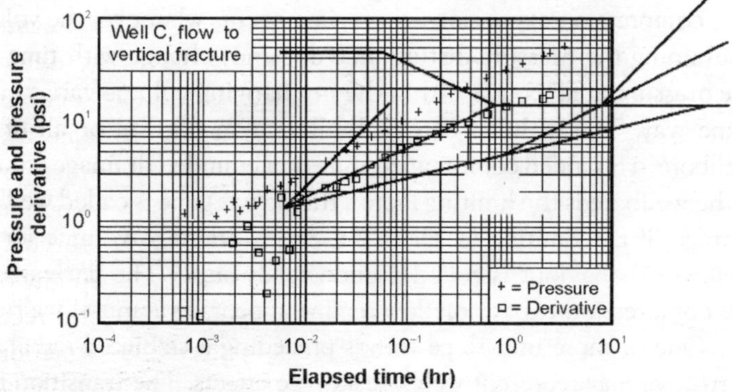

Figure 6.7: The linear flow regime has a positive half-slope trend in the derivative curve.

(e) *Bilinear Flow*

Hydraulically fractured wells may exhibit bilinear flow instead of, or in addition to, linear flow. The bilinear flow regime occurs because a pressure drop in the fracture itself results in parallel streamlines in the fracture at the same time as the streamlines in the formation become parallel as they converge to the fracture (Fig.). The term bilinear refers to the simultaneous occurrence of two linear flow patterns in normal directions. The derivative trend for this flow regime has a positive quarter slope. When the fracture half-length and formation permeability are known independently, the fracture conductivity *kfw* can be determined from the bilinear flow regime.

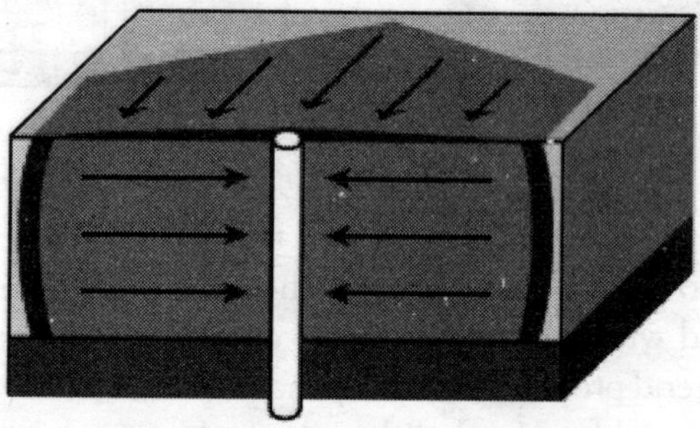

Figure 6.8: Bilinear flow regime commonly exhibited by hydraulically fractured wells.

(f) *Compression/Expansion*

The compression/expansion flow regime occurs whenever the volume containing the pressure disturbance does not change with time and the pressure at all points within the unchanging volume varies in the same way. This volume can be limited by a portion or all of the wellbore, a bounded commingled zone or a bounded drainage volume. If the wellbore is the limiting factor, the flow regime is called wellbore storage; if the limiting factor is the entire drainage volume for the well, this behaviour is called pseudosteady state. The derivative of the compression/expansion flow regime appears as a unit-slope trend.

One or more unit-slope trends preceding a stabilized radial flow derivative may represent wellbore storage effects. The transition from the wellbore storage unit-slope trend to another flow regime usually appears as a hump (Fig.). The wellbore storage flow regime represents a response that is effectively limited to the wellbore volume. Hence, it provides little information about the reservoir. Furthermore, wellbore storage effects may mask important early-time responses that characterize near-wellbore features, including partial penetration or a finite damage radius. This flow regime is minimized by shutting in the well near the production interval. This practice can reduce the portion of the data dominated by wellbore storage behaviour by two or more logarithmic cycles in time. In some wells tested without downhole shut-in, wellbore storage effects have lasted up to several days.

After radial flow has occurred, a unit-slope trend that is not the final observed behaviour may result from production from one zone into one or more other zones (or from multiple zones into a single zone) commingled in the wellbore. This behaviour is accompanied by crossflow in the wellbore, and it occurs when the commingled zones are differentially depleted. If unit slope occurs as the last observed trend (Fig. 6.9a), it is assumed to indicate pseudosteady-state conditions for the entire reservoir volume contained in the well drainage area. Late-time unit-slope behaviour caused by pseudosteady state occurs only during drawdown. If the unit slope develops after radial flow, either the zone (or reservoir) volume or its shape can be determined.

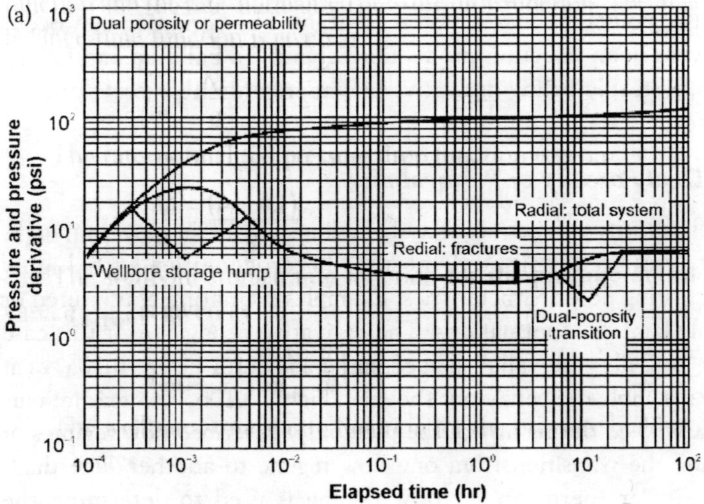

(b)

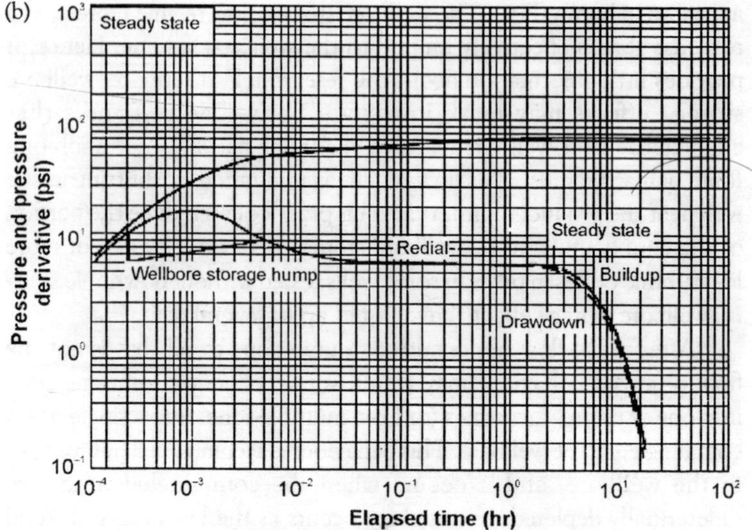

Figure 6.9: Flow regime trends exhibited by wellbore storage, boundaries, and pressure maintenance.

(g) Steady State

Steady state implies that pressure in the well drainage volume does not vary in time at any point and that the pressure gradient between any two points in the reservoir is constant. This condition may occur for wells in an injection-production scheme. In build-up and fall-off tests, a steeply falling derivative may represent either pseudosteady or steady state.

(h) Dual Porosity or Permeability

Dual-porosity or -permeability behaviour occurs in reservoir rocks that contain distributed internal heterogeneities with highly contrasting flow characteristics. Examples are naturally fractured or highly laminated formations. The derivative behaviour for this case may look like the valley-shaped trend shown in Figure 6.10a, or it may resemble the behaviour shown in Figure 6.10b. This feature may come and go during any of the previously described flow regimes or during the transition from one flow regime to another. The dual-porosity or -permeability flow regime is used to determine the parameters associated with internal heterogeneity, such as interporosity flow transmissibility, relative storativity of the contrasted heterogeneities, and geometric factors.

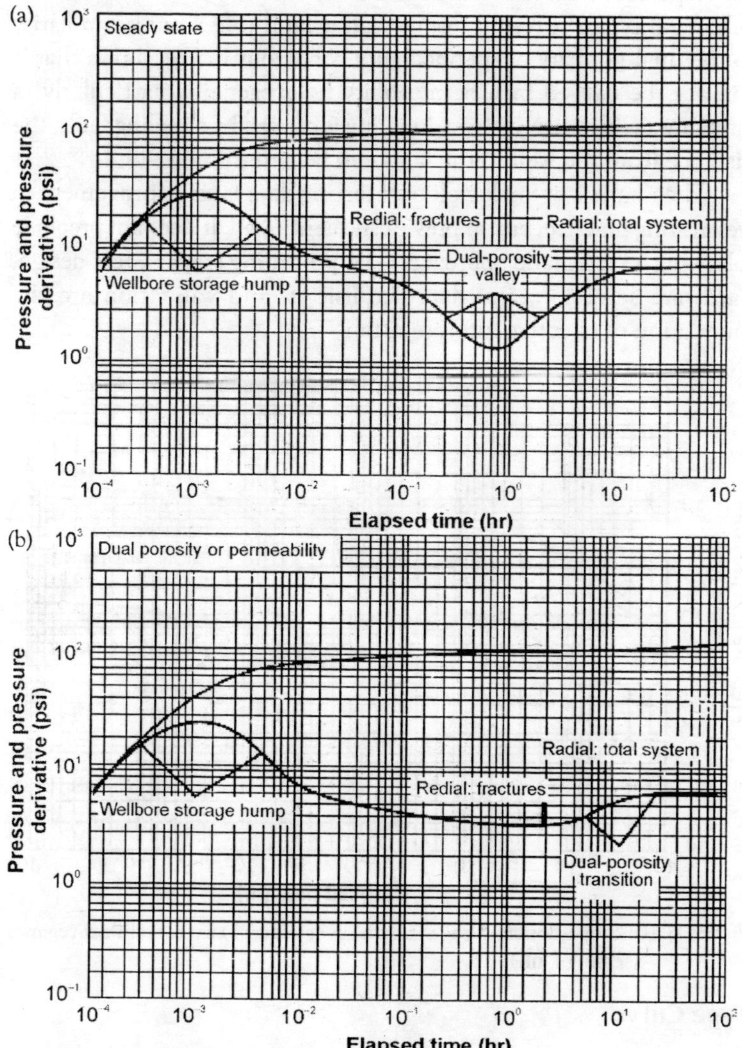

Figure 6.10: Characteristic patterns of naturally fractured and highly laminated formations.

(i) Slope Doubling

Slope doubling describes a succession of two radial flow regimes, with the slope of the second, which is exactly twice that of the first. This behaviour typically results from a sealing fault (Fig.), but its similarity to the dual-porosity or -permeability behaviour in Fig. shows that it can also be caused by a permeability heterogeneity, particularly in laminated reservoirs. If slope doubling is caused by a sealing fault, the distance from the well to the fault can be determined.

The analysis of log-log plots of testing data is an improvement in well testing practice, but, as previously mentioned, it does not preclude following a systematic approach. The preceding steps of test design, hardware selection, and data acquisition and validation are the foundation of effective interpretation.

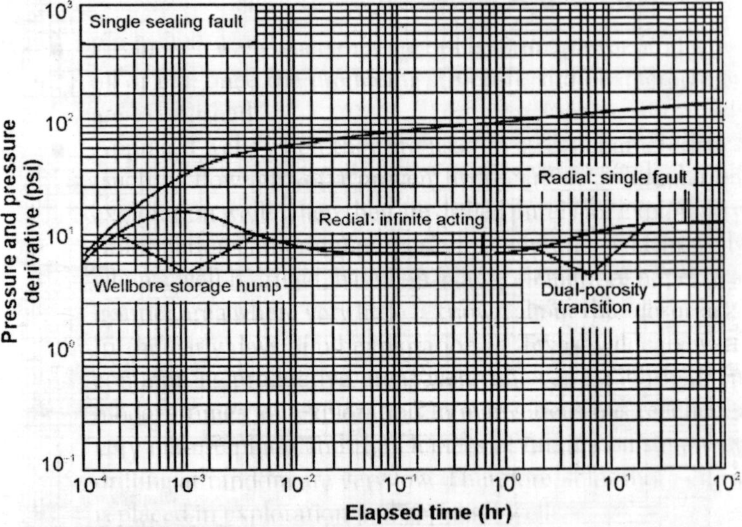

Figure 6.10: Slope doubling caused by a succession of two radial flow regimes (sealing fault).

Type Curve

In general, conducting the interpretation of transient tests preceded by a variable rate history requires computer processing. A customized type curve must be constructed for each well test, except for the analysis of pressure build-up tests of wells that have undergone a lengthy drawdown period before the test.

The type curves can be applied directly to drawdown periods at a constant flow rate or build-up tests performed with downhole shut-in devices and preceded by a long drawdown period.

In practice, drawdowns are short or exhibit widely varying flow rates before shut-in. Also, build-up tests are often conducted with surface shut-in, exhibiting variable wellbore storage.

Improved computing techniques have facilitated the development of custom curves, resulting in a major advance in well test interpretation. Analysts are also able to develop type curves that incorporate the potential effects of complex reservoir geometries on the pressure response of the reservoir. The computer-generated type curves are displayed simultaneously with the data and carefully matched to produce precise values for the reservoir parameters.

Type Curves 1— 4
Infinite-Acting Radial Flow Model

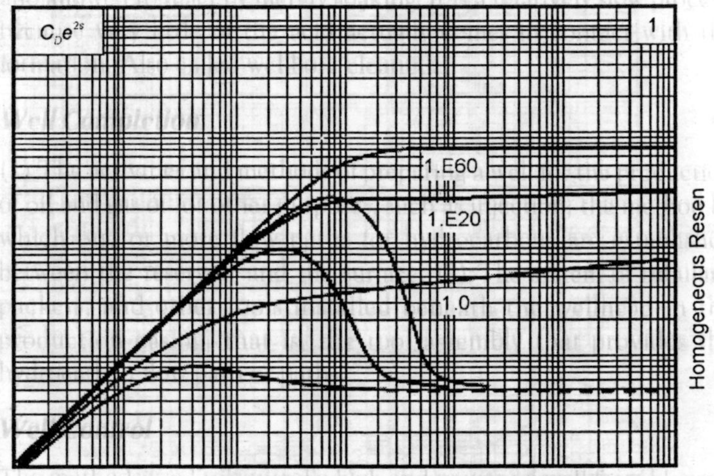

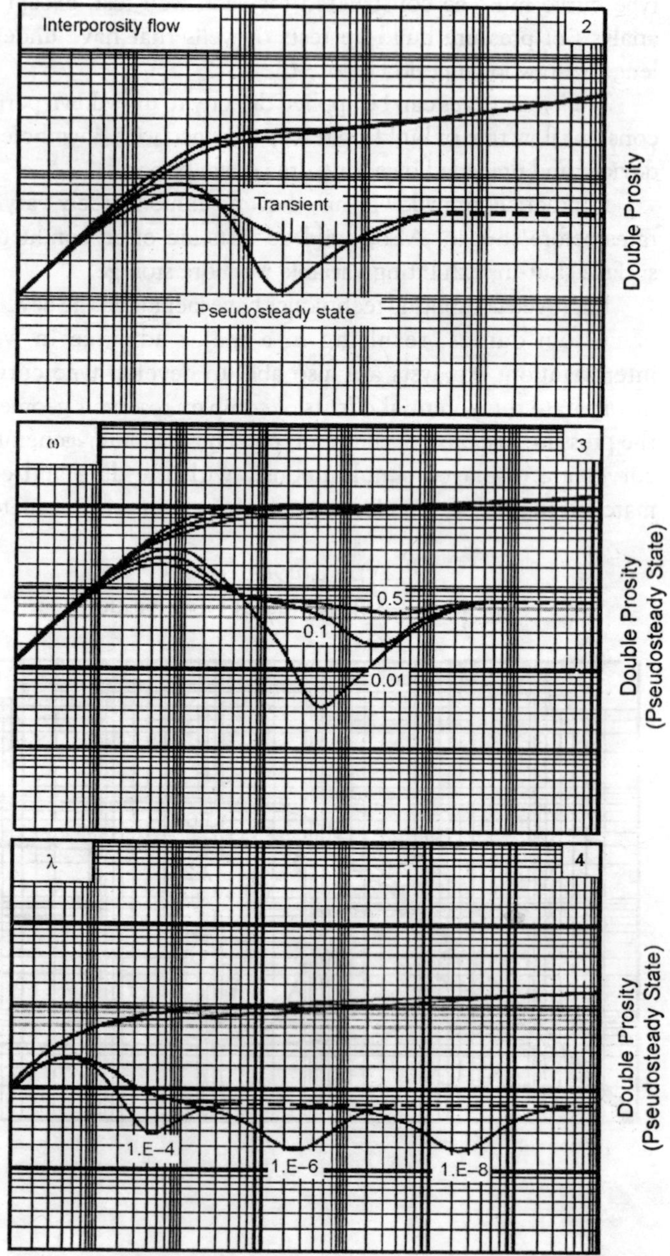
Interporosity flow
2
Transient
Pseudosteady state
Double Prosity
ω
3
0.5
0.1
0.01
Double Prosity
(Pseudosteady State)
λ
4
1.E–4
1.E–6
1.E–8
Double Prosity
(Pseudosteady State)

Type curves 5—8
Infinite-Acting Doublepermeability Model

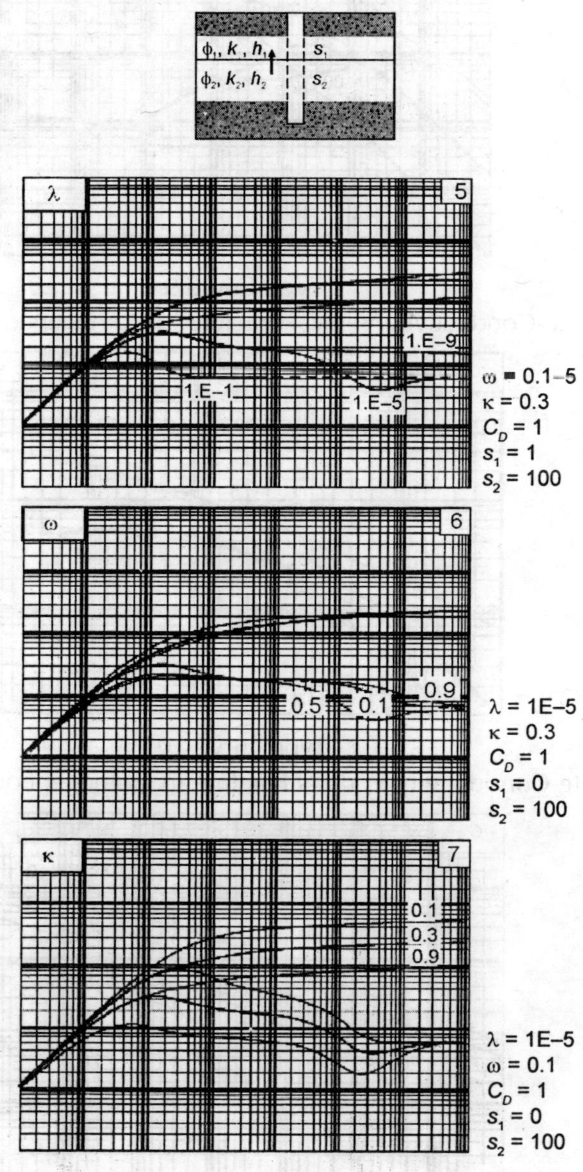

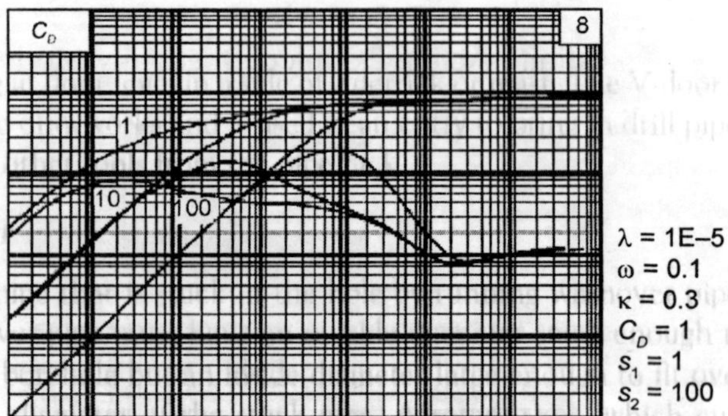

Type Curve 9

Infinite-Conductivity Vertical Fracture in Homogeneous Reservoir

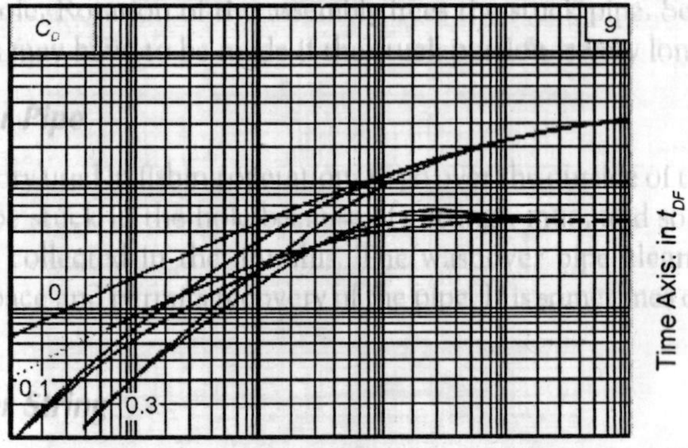

Type curve 10

Finite-Conductivity Vertical Fracture in Homogeneous Reservoir

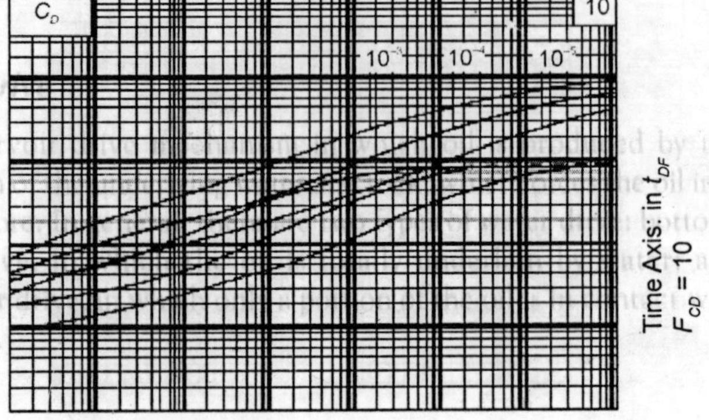

Type Curves 11—12
Partial Completion Near Gas Cap

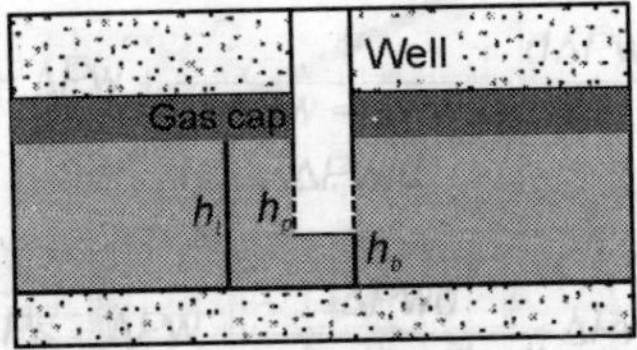

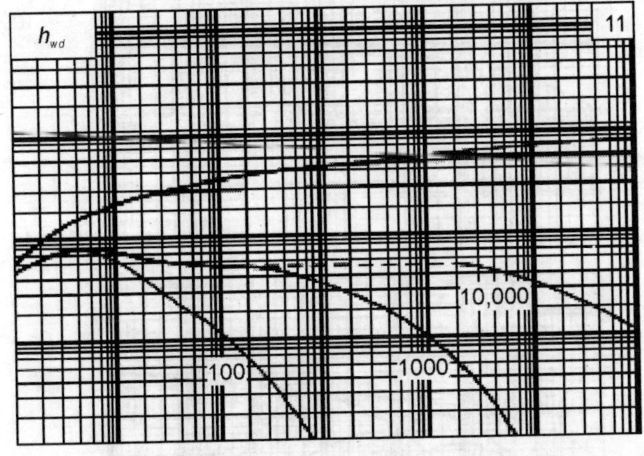

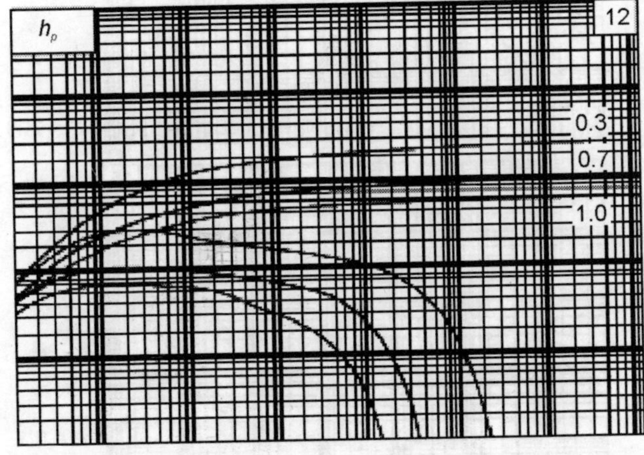

Type Curves 13—15
Well Near Impermeable Boundary

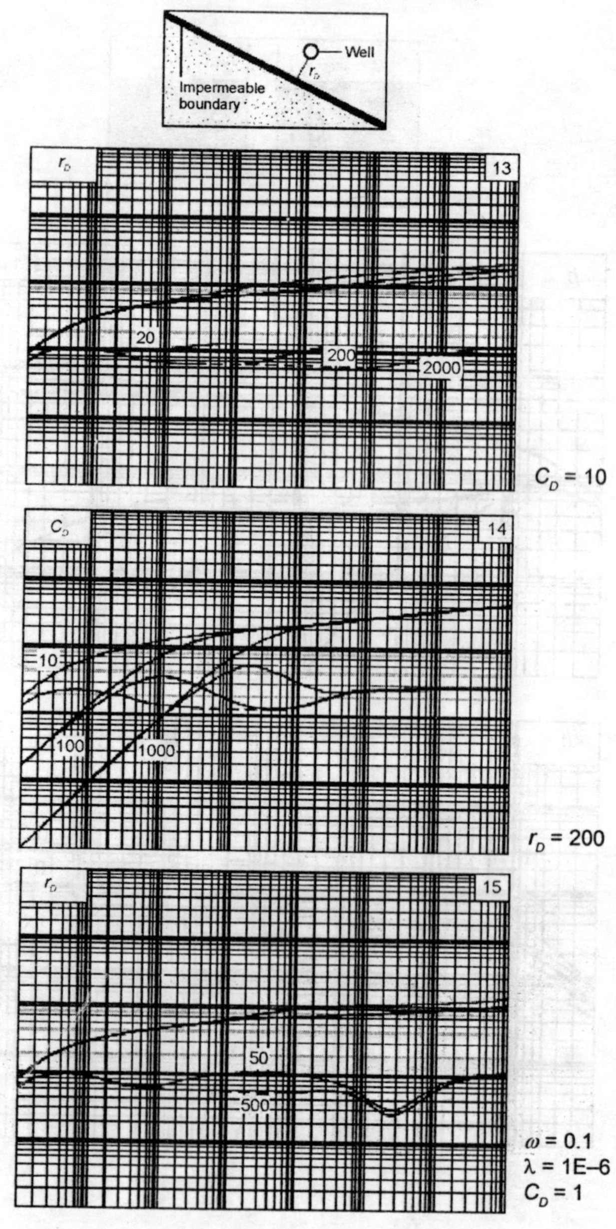

Type Curves 16—18
Well Near Partially Sealing Fault

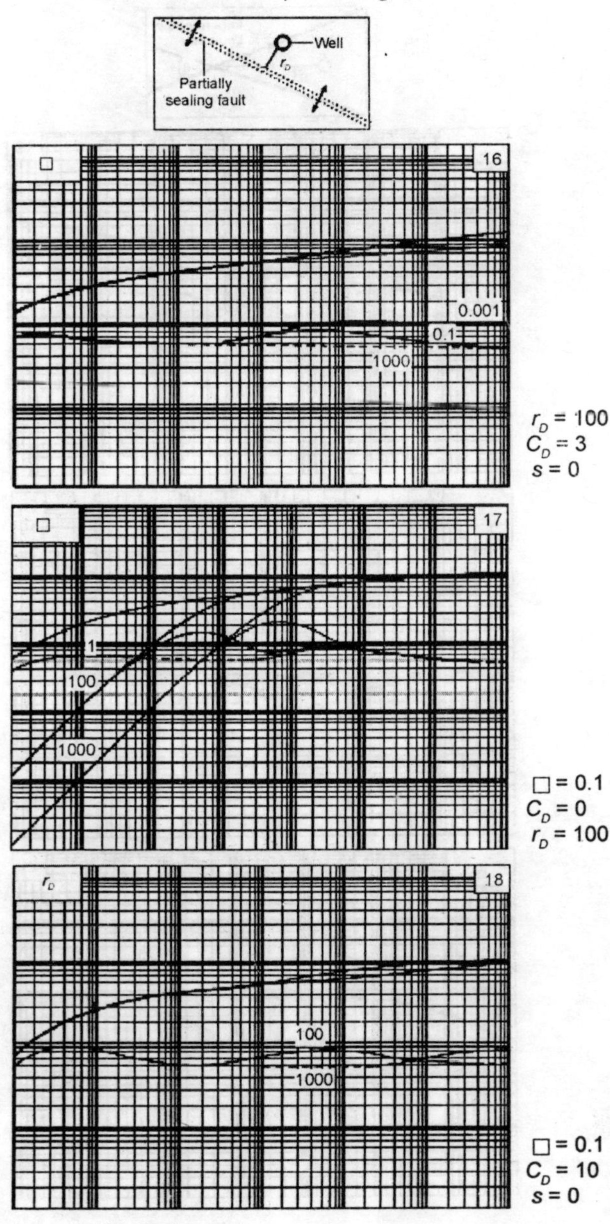

Type Curves 19—22
Well between Two Intersecting Impermeable Boundaries

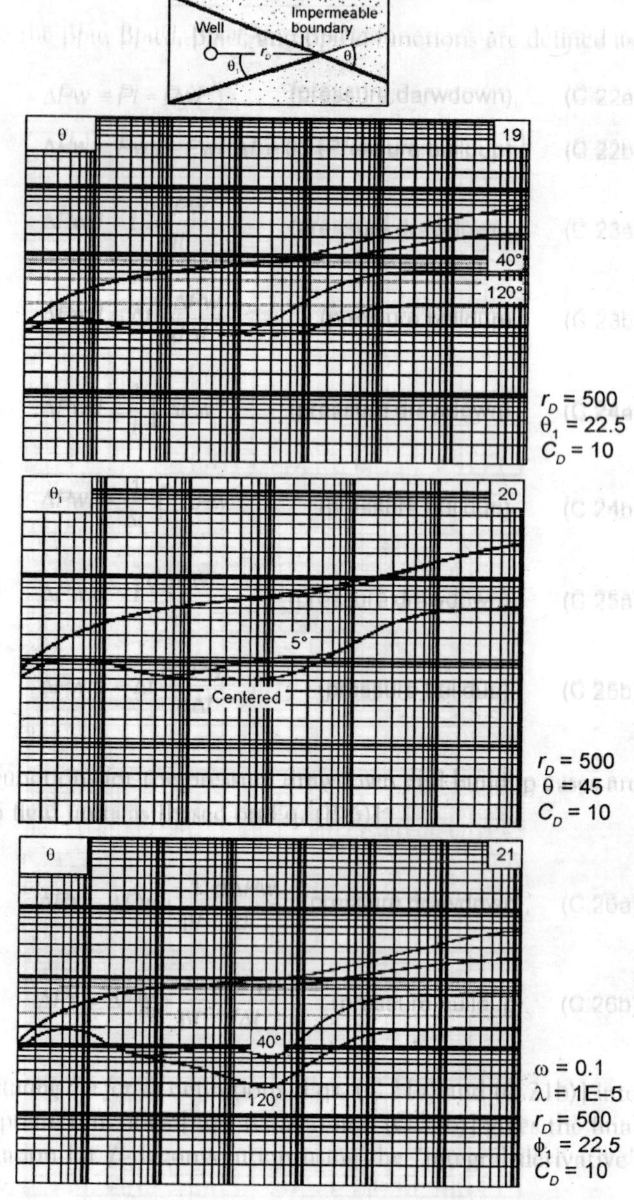

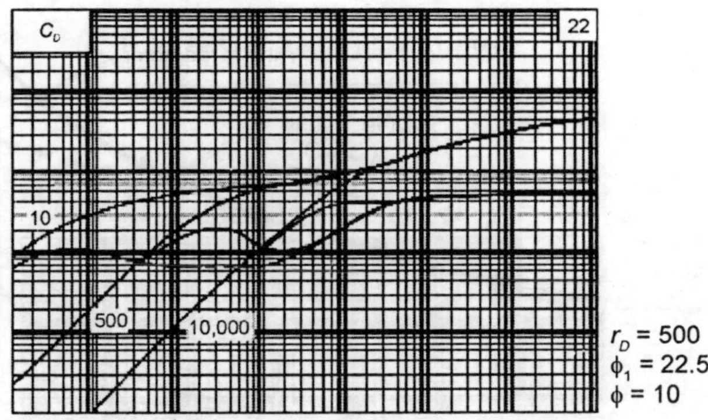

$r_D = 500$
$\phi_1 = 22.5$
$\phi = 10$

Type Curves 23—24

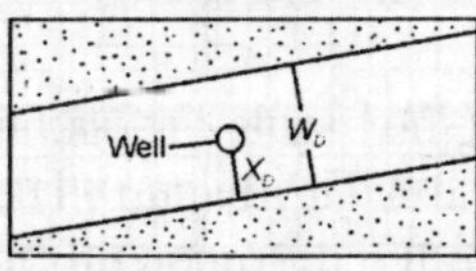

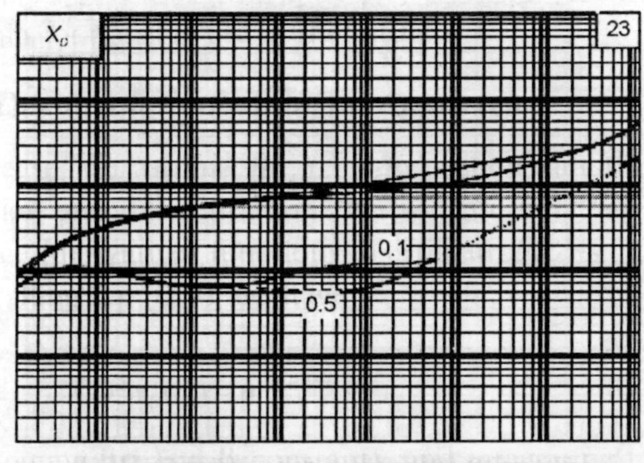

$W_D = 1000$
$C_D = 10$

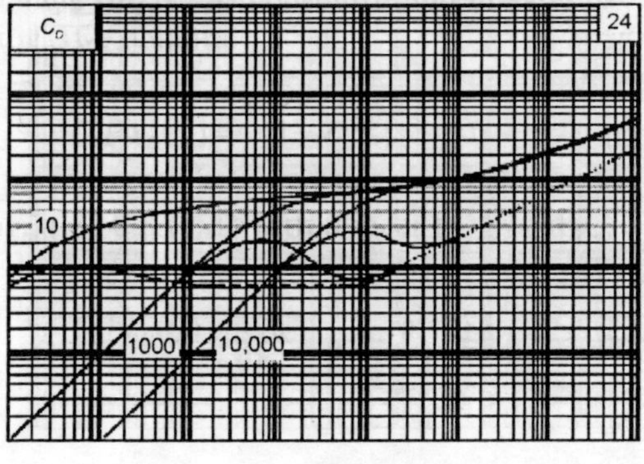

$W_D = 1000$
$X_D = 0.5$

Type Curves 25–27
Well in Truncated Channel

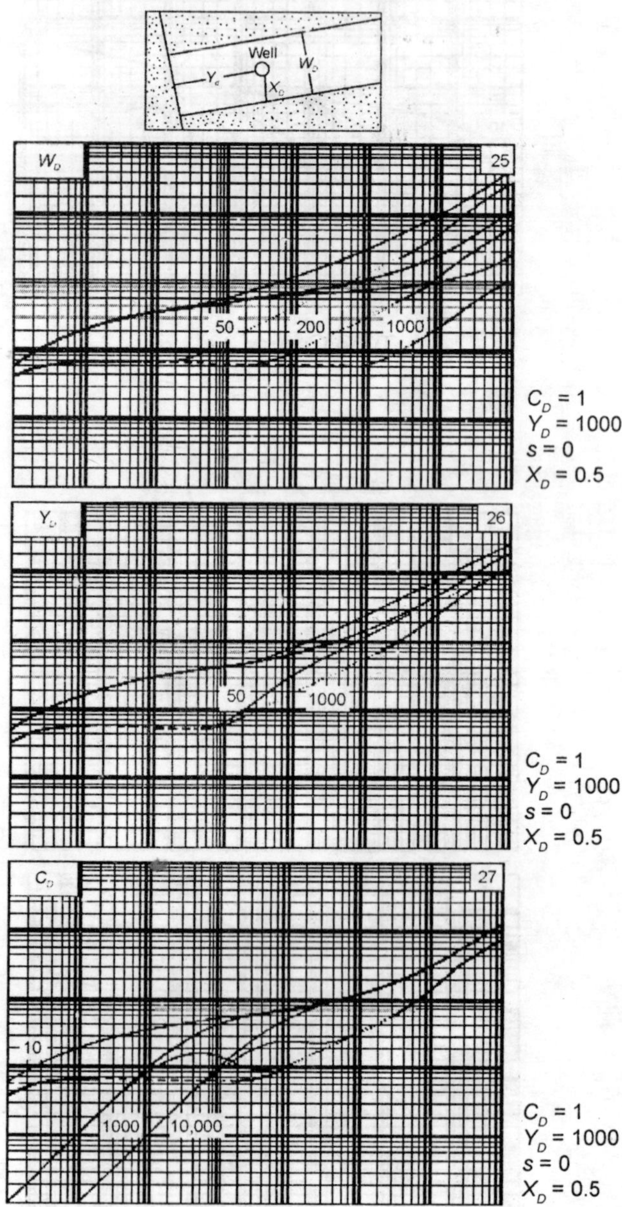

Type Curves 28

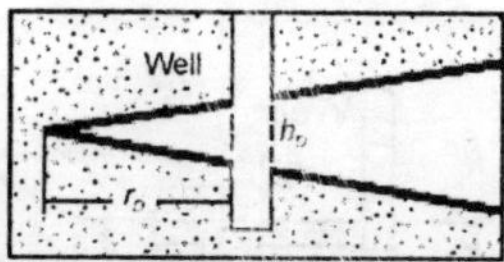

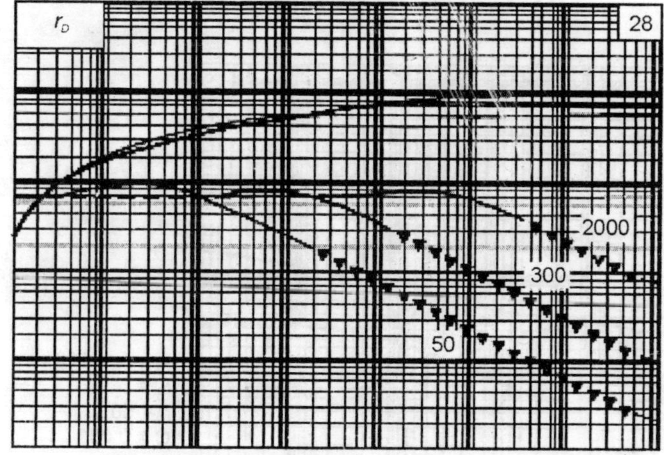

$h_D = 100$
$C_D = 0$
$s = 0$

Type Curves 29—30

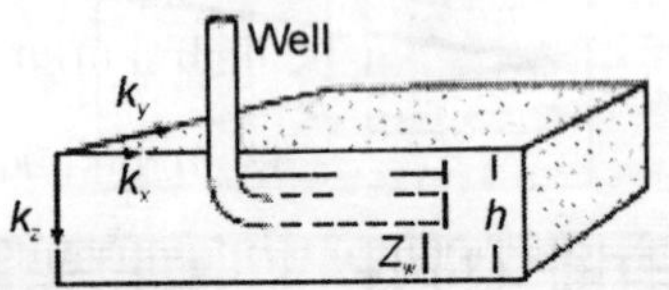

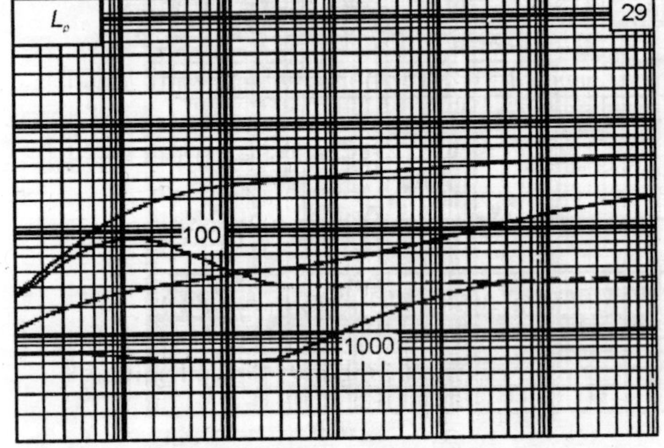

$k_x = k_y = 500$
$k_z = 50$
$h = 50$
$C = 0.001$
$Z_w = 25$

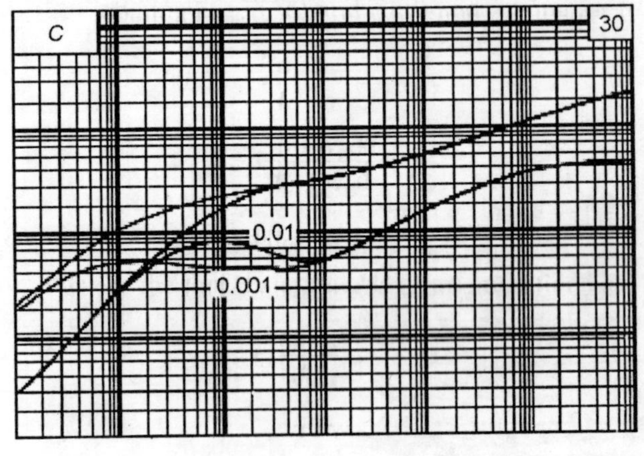

$k_x = k_y = 500$
$k_z = 50$
$h = 30$
$L_p = 1000$
$Z_w = 15$

Type Curves 31

Well in rectangular reservoir with one impermeable and three constant-pressure boundaries (rD = distance to impermeable boundary).

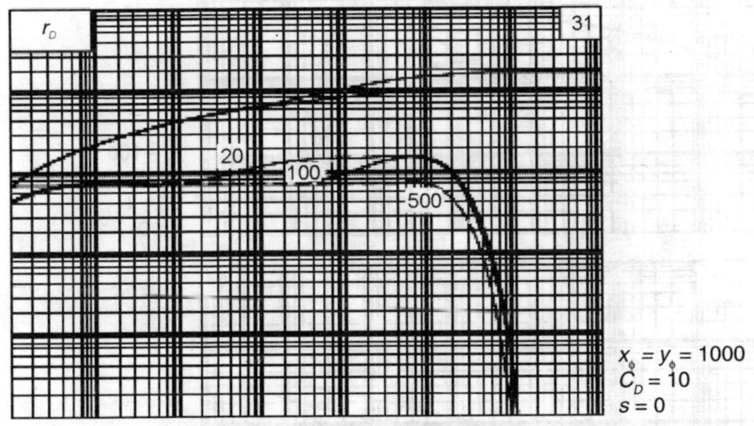

Type Curves 32—34

Well in Rectangle btween two Constant-Pressure Boundaries

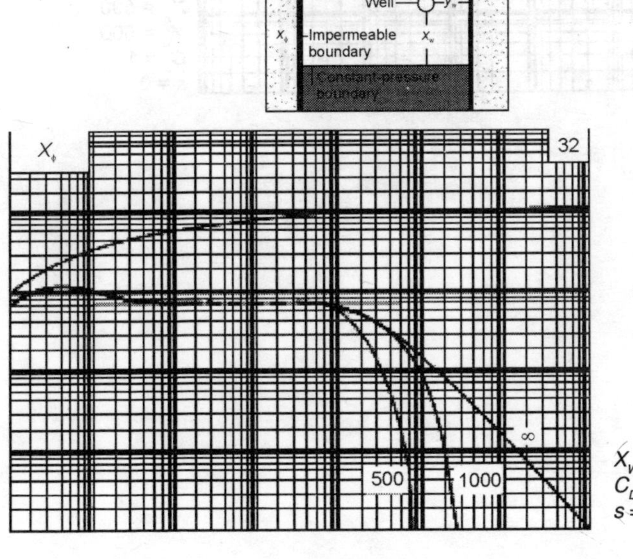

$X_W = 500$
$C_D = 10$
$s = 0$

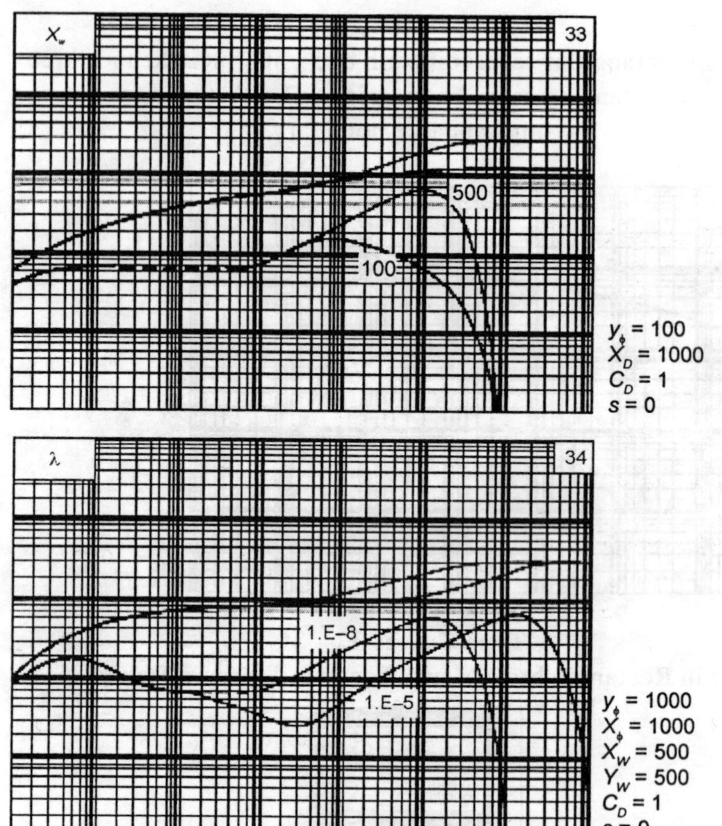

X_w
33
500
100
y_ϕ = 100
X_D = 1000
C_D = 1
s = 0
λ
34
1.E–8
1.E–5
y_ϕ = 1000
X_ϕ = 1000
X_W = 500
Y_W = 500
C_D = 1
s = 0

Type Curves 35—37
Well in Rectangle Near Constant Pressure Boundary

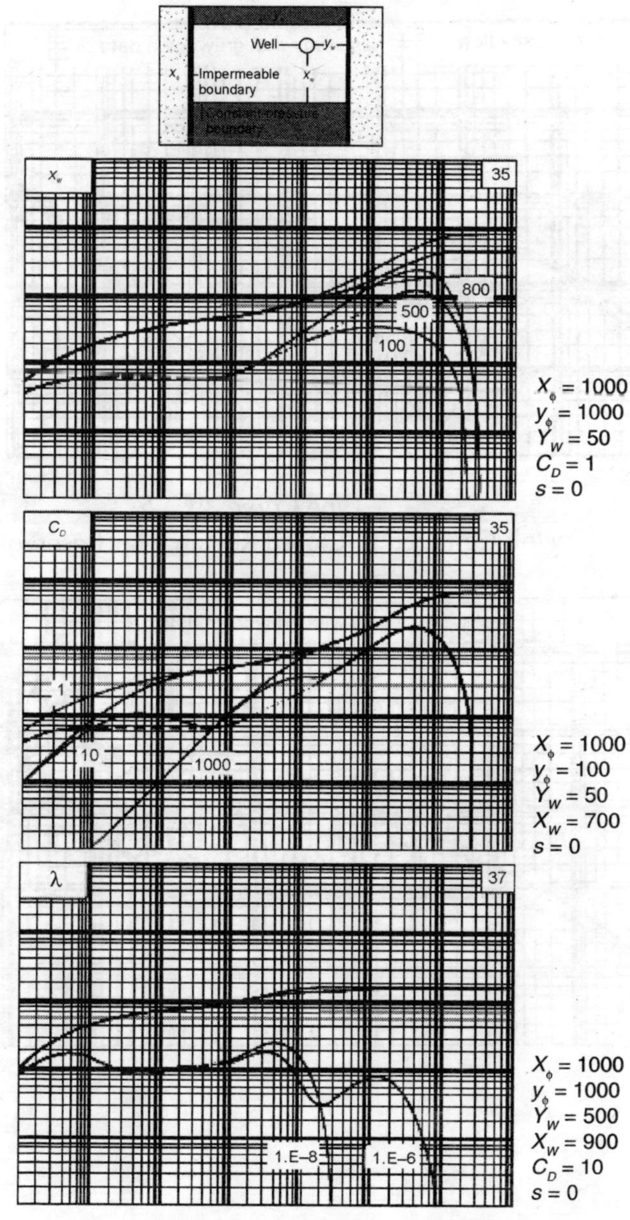

Type Curve 38
Well in Closed Circular Reservoir

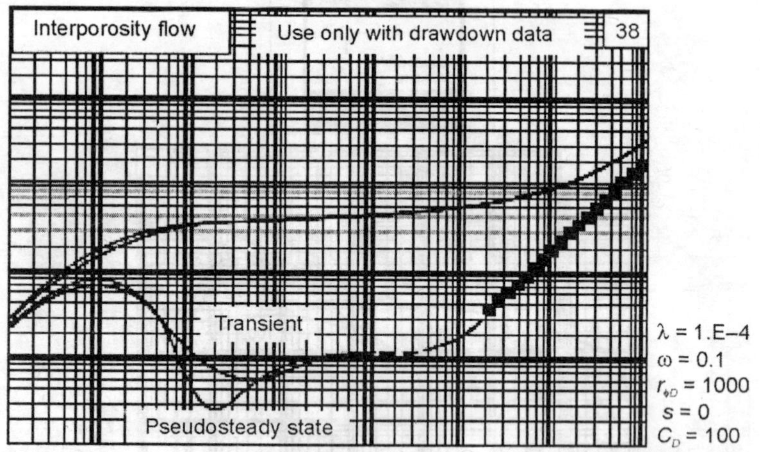

Type Curve 39
Well Centered in Closed Rectangular Reservoir

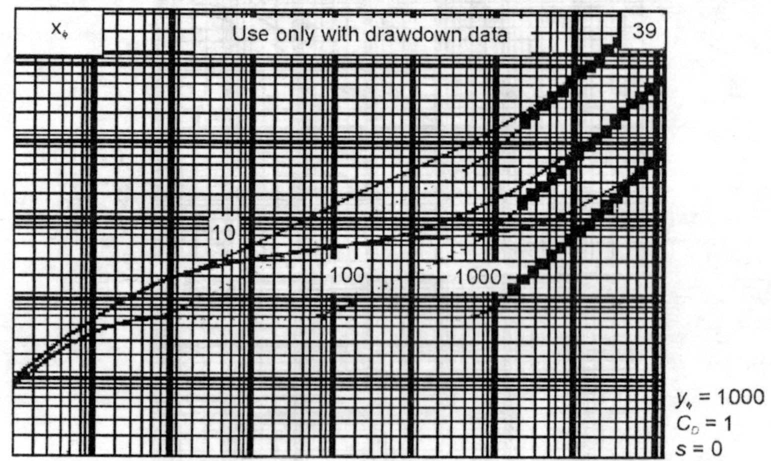

Type Curve 40
Injection Well

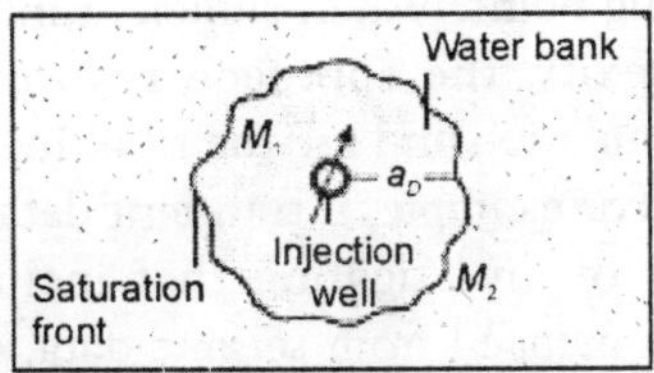

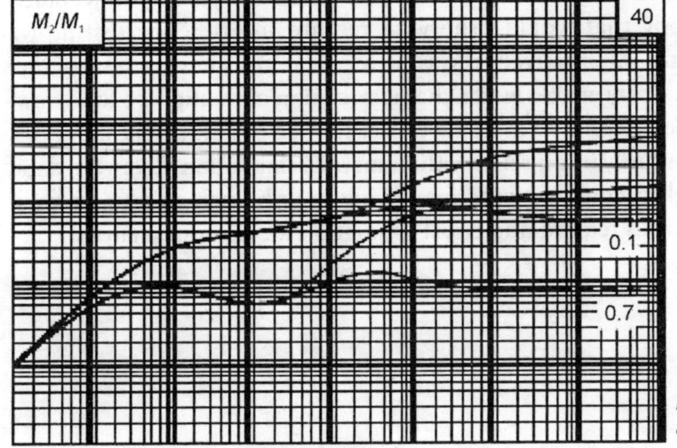

M_2 = 0.1
a_D = 100

Use of Numerical Simulation

Acquired transient data commonly contains behaviour dominated by effects that are not captured in analytical models. Typical departures from the analytical model assumptions are multiphase flow, non-Darcy flow, and complex boundary configurations that are not easily generalized in an analytical model catalog. Such features can be addressed with a numerical model, but commercial numerical simulators are designed for full-field simulation with multiple wells and do not readily adapt to the single-well focus and short-time frame inherent to well testing.

If they are adapted to focus on the short-term transient behaviour of a single well or a few wells, and also designed to present the data in the form used for well test interpretation, numerical models can provide considerable insight beyond that possible from analytical models. The extremely broad range of what can be modeled with numerical simulation makes this a tool used to refine the interpretation process, not a starting point. When sufficient information supports this level of complexity, the approach is to capture all known parameters in the simulation and use the resulting model to quantify what is not known. For example, if transient data are acquired that encompass a radius of investigation that includes structural or stratigraphic barriers mapped from seismic data, capturing these in the numerical model may enable quantification of areal permeability anisotropy that would otherwise require interference testing to determine. Alternatively, the same scenario in successive tests of the same well may enable *in situ* characterization of multiphase fluid flow properties. Data from multiple wells acquired by permanent monitors are more easily interpreted with numerical simulation. Likewise, data acquired in complex wells employing multibranch and smart well technologies require numerical simulation for rigorous analysis.

7 Modeling

Modern well test interpretation has three distinct stages. In the model identification stage, the analyst identifies a theoretical reservoir model with pressure trends that resemble those observed in the acquired data. Once the model has been chosen, the model parameters that produce the best match for the measured pressure data are determined in the parameter estimation stage. Finally, in the results verification stage the selected model and its parameters are used to demonstrate a satisfactory match for one or more transient tests in the well.

Model Identification

For the model identification stage, the analyst should recognize certain characteristic patterns displayed by the pressure transient data. This is greatly facilitated by a knowledge of straight-line pressure derivative response trends associated with the formation flow geometry. As previously discussed, spherical or hemispherical flow to a partial completion exhibits a derivative line with a negative half-slope. Linear flow to a hydraulic fracture or in an elongated reservoir is recognized as a straight trend in the derivative with a positive half-slope. Bilinear flow to a finiteconductivity hydraulic fracture has a derivative line with a positive quarter-slope. The dominant geometry of the flow streamlines in the formation determines which flow regime pattern appears in the pressure transient response at a given time. The presence of one or more of the recognized derivative patterns marks the need to select a model that accounts for the implied flow regimes.

Moreover, each of the several easily recognized derivative trends has a specialized plot that is used to estimate the parameters associated with the trend. The specialized plot for each straight derivative trend is merely a plot of the pressure change versus the elapsed time, raised to the same power as the slope of the derivative line on the log-log plot. The slopes and intercepts of these specialized plots provide the equations for parameter computations. Parameters estimated from a specialized plot may be used as starting values for computerized refinement of the model for the transient response in the second interpretation stage.

Reservoir information collected from geoscientists assists the selection of a reservoir model. The distinctions among the various model options consistent with the transient test data are not always clear-cut, and more than one model may provide similar responses. In this case, the analyst may rule out most model options by consulting with colleagues working with other, independent data. If the flow regime responses are poorly developed or nonexistent, interdisciplinary discussion may suggest the selection of an appropriate model and reasonable starting values for the parameter estimation stage of the interpretation.

Flow regime responses may be difficult to recognize because of a problem or procedure that could have been addressed before starting the test. This underscores the need for careful test design. For example, excessive wellbore storage resulting from shutting in the well at the surface can mask important flow regime trends. Furthermore, late-time trends may be distorted by superposition effects that could have been minimized with adjustments in the test sequence or by inadequate pressure gauge resolution that could have been avoided by using a more sensitive gauge. Missing or incomplete late-time trends may result from premature test termination that would have been avoided with real-time surface acquisition and on-site data validation.

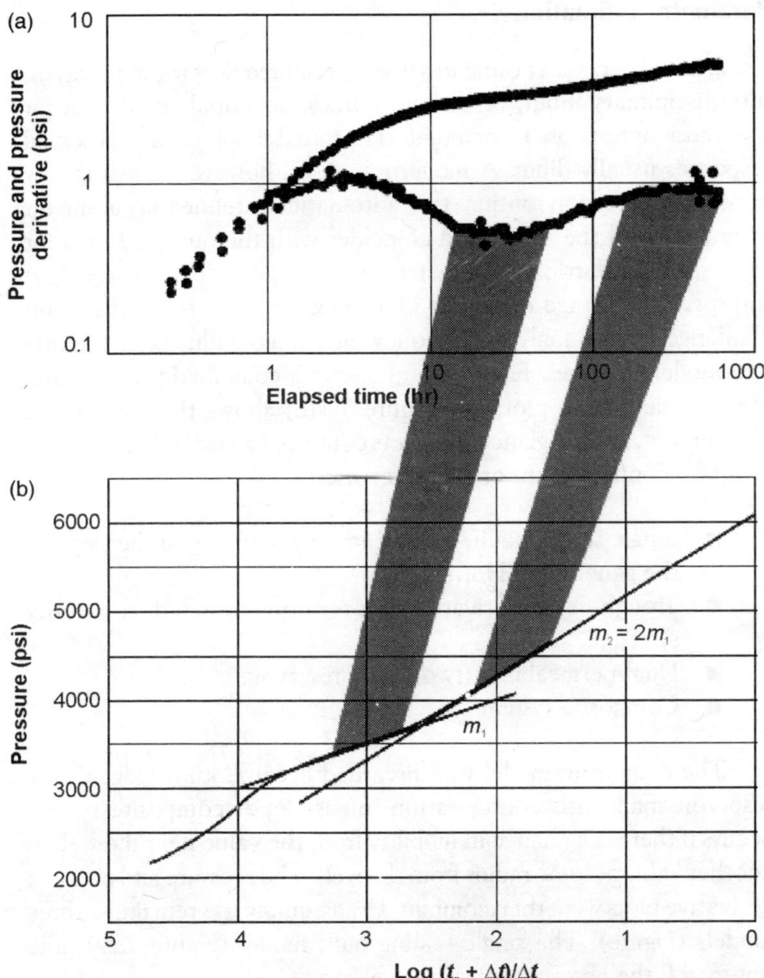

Figure 7.1: Pressure and pressure derivative (a) and Horner (b) plots of measured data for use in model identification and parameter computation. The doubling of the slope *m* on the Horner plot simplistically indicates that the sole cause is an impermeable barrier near the well, such as a sealing fault. Closer examination of the data using current computational techniques and interdisciplinary consultation identifies other factors that may cause the change in slope, such as a two-layer reservoir (dual permeability).

Parameter Estimation

Using initial parameter estimates from specialized flow regime analysis, interdisciplinary input, or both resources, an initial simulation for the transient response is computed. The initial simulated and observed responses usually differ. A modern analysis, however, is assisted by nonlinear regression routines that automatically refine the parameter estimates until the simulation coincides with the observed data for the essential portions of the transient response. Thus, the first interpretation stage of model identification represents the main challenge for the analyst. The following example illustrates the first two modeling stages. Figure 7.1(a) shows a combined pressure and pressure derivative plot, and Figure 7.1(b) shows the generalized Horner plot. At first glance, the plots could be caused by four possible reservoir configurations or characteristics:

- Single sealing fault, as indicated by doubling of the slope in the generalized Horner plot,
- Trough in the derivative plot resulting from a dual-porosity system,
- Dual-permeability (two-layer) reservoir,
- Composite system.

The composite model was discarded because knowledge of the reservoir made this configuration infeasible. A composite system occurs if there is a change in mobility from the value near the well to another value at some radius from the well. The pressure and pressure derivative plots were then computed by assuming the remaining three models (Figure). The single sealing fault model (Figure 7.2a) does not match the observed pressure transient.

Figures 7.2(b) and 7.2(c), derived assuming a dual-porosity system, provide a much better match than the two previous models, although they are still imperfect. Figure 7.2(d) confirms the extremely good fit of the dual-permeability or two-layer reservoir model with the pressure transient and derivative curves.

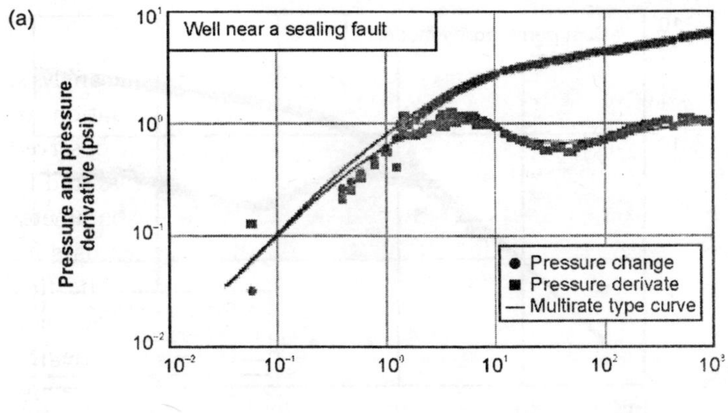

(a)
Well near a sealing fault
Pressure and pressure derivative (psi)
10¹
10⁰
10⁻¹
10⁻²
10⁻²
10⁻¹
10⁰
10¹
10²
10³
● Pressure change
■ Pressure derivate
— Multirate type curve

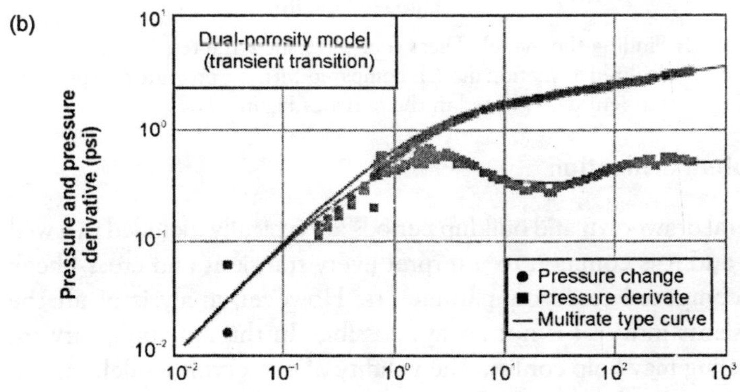

(b)
Dual-porosity model
(transient transition)
Pressure and pressure derivative (psi)
10¹
10⁰
10⁻¹
10⁻²
10⁻²
10⁻¹
10⁰
10¹
10²
10³
● Pressure change
■ Pressure derivate
— Multirate type curve

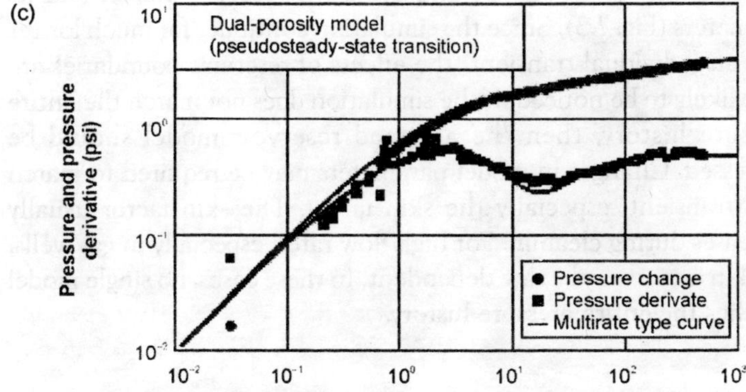

(c)
Dual-porosity model
(pseudosteady-state transition)
Pressure and pressure derivative (psi)
10¹
10⁰
10⁻¹
10⁻²
10⁻²
10⁻¹
10⁰
10¹
10²
10³
● Pressure change
■ Pressure derivate
— Multirate type curve

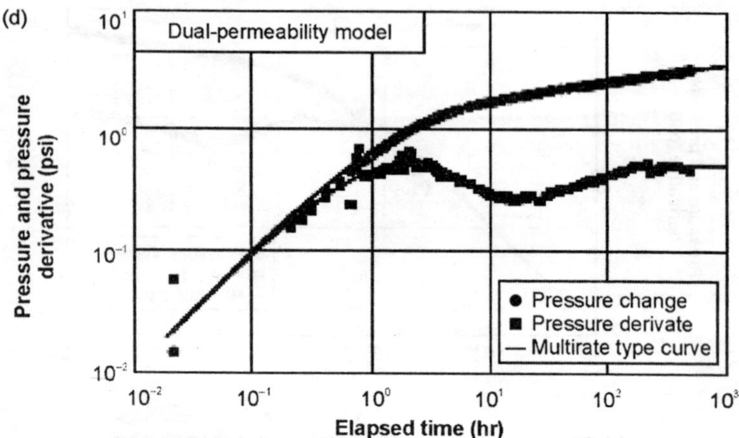

Figure 7.2: Finding the model. These four plots show the response of various idealized formation models compared with the pressure and pressure transient data plotted in the previous Figure.

Results Verification

Several drawdown and buildup periods are typically included in a well test, and it is common to interpret every transient and cross-check the computed reservoir parameters. However, analysis of all the transients in a test is not always possible. In this situation, forward modeling may help confirm the validity of a reservoir model.

Basically, forward modeling involves simulating the entire series of drawdowns and buildups and using the reservoir model and its parameters (Fig. 7.3). Since the simulation continues for much longer than an individual transient, the effects of reservoir boundaries are more likely to be noticed. If the simulation does not match the entire pressure history, then the assumed reservoir model should be reassessed. Changes in model parameters may be required to match each transient, especially the skin factor. The skin factor usually decreases during cleanup. For high flow rates, especially in gas wells, the skin factor may be rate dependent. In these cases, no single model matches the entire pressure history.

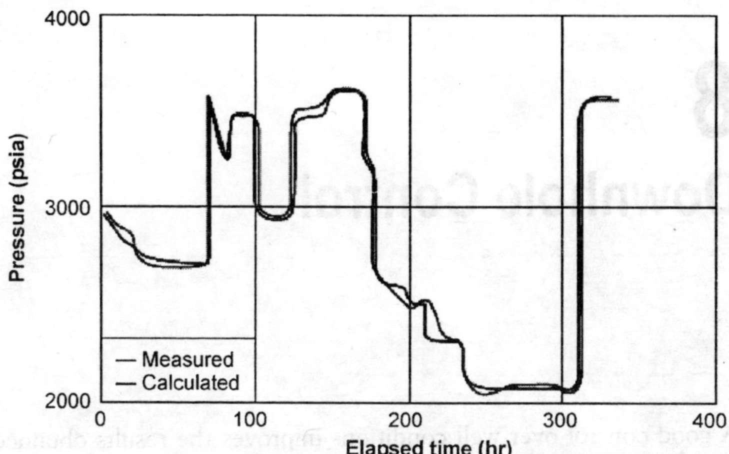

Figure 7.3: Forward modeling used to reproduce the entire data set. The model and parameters were selected by analyzing one of the pressure transients.

8
Downhole Control

A good control over well conditions improves the results obtained from well testing. Two important advances that have significantly improved control during well testing are downhole shut-in valves and downhole flow measurements. These techniques have eliminated most of the drawbacks inherent in surface shut-in testing. Another factor that has contributed to improved well testing practices is the advent of surface readout in real time. This enables the detection of problems that can be corrected to avoid data loss or improve data quality.

Downhole Shut-in Techniques

Downhole shut-in techniques play a critical role in modern well testing. The schematic diagram of a downhole shut-in valve in Figure 8.1 shows how the pressure gauge monitors pressure in the wellbore chamber created beneath the closed valve.

The main advantages of using downhole shut-in are the minimization of both wellbore storage effects and the duration of the afterflow period.

When the downhole shut-in valve is closed, flow up the well is interrupted. Meanwhile, flow continues to enter the chamber below at an exponentially decreasing rate. Figure shows a typical response during a build-up test using the downhole shut-in technique and also illustrates how flow into the well does not immediately cease after shut-in. Continued flow into the well undermines the assumptions made in the well testing solutions.

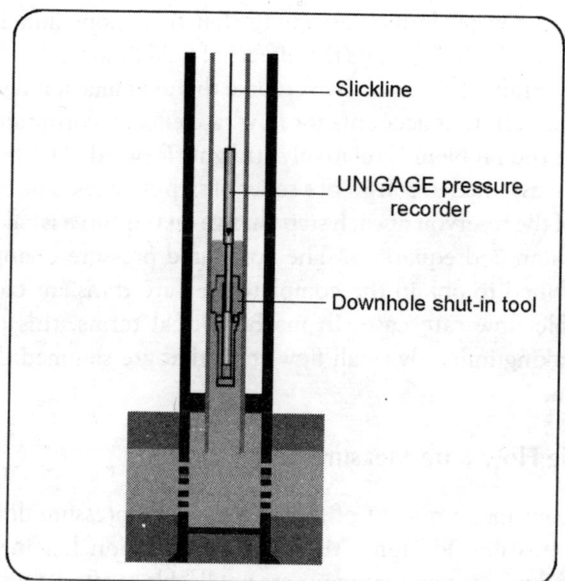

Figure 8.1: Downhole shut-in valve is used during pressure buildup tests to provide excellent downhole control.

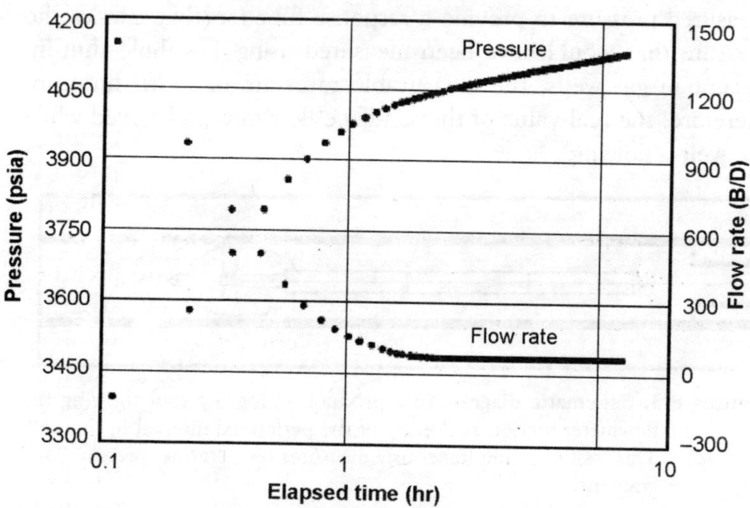

Figure 8.2: Pressure and flow rate variations that occur with the use of a downhole shut-in valve.

Equations were derived assuming that flow stops immediately upon shut-in, which discounts the effects of fluid flow on the shape of the pressure transient curve. To overcome this dilemma, it is necessary to find a solution that accounts for flow rate effects. Fortunately, the solution to the problem is relatively straights forward. The flow rate curve is first assumed to consist of a series of step changes. The pressure response of the reservoir at each step change on the curve is calculated using the standard equations. The computed pressure changes are then combined to obtain the complete pressure transient curve for the variable flow rate case. In mathematical terms, this process involves taking infinitely small flow steps that are summed through integration.

Downhole Flow Rate Measurement

Simultaneous measurement of the flow rate and pressure downhole has been possible for some time with production logging tools. Downhole flow rate measurements are applicable to afterflow analysis, drawdown and injectivity tests, and layered reservoir testing (LRT). The continuously measured flow rate can be processed with the measured pressure to provide a response function that mimics the pressure that would have been measured using downhole shut-in. Except in gas wells, the measurable rates are of short duration; therefore, the real value of the sandface flow rate is observed while the well is flowing.

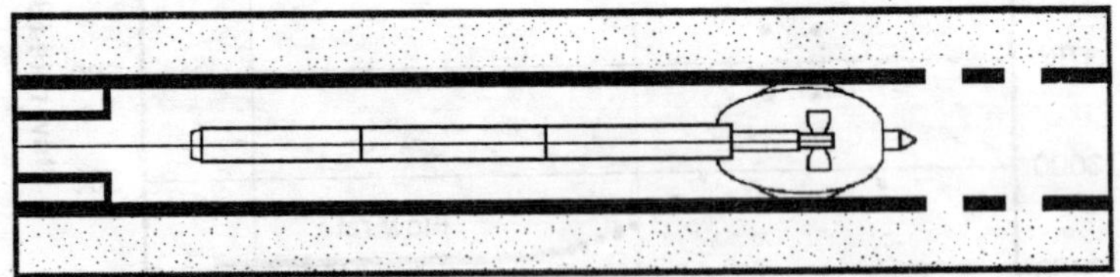

Figures 8.3: Schematic diagram of a production logging tool showing the flowmeter section at the top of the perforated interval in the well. This tool also simultaneously measures temperature, pressure, and gradient.

In many cases, particularly in thick or layered formations, only a small percentage of the perforated interval may be producing. This condition can result from blocked perforations or the presence of low-permeability layers. A conventional surface well test may incorrectly indicate that there are major skin effects caused by formation damage throughout the well. Downhole flow measurement enables measurement of the flow profile in a stabilized well for calculation of the skin effects caused by flow convergence. This technique makes it possible to infer the actual contribution of formation damage to the overall skin effect.

Downhole Flow Rate Measurements

The techniques described for analyzing transient tests rely on only pressure measurements and were derived assuming a constant flow rate during the analyzed test period. The constant flow rate situation, in practice, prevails only during shut-in conditions. Because of this, build-up tests are the most commonly practiced well testing method.

A build-up test is undesirable if the operator cannot afford the lost production associated with the test or because the well would not flow again if shut-in. For these circumstances, drawdown tests are preferable. In practice, however, it is difficult to achieve a constant flow rate out of the well, so these tests were traditionally ruled out.

Advances in measurement and interpretation techniques now enable the analysis of tests that exhibit variable flow rate conditions to obtain the same information furnished by build-up tests, provided that the flow rate variations are measured in tandem with changes in pressure. Today, pressure transient tests can be run in almost any production or injection well without shutting in the well and halting production.

Drawdown data are not ambiguous like build-up data (varying between steady state and pseudosteady-state responses). Boundary geometries are easier to diagnose because there is less distortion caused by superposition, provided that the downhole flow rate is measured. Consequently, the results are more definitive. Let us study a procedure for well test analysis in a single-layer reservoir with combined downhole flow rate and pressure measurements. The method enables the analysis of drawdown periods and the afterflow-dominated portion of a build-up test.

Problem

Flow rates and pressure changes are closely associated: any change in the flow rate produces a corresponding change in pressure and vice versa. The challenge for the analyst is to distinguish the changes in the pressure response curve that have been caused by a genuine reservoir characteristic from those created by varying wellbore flow rates (i.e., the pure reservoir signal versus noise).

The pure reservoir signal can be separated from the noise by acquiring simultaneous measurements of flow and pressure. Production logging tools can acquire both variables simultaneously and accurately, extending the range of wells in which well testing can be successfully performed.

In a typical test, a production logging tool is positioned at the top of the producing interval (Figure 8.4). The tool records flow and pressure data for the duration of the test. Figure shows a typical dataset acquired during a drawdown test, with changes in the shape of the pressure curve matching those on the flow rate curve.

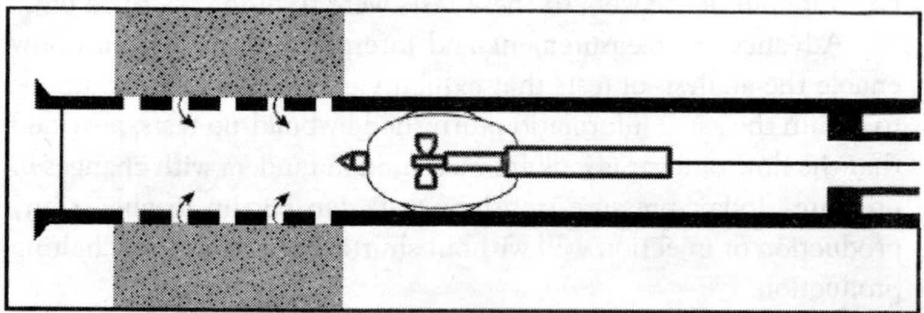

Figure 8.4: Production logging tool in position for a well test in a single-layer reservoir.

The analysis of transient tests with simultaneously recorded flow rate and pressure measurements involves the same three basic stages as pressure data analysis—model identification, parameter estimation, and verification. The same plotting techniques are used, except that the scales contain functions that account for all observed flow rate changes.

Model Identification

Measured pressure values can be compared directly with the theoretical curves only when the flow rate from the reservoir is constant, the curves can also be used for variable rate cases if mathematical transforms are applied to the test data. The transforms account for the flow rate variations observed during the transient.

Figure 8.5 shows the log-log plot of the pressure and pressure derivative curves of the data shown in fig. The data are from a well in which the flow rates were changing before and during the test. The flow rate changes had a dominating effect on the well pressure, to the point where the pressure and pressure derivative curves lack any distinct shape that could be used for model identification. It would be incorrect to attempt identification of the reservoir model by comparing these raw data with the library of type curves, which were constructed using a single-step change, constant flow rate.

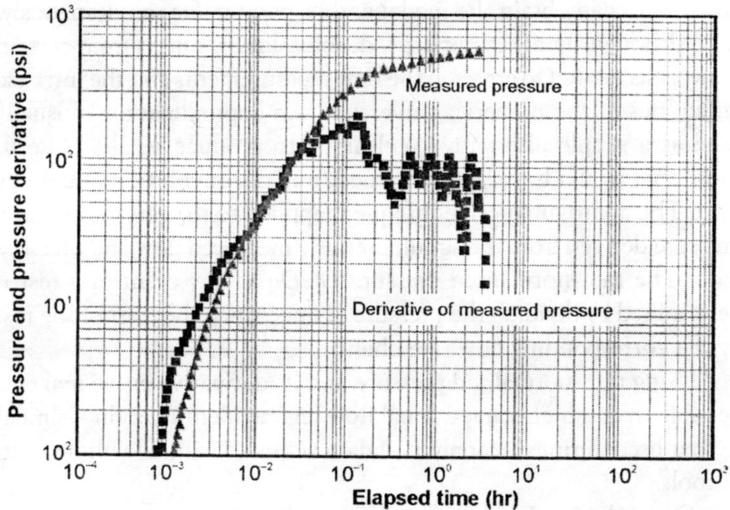

Figure 8.5: Flow rate changes before and during a well test can dominate the measured well pressure. Because the pressure and pressure derivative curves lack any distinct shapes, they cannot be compared with the published type curves to identify the reservoir model.

Rather, the data are transformed to a form that can be more readily analyzed. One such transform is deconvolution—a process that enables construction of the raw pressure curve that would have occurred in response to a single-step change, constant flow rate.

The pressure response for a transient test under variable flow rate conditions is given by the convolution integral, which can be expressed in dimensionless variables as—

$$P_{wbD}(t_D) = \int_0^{t_D} q_D(\tau) P_{wD}'(t_D - \tau) d\tau.$$

Mathematically, deconvolution is the inversion of the convolution integral. The constant flow rate response (including wellbore storage and skin effects) is computed from measurements of the wellbore flowing pressure *pwbf* and flow rate *qwbf*. Ideally, deconvolved pressure data can be compared directly with the published type curves. Then, straightforward conventional interpretation techniques and matching procedures can obtain the model and its parameters simultaneously.

Although simple in concept, deconvolution suffers from certain drawbacks related to errors in the flow measurements and the intrinsic difficulties of the numerical inversion. An approximation is usually used as a simple alternative technique to produce results close to those that would have been obtained from deconvolution of the raw data. The approximation technique is applied to the rate-normalized pressure derived from the simultaneously measured flow and pressure data. The rate-normalized pressure *Dp/Dq* at any point in a test is determined by dividing the pressure change since the start of the test by the corresponding flow rate change.

Using rate-normalized pressure and its derivative curve makes it possible to conduct conventional flow regime identification—similar to that used during the analysis of data acquired with downhole shut-in tools.

Once the model that suites the wellbore reservoir system has been identified using the deconvolution approximation, the interpretation proceeds to the quantification of model parameters such as *k*, *s*, and the distance from the well to the nearest faults.

Parameter Estimation

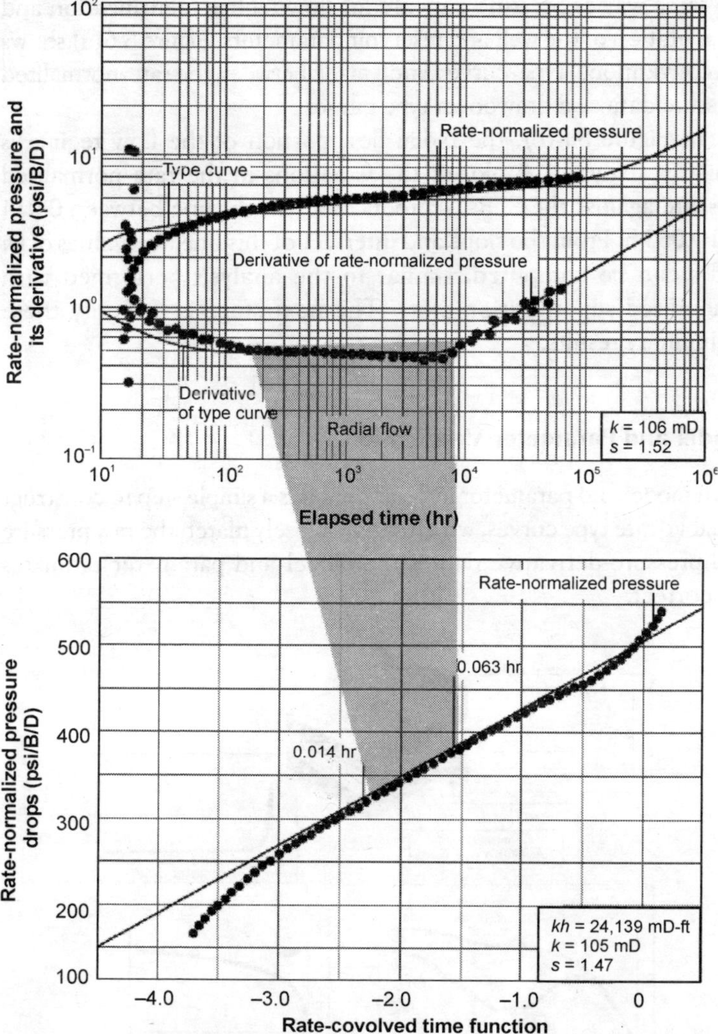

Figure 8.6: (a) Log-log plot of rate-normalized pressure and its derivative curve used for flow regime identification and type-curve matching analysis. This method is similar to that used for the analysis of data acquired at a constant flow rate. (b) Sandface rate convolution plot of pressure data normalized with flow rate data versus a time function that accounts for all observed flow rate changes.

Initial estimates of the model parameters are determined in this stage of the analysis. The rate-normalized pressure data are used in the same way as pressure data are for flow regime identification and computation of the well and reservoir parameters. Figure 8.6(a) shows the conventional type-curve match made between the rate-normalized pressure data and drawdown type curves.

In Figure 8.6(b), the radial flow portion of the flow regime is similarly analyzed. A plot of the variations in the rate-normalized pressure against the SFRCT produces a straight line between 0.014 and 0.063 h. From the slope and intersect of this line, the values of kh and s can be computed, similar to the analysis performed with generalized superposition plots. The next stage is to verify these preliminary results.

Model and Parameter Verification

With model and parameter information, it is a simple step to construct variable-rate type curves, which should closely match the raw pressure and pressure derivative data if the model and parameter estimates are correct.

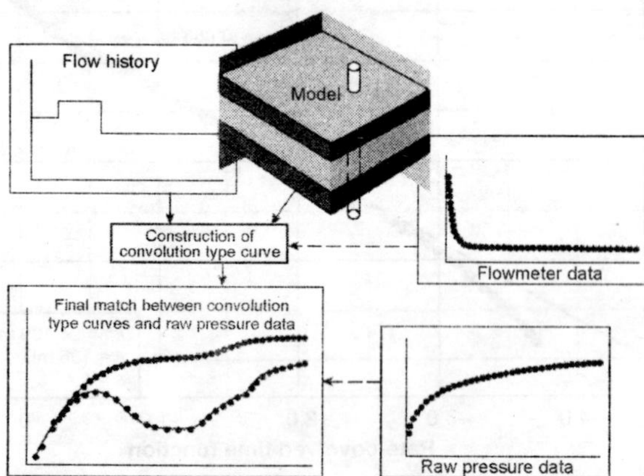

Figure 8.7: The construction of convolution type curves. Pressure is computed from flow rate data and from the theoretical pressure response (model) to a single-step rate change. The CTC accounts for all rate variations before and during the test.

To produce a variable-rate type curve, the model uses the actual flow history of the well. The measured flow rate during the transient is convolved with the selected model pressure response, and the effects of the flow rate changes before the test are added. The resulting curve has been called a convolution type curve (CTC).

9
Horizontal Wells

With the significant increase in horizontal drilling activity during recent years, pressure transient behaviour in horizontal wells has received considerable attention. Pressure transient behaviour in a horizontal well test is considerably more complex than in a conventional vertical well test because of its three-dimensional nature. In a horizontal well, instead of the radial flow regime that develops for a conventional test, three flow regimes may occur after the effects of wellbore storage disappear.

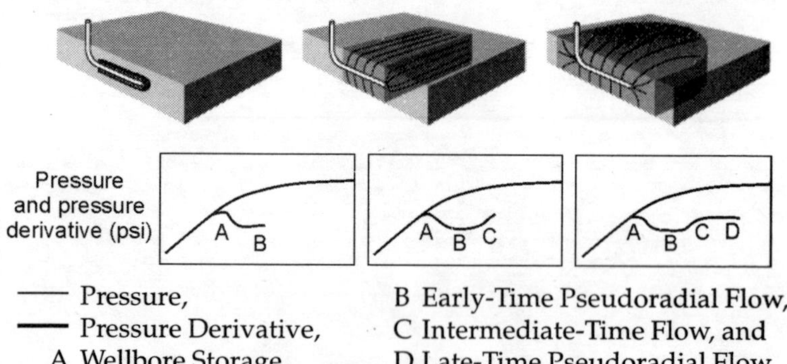

—— Pressure,
—— Pressure Derivative,
A Wellbore Storage,
B Early-Time Pseudoradial Flow,
C Intermediate-Time Flow, and
D Late-Time Pseudoradial Flow.

Figure 9.1: Phases in a horizontal well transient test. After wellbore storage effects have disappeared, the flow is radial toward the well in the vertical *y-z* plane (first plateau in the derivative curve). The next phase is linear flow in the *y-z* plane (straight line with half-slope in the derivative curve). Finally flow is radial in the *x-y* plane (second plateau in the derivative curve).

Initially, flow occurs radially in a vertical plane toward the well, indicated by a plateau on the derivative curve of the log-log plot. This regime is termed early-time pseudoradial flow because of the elliptical flow pattern resulting from the vertical to horizontal permeability anisotropy. The second flow regime begins when the transient reaches the upper and lower boundaries of the producing interval, and flow becomes linear toward the well within a horizontal plane. This intermediate-time regime is characterized by a half-slope trend in the derivative curve. The third flow regime occurs as the transient moves deeper into the reservoir and the flow becomes radial again, but in the horizontal plane. This late-time regime is indicated by a second plateau in the derivative curve.

The first radial flow regime yields the mechanical skin factor and the geometric average of the vertical and horizontal permeabilities. The intermediate-time linear flow regime can be analyzed to estimate the length of the producing interval, as long as the horizontal plane can be considered isotropic. The late-time radial flow yields the average permeability in the horizontal plane and the total skin factor (mechanical and geometrical skin factors).

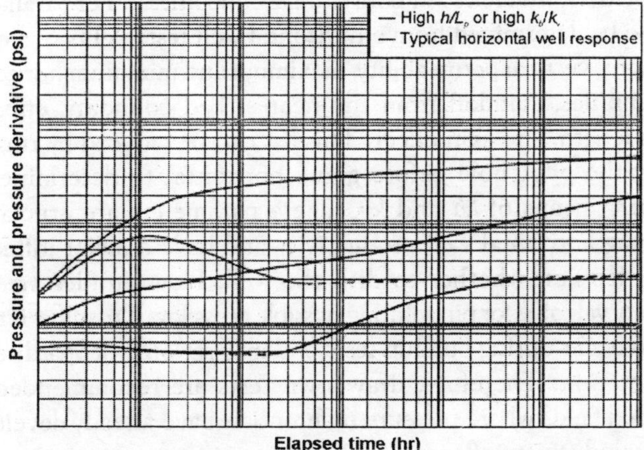

Figure 9.2: Theoretical pressure response of a horizontal well drilled in a thick reservoir or in a reservoir with high vertical to horizontal permeability anisotropy. h/Lp = ratio of reservoir height to length of the horizontal well perforated interval.

The geometrical skin factor is important for horizontal wells drilled in thick formations or in formations that exhibit a high contrast between *kh* and *kv*. Furthermore, in these circumstances neither the early-time flow regime nor the linear one develops.

The identification of the first pseudoradial flow is crucial for a complete interpretation because it provides the formation damage. This regime is often masked by the unavoidably large wellbore storage effects in horizontal wells. The key to successful horizontal well testing is the full control of the downhole environment.

Full control can be achieved by using simultaneous measurements of flow rate and either pressure or downhole shut-in or both. Moreover, the identification of all three flow regimes is not always possible from one transient. Combining drawdown tests in which the flow rate and pressure are measured simultaneously with buildup tests using downhole shut-in maximizes the likelihood of identifying all three flow regimes.

Supplementing the transient test data with flow profiles along the trajectory of the horizontal well facilitates identifying the producing zones and determining the effective flowing interval. Deriving this parameter from the transient data is more complicated because, in addition to the inherent wellbore storage difficulties, other parameters may also be determined from a horizontal well test: wellbore storage coefficient, vertical permeability, maximum and minimum horizontal permeabilities, standoff from the nearest bed boundary, effective flowing length, and skin effect. This list can be reduced by running tests in the pilot hole before going horizontal to determine the geometric means of *kh* and *kv*. These parameters are crucial for estimating horizontal well productivity and have a major influence on the decision whether to drill the well. Flow profiles are also extremely valuable for pinpointing possible crossflow. Crossflow is more likely to occur during buildup tests and may seriously jeopardize the interpretation. Therefore, drawdown tests are recommended for developed fields where pressure differentials have already developed and may induce crossflow.

The interpretation of horizontal well test pressure measurements involves the same three stages used for vertical well test analysis. First, the pressure response and its derivative are analyzed to diagnose the characteristic behaviour of the system and identify specific flow regimes. Second, specialized plots are used to extract the effective parameters for each flow regime, typically the values of *k* and *s*. Third, these reservoir parameter estimates are refined by history matching the measured transient response to that predicted by a mathematical model for the well and reservoir system.

As always, history matching is expected to produce more accurate results because the features of the various flow patterns are rigorously taken into account. Moreover, the match involves the entire set of transient data, including transition periods between specific flow regimes, whereas direct analysis uses only the data subset of identifiable flow regimes. This stage also offers the possibility of simultaneously matching more than one transient, which further constrains the model to accurately represent the well and reservoir system.

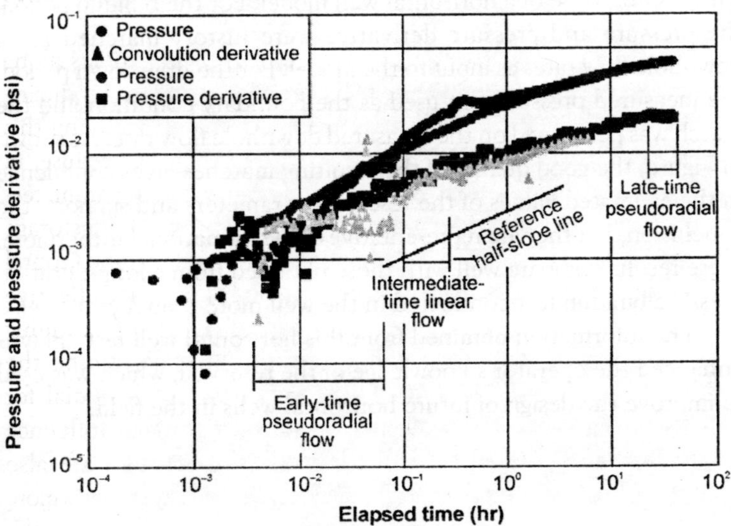

Figure 9.3: Comparison diagnostic plot used for horizontal well flow regime identification.

Figure 9.3 shows the comparative log-log plot of both transients from a drawdown and buildup test conducted in a well in India. The data are noisy and do not display sufficient character to indicate a unique solution, but knowing that these data were acquired in a horizontal well makes a reasonable flow regime identification feasible. The derivative and convolution derivative curves in Fig. exhibit plateaus that suggest the existence of two pseudoradial flow regimes. The first plateau, indicative of early-time pseudoradial flow, is visible only in the convolution derivative of the drawdown transient. This plateau should also have developed during the buildup, but it is masked by wellbore storage. On the other hand, the second plateau is visible only in the derivative curve of the buildup, which lasted long enough for radial flow to develop. Between these plateaus, the derivative curves of both transients exhibit slopes close to a half-slope trend, indicating the presence of linear flow.

Analysis of these individual flow regimes yielded values for the vertical and horizontal permeabilities and mechanical skin factor. These parameters were refined by history matching both transients with the response of a horizontal well model. For the buildup period, the pressure and pressure derivative were history matched using downhole flow rates as input to the model. For the drawdown period, the measured pressure was used as the boundary condition and the match was performed on the measured downhole flow rate. As shown in Figure, the good quality of the resulting matches gives confidence in the estimated values of the reservoir parameters and supports the conclusion that they are representative of the formation. Furthermore, these results compare well with those obtained from a long-duration pressure buildup test conducted in the well more than a year later.

The information obtained from this horizontal well test analysis enhanced the operator's knowledge of the reservoir, which was used to improve the design of future horizontal wells in the field.

10
Wellbore Storage

The analysis/interpretation of wellbore storage distorted pressure transient test data remains one of the most significant challenges in well test analysis. Deconvolution (i.e., the "conversion" of a variable-rate distorted pressure profile into the pressure profile for an equivalent constant rate production sequence) has been in limited use as a "conversion" mechanism for the last 25 years. Unfortunately, standard deconvolution techniques require accurate measurements of flow-rate and pressure—at downhole (or sandface) conditions. While accurate pressure measurements are commonplace, the measurement of sandface flow rates is rare, essentially non-existent in practice. As such, the "deconvolution" of wellbore storage distorted pressure test data is problematic.

Wellbore Effects on a Well Test

A pressure recorder, as accurate as it may be (nowadays the error can be less than 1/100 of a psi), generally performs its measurements in somewhere between the sandface and wellbore. This must be acknowledged when using pressure data for the characterization of a reservoir, since the pressure transient test data are the result of a combination of wellbore and reservoir effects. For most of the life of a reservoir, reservoir effects dominate the pressure response of the system, and the conventional pressure transient test equations and analyses apply accurately. However, for cases of transient flow, wellbore effects (i.e., storage of the fluid in the wellbore or wellbore storage) distort and even dominate the reservoir pressure and rate response particularly at early times.

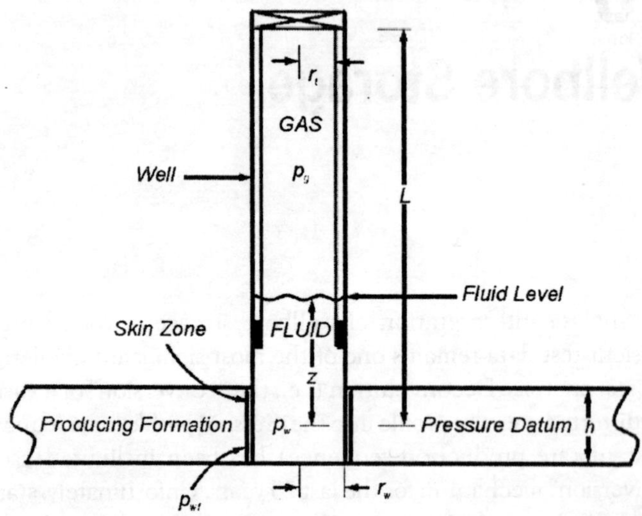

Figure 10.1: Schematic diagram of well and formation during pressure build-up.

A schematic case of wellbore storage effects imposed on a system is illustrated in the pressure response shown in Fig. A complete knowledge of these "wellbore effects" would permit the "correction" of these effects (using a process known as "deconvolution") which would provide interpretation and analysis of well tests for early and very early data (as these are the most distorted data). Simply put, the goal of this work (and of deconvolution in general) is to correct the pressure data taken at early times which are affected by "wellbore storage." Lacking the ability to "correct" these data means that we must wait for the distortion of the data to diminish (sometimes only a few hours, but possibly months or years for very low permeability gas reservoirs). As well tests are often run for as short as economically feasible for a particular well, many well tests are often completely distorted by wellbore storage effects.

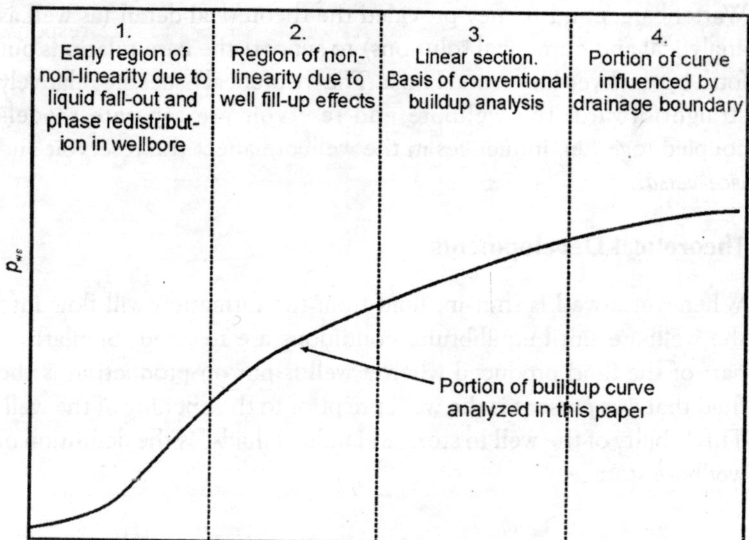

Figure 10.2: Typical pressure build-up plot.

These "wellbore" effects have been labeled as "wellbore dynamics" by Mattar and Santo, and these effects include the following components (one or more effects may act at any given time):

- Liquid influx/efflux.
- Phase redistribution.
- Wellbore and near-wellbore cleanup.
- Plugging.
- Recorder effects: drift, hysteresis, malfunction, temperature sensitivity, and fluid PVT changes.
- Gas/oil solution/liberation.
- Retrograde condensation.
- Diverse effects such as leaks, geotidal/microseismic.

The Wellbore Storage Effect

Since its introduction by van Everdingen and Hurst in 1949, the issue of wellbore storage distortion has been extensively treated in the Petroleum Engineering literature. In 1970, Agarwal *et al.* and

Wattenbarger and Ramey provided the theoretical detail (as well as analytical and numerical solutions) to support the base relations put forth by van Everdingen and Hurst. The theoretical issues are relatively straightforward, the wellbore and reservoir are separate models coupled together, influences in the wellbore affect the reservoir and *vice-versa*.

Theoretical Developments

Whenever a well is shut-in, fluid from the formation will flow into the wellbore until equilibrium conditions are reached. Similarly, a part of the fluid produced when a well is put on production is the fluid that was present is the wellbore prior to the opening of the well. This "ability of the well to store and unload fluids" is the definition of wellbore storage:

$$q_{wd} = \frac{c}{b}\frac{dp_{wf}}{dt}, \qquad \text{..... (1)}$$

where *qwb* represents the rate at which the wellbore "unloads" fluids, and C represents the storage constant of the well. In the specific case where the wellbore unloading is entirely due to fluid expansion, the wellbore storage constant is defined by

$$C = \frac{dV}{dp}, \qquad \text{..... (2)}$$

where ?*V* is the change in volume of fluid in the wellbore—at wellbore conditions—and ?*p* is the change in bottom-hole pressure.

When the wellbore is filled with a single fluid phase, Eq. (2) becomes—

$$C = V_w c, \qquad \text{..... (3)}$$

where V_w is the total wellbore volume and *c* is the compressiblility of the fluid in the wellbore at wellbore conditions. The use of dimensionless pressure functions in most of the derivations of this work leads to the use of a dimensionless wellbore storage coefficient C_D:

$$C_D = 0.894 \frac{C}{fc_t h r_w^2}, \qquad \text{..... (4)}$$

As such, wellbore storage affects the sandface flow rate, causing a lag in the sandface flow rate relative to any change in the surface flow rate. The surface flowrate is the sum of the wellbore rate (q_{wb}) and the sandface rate (q_{sf})—i.e., the sum of the wellbore (unloading) rate and the sandface flowrate:

$$q = q_s f + q_{wb}. \qquad \text{..... (5)}$$

van Everdigen and Hurst expressed the rigorous sandface flow rate relation for wellbore storage and skin using constant wellbore storage coefficient. The relation is given in dimensionless form as—

$$q_D(t_D) = 1 - C_D \frac{dp_w D}{dt_D}.$$

We will make frequent use of this relation in this study, since it directly links the sandface flow rate (for which we do not have any direct measurements) to the wellbore pressure (for which we typically do have direct and accurate measurements).

Sandface Flowrate Estimators

Blasingame *et al.* proposed five different methods of calculating sandface rates from pressure data for the constant wellbore storage case. These methods will be useful in the implementation of the computational module since most of the implemented methods require the knowledge (or an estimate) of the sandface flowrates.

Method 1

Definition of sandface flowrate (exact)

$$q_D = 1 - C_D \frac{dp_w D}{dt_D} = 1 - \frac{\frac{d}{dt}[\Delta p_w]}{m_{wbs}}.$$

Method 2

Alternative calculation of sandface flowrate based on Method 1 (exact)

$$Q_D = t_D - C_D P_{wD} = t - \frac{\Delta P_w}{m_{wbs}},$$

$$q_{D_1} = \frac{d}{dt}[Q_D(t)].$$

Method 3

Average sandface flowrate calculation (exact)

$$q_{Di} = 1 - C_D \frac{P_{wD}}{t_D} = 1 - \frac{1}{m_{wbs}} \frac{\Delta p_w}{t},$$

$$t_{Di} = \frac{t_D}{2}.$$

Method 4

Semi-empirical sandface flowrate calculation—assumes $C_D = t_D/p_{wD}$ (approximate)

$$q_{D2} = 1 - \frac{t_D}{p_{wD}} \frac{dp_{wD}}{dt_D} = 1 - \frac{t}{\Delta p_w} \frac{d}{dt}[\Delta p],$$

$$t_{D2} = 1 - \frac{t_D}{2}.$$

Method 5

Semi-empirical sandface flowrate calculation—assumes $C_D = t_D/p_{wDi}$ (approximate)

$$q_{D3} = 1 - \frac{p_{wDid}}{p_{wDi}} = 1 - \frac{p_{wD} - p_{wDi}}{p_{wDi}} = 1 - \frac{t}{\Delta p_{wi}} \frac{d}{dt}[\Delta p_{wi}],$$

$$t_D3 = \frac{t_D}{4}.$$

Theoretical Development: Superposition Principle and Convolution

Convolution is a mathematical operator which, using two functions f and g, produces a third function commonly noted as $f*g$ representing the amount of overlap between f and a reversed and shifted version of g. The convolution operation is defined as

$$(f \times g)(t) = \int_0^t f(\tau)g(t-\tau)d\tau.$$

The convolution operation can by expressed in discrete form as

$$(f \times g)(t) \approx \sum_{i=1}^{n} f(\tau_{i-1})g(t-\tau_{i-1})\Delta\tau.$$

The principle of superposition (or convolution) states that, for a linear system, a linear combination of solutions for a system is also a solution to the same linear system. The superposition (or convolution) principle applies to linear systems of algebraic equations and for our field of study—linear partial differential equations (i.e., the diffusivity equation for flow in porous media). In well test analysis, the superposition principle is used to construct reservoir response functions, to represent various reservoir boundaries (by superposition in space), and to determine variable rate reservoir responses (using superposition in time). However, we must always keep in mind when applying this principle that it is only valid for linear systems, that is, when nonlinearities are present (e.g., gas flow), principle of superposition is not directly applicable. In those cases, linearization (via the pseudopressure transform) must be performed in order to apply the superposition principle to the tranformed system. The early work by Duhamel on heat transfer has since then been used in numerous engineering domains. Adapted to our domain, petroleum engineering, Duhamel's principle states that the observed pressure drop is the convolution of the input rate function and the derivative of the constant-rate pressure response—at $t = 0$, the system is assumed to be in equilibrium [i.e., $p\ (r, t = 0) = p_i$].

For reference, the convolution integral is defined as

$$\Delta p(t) = \int_0^t q(t-\tau)\, p_u'(\tau)\, d\tau.$$

The above equation can be written in a discrete form by assuming that the rate change can be discretized as a series of rate changes:

$$\Delta p(t) = \sum_{i=1}^{n} (q_i - q_{i-1})\left[p_u(t - t_{i-1})\right].$$

van Everdingen and Hurst introduced the use of Duhamel's principle in the analysis of variable-rate welltest data, and they utilized Duhamel's principle to obtain dimensionless wellbore pressure-drop responses for a continuously (smoothly) varying flowrate. The underlying idea was to introduce a method to convolve/superimpose the constant rate pressure response with a continuous (smooth) rate profile to produce the variable rate wellbore pressure-drop response.

Odeh and Jones, Agarwal, Soliman, Stewart, Wittman and Meunier, Fetkovich and Vienot, among others, applied the convolution guidelines in various settings. However, these methods are inherently restricted by the use of a particular model for the constant rate pressure function (i.e., presumed reservoir model) used in the convolution integral.

Explicit Methods for the Analysis of Wellbore Storage Distorted Well Test Data

Russell Method (1966): The pressure "correction" function given by Russell1 is given as

$$\frac{\left[p_{ws}(\Delta t) - p_{wf}(\Delta t = 0)\right]}{\left[1 - \dfrac{1}{C_2 \Delta t}\right]} = f(\Delta t = 1\text{hr}) + m_{sl}\log(\Delta t),$$

where the C_2-term is derived rigorously using Russell's assumptions of the system. The C_2-term is used as an arbitrary constant to be optimized. In short, the Russell method has an elegant mathematical formulation, but ultimately, we believe that this formulation does not represent the wellbore storage condition, and hence, we do not recommend the Russell method under any circumstances.

Russell made the following assumptions in the derivation of his wellbore storage "correction" solution:

- Completely penetrating well in an infinite reservoir.
- Slightly compressible liquid (constant compressibility).
- Constant fluid viscosity.
- Single-phase liquid flow in the reservoir.
- Gravity and capillary pressure neglected.
- Constant permeability.
- Horizontal radial flow (no vertical flow).
- Ideal gas (for the gas cushion in the well).

Although the Russell method was derived from analytical considerations, the problem actually solved is a variation of the true wellbore storage problem, derived using Russell's representation of the gas and liquid volume in the wellbore as the "wellbore storage" term. This formulation is not based on the same physics as the wellbore storage problem where the wellbore production (at the start of production or shut-in) is inversely proportional to the compressibility of the fluids (or the influence of a rising/falling liquid level). In short, Russell approximated the wellbore storage concept in order to develop his "storage" function, presumably for the correction of wellbore storage distortion in pressure build-up tests.

Russell also proposed a methodology to obtain the "extrapolated" pressure using the results of his correction procedure.

Rate Normalization

Gladfelter, Tracy and Wilsey introduced the "rate-normalization" deconvolution approach—which, in their words, "permits direct measurement of the cause of low well productivity." The objective of rate normalization is to remove/correct the effects of the variable rate from the observed pressure data. Rate normalization can also be defined as an approximation to convolution integral:

$$\Delta p(t) \approx q(t)\, pu(t),$$

where p_u is the constant rate pressure response. Rate normalization has been employed for a number of applications in well test analysis. For the specific application of "rate-normalization" deconvolution, we must recognize that the approach is approximate—and while this method does provide some "correction" capabilities, it is basically a technique that can be used for pressure data influenced by continuously varying flow rates. Most notably, Fetkovich and Vienot, Winestock and Colpitts (transient test analysis), and Doublet *et al.* have demonstrated the effectiveness of "rate-normalization" deconvolution.

In particular, for the wellbore storage domination and distortion regimes, rate normalization can provide a reasonable approximation of the no wellbore storage solution. For this inifinite-acting radial flow case, rate normalization yields an erroneous estimate of the skin factor by introducing a shift on the semilog straight line (obvioulsy, the sandface rate profile must be known). This last point, however, makes the application of rate-normalization techniques very limited in our particular problem—we do not have measurements of sandface flow rate. Therefore, this method must be applied using an estimate of the downhole rate which will definitely introduce errors in the deconvolution process. Such issues make rate normalization a "zero-order" approximation—that is, rate-normalization results should be considered as a guide, but not relied upon as the best methodology.

Material Balance Deconvolution

The wellbore storage-based, material balance time function for the pressure buildup case is given as

$$\Delta t_{mb,BU} = \frac{N_{p,wbs,BU}}{1 - q_{wbs,BU}} = \frac{\Delta t - \dfrac{1}{m_{wbs}} \Delta p_{ws}}{1 - \dfrac{1}{m_{wbs}} \dfrac{d}{d\Delta t}[\Delta p_{ws}]}.$$

And the wellbore storage-based, rate-normalized pressure drop function for the pressure buildup case is given as

$$\Delta p_{s,BU} = \frac{\Delta p_{ws}}{1 - q_{wbs,BU}} = \frac{1}{1 - \dfrac{1}{m_{wbs}} \dfrac{d}{d\Delta t}[\Delta p_{ws}]} \Delta p_{ws}.$$

In the material balance deconvolution formulation, the function is used in place of the time function, in whatever fashion is required—plotting data functions, modeling, etc. And the function is used as a pressure drop function—in any appropriate manner that pressure drop would be employed.

β ("Beta") Deconvolution

We also present the application of our new ß-deconvolution algorithm derived from wellbore-storage distorted pressure functions. The final result developed for application in our present work is given by (this is the general form for pressure drawdown or build-up cases)

$$\Delta p_s = \Delta p_w + \frac{\Delta p_{wd}}{(\Delta p_w - \Delta p_{wd})} \Delta p_{wid},$$

where, for the pressure buildup case, we have

$$\Delta_{pw} = p_{ws} - p_{wf}(\Delta t = 0) \quad \text{(pressure drop)},$$

$$\Delta_{pwd} = \Delta t \frac{d\Delta p_w}{d\Delta t} \quad \text{(Pressure drop derivative)},$$

$$\Delta_{pwi} = \frac{1}{\Delta t} \int_0^{\Delta t} \Delta p_w d\tau \quad \text{(ressure drop integral)},$$

$$\Delta_{pwi} = \Delta t \frac{d\Delta p_{wi}}{d\Delta t} \quad \text{(pressure drop integral-derivative)}.$$

The more "rigorous" ß-deconvolution algorithm (i.e., where an exponential rate profile is required), and the β-term is constant (i.e., not time dependent as we have derived in this case), could be applied but the constant β formulation will not perform as well as the time-dependent (and approximate) β-deconvolution algorithm that we have proposed in this work.

Of the methods reviewed/developed in this work, we believe that our modifications of the "material balance deconvolution" approach and the ß-deconvolution algorithm should perform well in field applications. We note that both of these methods have been specifically formulated for the analysis of wellbore storage distorted pressure transient test data—the relations in this chapter are presented for the purpose of field analysis. For a complete treatment of the β-deconvolution algorithm, see Appendices B and C; and for a complete treatment of the material balance deconvolution method.

Material Balance Deconvolution Relations For Wellbore Storage Distorted Pressure Transient Data

Material balance deconvolution is an extension of the rate-normalization method. Johnston defines a new *x*-axis plotting function (material balance time) which provides an approximate deconvolution of the variable-rate pressure transient problem. There are numerous assumptions associated with the "material balance deconvolution" methods—one of the most widely accepted assumptions is that the rate profile must change smoothly and monotonically. In practical terms, this condition should be met for the wellbore storage problem.

The general form of material balance deconvolution is provided for the pressure drawdown case in terms of the material balance time function and the rate-normalized pressure drop function.

Plotting the rate-normalized pressure function versus the material balance time function [on log *(tmb)* scales] shows that the material balance time function does correct the erroneous shift in the semilog straight line obtained by rate normalization.

Structured Analysis

Structured Analysis and Design Technique, introduced by Ross and Schoman to describe in depth the structure of computational module:

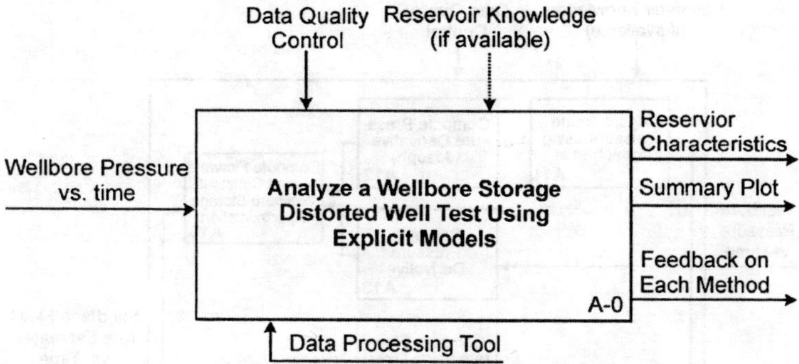

Figure 10.1: Structured analysis of the data processing tool—level A-0.

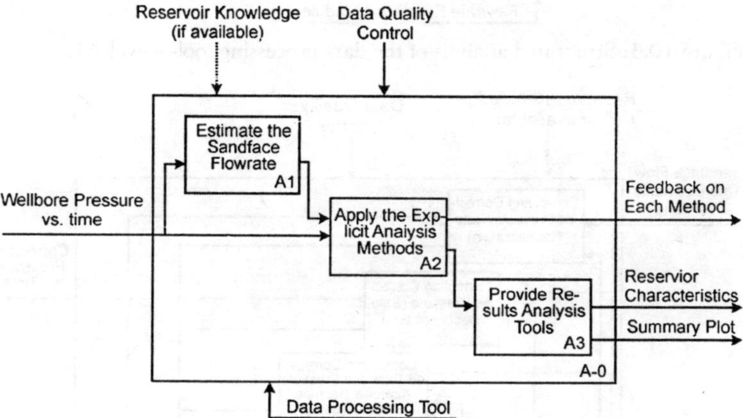

Figure 10.2: Structured analysis of the data processing tool—level A0.

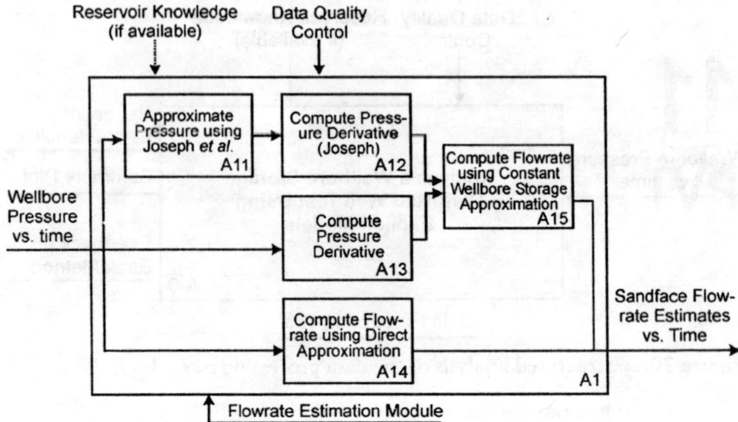

Figure 10.3: Structured analysis of the data processing tool—level A1.

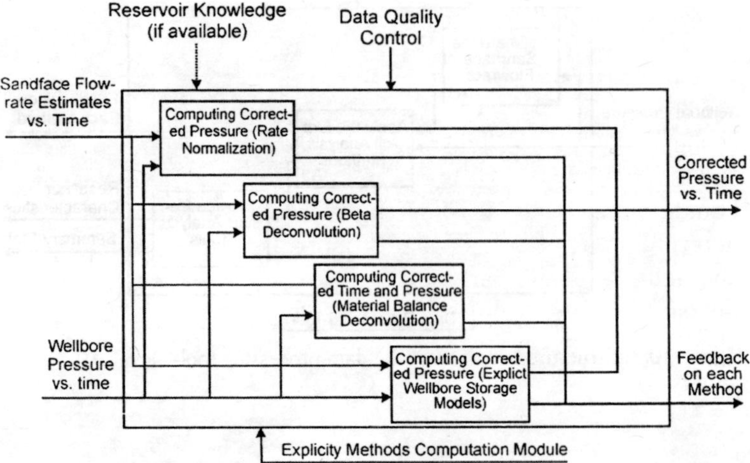

Figure 10.4: Structured analysis of the data processing tool—level A2.

11
PVT Analysis

Pressure-volume-temperature (PVT) system is the most versatile system available for the study of vapor-liquid-aqueous-solid equilibria for gas-condensate and oil systems.

The mercury-free PVT cell analyzes all fluid types in a single system. Although ideally suited for black oil studies, the system is equally capable of performing precise studies of gas-condensate systems by simply inverting the cell with the motorized cell-positioning device and using the truncated cone piston. In addition to performing vapor-liquid equilibrium and hydrate studies, the system is capable of determining live-fluid asphaltene precipitation onset and wax appearance temperature using the solid detection component. The full sample visibility of the PVT cell allows for direct measurement of phase volumes to be more accurately performed and eliminates errors caused by the liquid hang-up factor of partially blind systems.

The magnetic mixer ensures complete equilibrium of sample phases in a fraction of the time (~1/15) of conventional methods and is shielded to eliminate errors caused by traditional magnetic mixers that alter asphaltene behaviour. The mixer enhances system ability to quickly and precisely define saturation conditions. The mixer design reduces system dead volume and therefore increases the accuracy of work performed.

Physical property and phase behaviour PVT data provide the information required to properly manage reservoir production. Initial measurements of fluid compressibility and shrinkage factors are required to determine OIP/GIP, provide input for recovery estimates, and evaluate reservoir material balance calculations. CCE, DL or CVD, and viscosity measurements are required to understand fluid behaviour in the reservoir which influences both recovery and economics. Aompositional analysis combined with the physically measured fluid properties is used as input and basis for tuning of Equation of State (EOS) modeling software. This complete dataset can now be used to understand the phase behaviour, evaluate various production scenarios, optimize reservoir production and IOR schemes, maximize ultimate recovery, and optimize production economics.

Pvt Cell

The variable volume DBR PVT Cell is the heart of the phase behaviour (PVT) System. This fully visual cell provides confirmation of dew point and bubble point pressure, and is the only cell that allows direct measurement of the phase volumes. The DBR PVT cell is equipped with the DBR Magnetic Mixer that provides vigorous mixing and ensures proper establishment of phase equilibrium while reducing the total experimental time required. The video-based cathetometer provides accurate direct measurements of phase volumes. A precise quantification of low liquid volumes such as those found in lean gas-condensate systems is accomplished by using the electronic cathetometer in conjunction with the truncated cone piston.

The design of the PVT cell incorporates numerous features that provide improved phase volume measurements and enhanced sample visibility. The dominant feature is the glass cylinder that encapsulates the fluid sample. During operation, the structural integrity of the glass cylinder is maintained by exerting an overburden pressure to the exterior surface of the cylinder.

Among the many advantages of the mercury-free PVT cell is the reduced exposure of the sample to metal components. Contact is limited to the endcap surfaces, which can be custom manufactured from specialty alloys. This allows the cell to be readily and economically modified to handle samples containing the most troublesome components.

Solids Detection

The solid detection system (SDS) uses the principles of light transmission to accurately determine the conditions of solid (asphaltene and paraffin) formation. Low-intensity laser light is passed through fiber-optic transmission probes mounted across a visual phase behaviour cell and measured by a power level detector. The SDS is ideally suited for concurrent measurement of fluid phase behaviour and solid formation conditions. It is particularly useful for the study of petroleum fluids. The SDS consists of two subsystems: the source and the detector. Within the source subsystem, light from the laser source travels through a fiber-optic cable and is focused with a collimating lens mounted on the front sight glass of the pressurevolume-temperature (PVT) cell. After traversing the test fluid inside the cell, the power of the electromagnetic wave is measured with the detector subsystem, which consists of a second collimating lens located on the rear sight-glass of the cell, another fiber-optic cable, and a power meter. The entire system is controlled by a software package that adjusts the computerized pump. The pump controls system pressure or solvent addition at a defined rate or at programmed pressure or titration steps, and manages the real-time recording and graphical display of the system temperature, pressure, solvent volume, time, and transmitted power level from the detector. At the precise point of solid onset, the formation of precipitates causes a sharp drop in the transmitted power, which is shown on the graphical display.

Applications

Detection of solid-phase formation in hydrocarbon fluids at high pressure and temperature.

Benefits

- Accurately detects appearance of solid phase (wax and asphaltene) in opaque fluids.
- Accurately detects saturation pressure in reservoir oils.
- Solid detection data can be generated concurrent to normal PVT tests without affecting sample properties.

- Constant composition expansion (CCE) measures the saturation pressure (bubble or dew point) of the reservoir fluid including live fluid densities and compressibilities in the single-phase region. Below the saturation pressure, liquid/vapor volume fractions are accurately measured, which are typically required for equation-of-state modeling.
- Differential liberation (DL) simulates the gas liberation process from the oil in the reservoir and is conducted at reservoir temperature. Data reported include solution gas-oil ratio (R_s), liquid formation volume factor (B_o), viscosity, and density of liquid and/or gas phases.
- Constant volume depletion (CVD) is performed to simulate the pressure depletion process in a gas condensate or volatile oil reservoir. Data reported include the total well stream recovery, produced gas properties, and retrograde liquid accumulation in the reservoir, all as a function of pressure.

Separation Tests

Simulate the gas-liquid separation of a reservoir fluid that takes place at the surface separator conditions. Results generated include gas-oil ratio (GOR) for each separator stage, liquid shrinkage factor, and evolved gas properties at each stage. These data are often used in an equation-of-state simulator to optimize separator conditions for maximizing oil production.

Applications

- Description of phase behaviour.
- Complete PVT dataset.
- Identification of potential solids problems.
- Measurement of viscosity for fluid mobility and fractional flow.
- GOR, compressibility, and shrinkage data for reservoir recovery estimates.
- Ideal for unaltered sample analysis of sour fluids.
- Input for EOS and reservoir modeling.

Benefits

- Provides dependable, accurate data.
- Offers minimum turn around time.
- Accurate quantification of dew point pressure and low liquid volumes in lean gas condensates.
- Expert interpretation of results.
- Allows early detection of potential solids (wax or asphaltene) flow assurance problems.
- Provides definition of second immiscible liquid phase or occurrence of solid phase.
- Maximized production economics.
- Minimum sample volumes required.

PVT Express

The PVT Express (Mark of Schlumberger) onsite well fluid analysis service is based on a revolutionary hardware and software platform that can deliver comprehensive fluid analysis data in a matter of hours. With applications in exploration, development, and production environments, this system has many advantages over PVT analysis equipment and services. By using mercury-free and hydrogen-free technologies, the inherent HSE risks associated with the use and transportation of these materials are eliminated.

The mobility and flexibility of the well fluid analysis system eliminates long sample wait times, allowing accurate results to be delivered rapidly. The system's capacity to acquire data, confirm sample quality, and measure reservoir fluid properties eliminates waiting to determine if the sampling objectives were achieved. This is valuable during wireline formation testing or drillstem testing (DST) operations.

The PVT Express service works with the MDT tester and downhole fluid analysis (DFA) to validate measurements.

Fluid properties identified by the service are critical to well production and optimization. In many cases, analysis at the wellsite enables decisions about additional wireline formation testing or DST operations before the services leave the well.

In addition, directly transferring the samples to the PVT Express cell saves time. With the current emphasis on fast-track field development, swift results are critical.

It enables rapid mobilization to any location Using a single-phase or conventional sample, the PVT Express system uses advanced technology to measure some properties and predict others. Some examples of single-phase samplers used include the following:

- MDT tester with single-phase multisample chamber or multisample production sample receptacle.
- Single-phase reservoir sampler or slimline single-phase sampler within the sample carrier.
- CHDT (Mark of Schlumberger) Cased Hole Dynamics Tester.

The PVT Express system can analyze samples by recombining the samples and bringing them to single-phase conditions. These samples can be collected from the PhaseWatcher flowmeter, PhaseTester flowmeter, or test separator. The system features a high-pressure cell that measures the saturation pressure of the reservoir fluid at reservoir temperature. Additionally, accurate measurements of bubble point and dew point pressures are made possible by optical signal technology. This technology enables measurement of the first bubble of gas liberated from oil and the first trace of condensable liquid in a gas during constant composition expansion from reservoir pressure.

The cell can produce a comprehensive fluid analysis report with less than 50 cm^3 of single-phase reservoir fluid. This ability allows multiple tests to be performed from the same sample bottle. Traditional PVT services require larger sample volume; therefore, running multiple tests may not be possible. All data measured by the cell are displayed and stored in real time by a digital interface module. In addition to interpreting and reporting the measured data, the digital interface module also links to the prediction model in the PVT Expert* well fluid analysis software application. Flashing the single-phase sample to atmospheric conditions separates the liquid and gases for GOR measurement. A dual chromatograph for oil and gas, featuring helium ionization detectors, is used to deliver compositional data. While flame ionization detectors typically use hydrogen gas, helium ionization technology does not use hydrogen and enhances the safety and mobility of the service.

It provides accurate, predictive PVT data rapidly. The PVT Expert software application is an operator-independent, multidimensional prediction model that delivers instant and reliable volumetric, phase-behaviour fluid properties from a specific set of measured data. In contrast to equation-of-state prediction models, the system is ideally suited to wellsite operations because it does not require time-consuming tuning operations. Additionally, this prediction model includes a quality assurance tool that provides instant evaluation of the fluid property predictions.

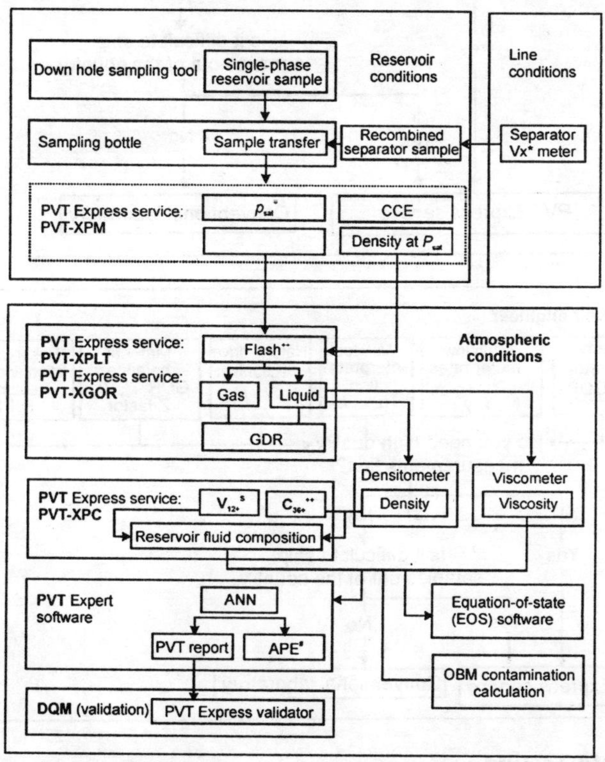

\+ P_{sat} is the saturation pressure. The saturation pressure is the bubblepoint pressure for liquid hydrocarbon samples and the dewpoint pressure for gaseous hydrocarbon samples.

++ Flash—hydrocarbon separates into gas and liquid at standard atmospheric conditions.

s Separation of hydrocarbon gas into its fractions upto C_{12+}.

\# Separation of hydrocarbon liquid into its fractions up to C_{36+}.

\# ANN predictor evaluator (APE) checks the accuracy of the ANN predictions.

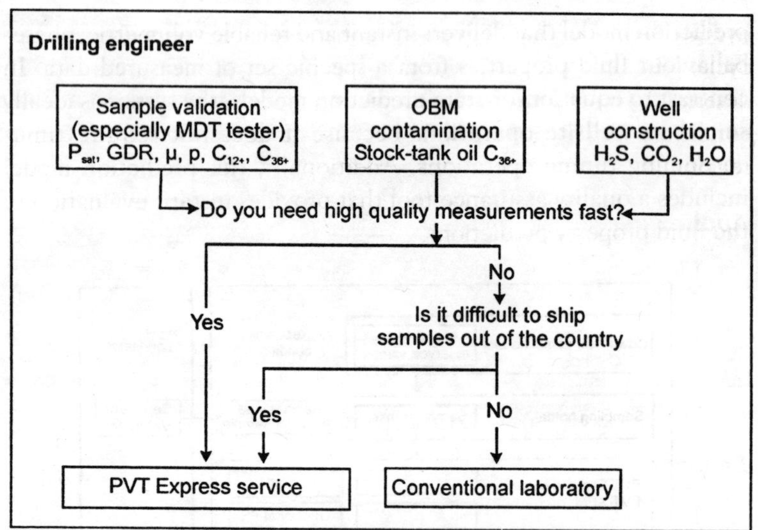

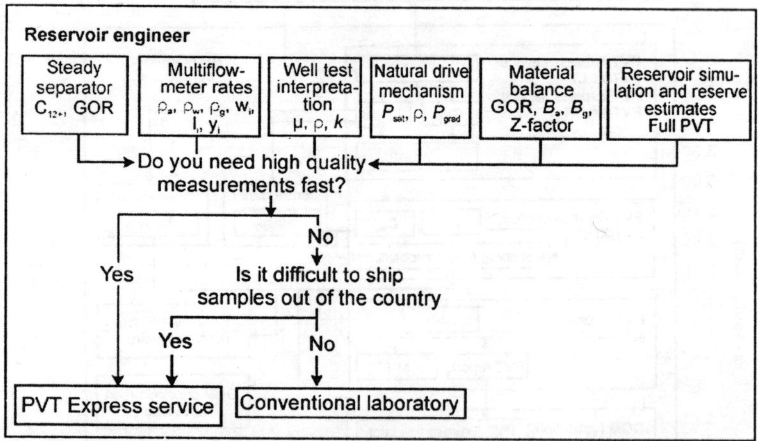

Hydrate Testing

A mercury-free Sapphire* pressure gauge is used to study hydrate formation at pressures to 3,000 psia and a visual PVT cell for studies to 15,000 psia. Testing entails charging known quantities of hydrocarbon and aqueous fluids to the cell. At constant pressure, the cell is cooled until a small amount of hydrate crystal is formed. The hydrate is then melted during the heating portion of the temperature cycle. Visual detection of the melting of hydrate crystals is used to determine the hydrate formation conditions. The hydrate formation conditions can be measured in both the single-phase and two-phase regions.

Applications

1. Identification of potential flow assurance problems caused by hydrate formation.
2. Determination of hydrate formation conditions.
3. Evaluation of the effectiveness of hydrate inhibitors.
4. Customized hydrate studies.

Benefits

1. Avoid production loss and service costs caused by unexpected hydrate problems.
2. Minimize cost of chemical inhibitors.
3. Identify and preclude hydrate formation caused by comingling gas streams.

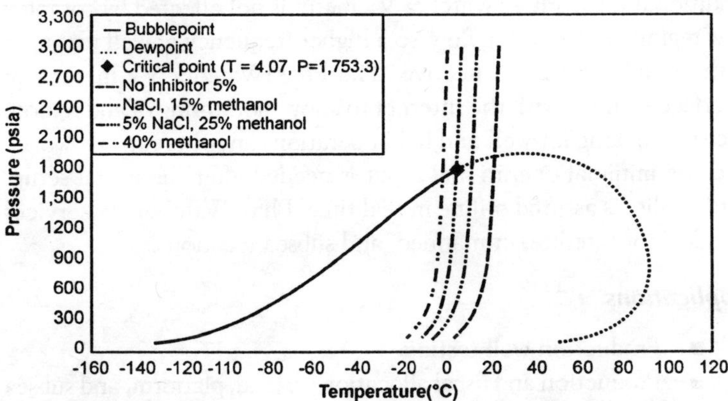

Phasewatcher

Vx (Mark of Schlumberger) multiphase measurement technology combines an instrumented venturi with a dual-energy fraction meter.

This combination measures the total mass flow rate and the fractions of gas, oil, and water, which in turn determine the oil, water, and gas flow rates. Vx technology functions without the need for separation or an upstream mixing device, which minimizes the size and weight of the equipment. The technology has no moving parts and is essentially maintenance-free. The PhaseWatcher permanent multiphase flowmeter uses Vx technology to continuously measure flow rates in wells exhibiting one-, two-, or three-phase flow for production monitoring on land, platform, and subsea wells. The PhaseWatcher Vx meter operates equally well in both oil and gas wells, making it possible to test dry gas, condensate, and oil wells with a single meter.

Because there is no need for separators, this significantly reduces space, load, and maintenance requirements in offshore applications and decreases the footprint in land-based applications. The PhaseWatcher Vx meter enables safer, more efficient installations while reducing field development costs. A superior dynamic response enables the PhaseWatcher Vx meter to take accurate and repeatable measurements in less time than required for flow stabilization. These measurements enable continuous diagnosis of production anomalies for fine-tuning of artificial lift systems and well performance. Additionally, the PhaseWatcher Vx meter is not affected by complex flow regimes such as slug flow, so a higher frequency of well testing is both feasible and cost effective. The PhaseWatcher Vx meter can interface securely with the Internet to allow monitoring of and remote decision making for well and field operations anywhere in the world. Because minimal operational input is needed after the initial setup, data quality is assured online in real time. PhaseWatcher Vx services are ideal for satellite, unmanned, and subsea locations.

Applications

- Production well testing.
- Production and fiscal allocation on land, platform, and subsea wells.
- Production trending.
- Artificial lift system optimization.
- Oil, water, and gas measurements for any given gas volume fraction.

Benefits

- Quicker, more efficient well testing, saving response time and costs.
- Lower field development costs.
- Safer installation and operation.
- Better flow rate accuracy enabled by fluid characterization services.

CONSTANT TEMPERATURE

Airbath

The study of the thermodynamic phase behaviour of fluids requires the accurate control and measurement of pressure, temperature, and composition. To provide superior temperature control for phase behaviour experiments, Schlumberger developed the constant temperature airbath.

Electrically powered, finned, air-immersion heaters situated in a high-flow recirculating airflow provide efficient air mixing and uniform heat distribution throughout the entire working volume of the airbath. The airbath temperature is monitored and controlled using a microprocessor-based controller in conjunction with a resistance temperature detector sensor. The integrated refrigeration system completes the package by providing the ability to conduct ambient and subambient studies of wax precipitation and hydrates.

Oilphase-DBR offers two versions of the airbath depending on the range of experiments the system will be used for. The refrigerated airbath operates from -31°F to 392°F. The nonrefrigerated airbath operates from 150°F [65°C] to 392°F [200°C]. The nonrefrigerated system can be be brought down to 60°F with a cooling coil.

Applications

- Phase behaviour PVT systems.
- Rising bubble apparatus.
- Slim-tube miscibility apparatus.
- Core-flood system.

Benefits

- Automatic temperature limits.
- Integrated refrigeration system.
- Robust design.

Magnetic Mixer

Mixing is a critical factor in the time taken to reach equilibrium when performing PVT and enhanced oil recovery studies. The mixer, magnetically coupled to a drive system through the PVT end cap, is capable of mixing fluids in PVT cells up to 15 times more efficiently than the traditional rocking method. Aignificant reduction in equilibration time can improve laboratory staff productivity by increasing the number of data points that can be measured in a day.

The magnetic components are shielded to prevent sample alteration. The mixer performs in upright (mixer cap on top of the cell) or inverted positions and can be run at intermediate angles. This can be useful when mixing a large volume of high-viscosity liquid that may not normally be capable of forming a vortex deep enough to contact the impeller blades when the cell is in the inverted position.

Application

- Mixing hydrocarbon fluids within Oilphase-DBR Mercuryfree PVT cells.

Benefits

- Reduces operating time for establishing phase equilibrium on sample.
- Allows equilibrium to be reached in minimal time.
- Capable of mixing high-viscosity samples.
- Minimal dead volume.
- Magnetic isolation eliminates heat transfer and sample alteration of polar materials.

Data Acquisition Syste

The data acquisition system provides instrument control, data capture, and data display for the phase behaviour PVT system. The computer-based data acquisition system provides flexibility in the configuration of data capture as well as user-customizable data logging and display. The data acquisition system supports all of the standard instrumentation in the PVT system, including pressure, temperature, and volume measurements, and provides full control of the pump module. In addition, the software is factory-configured to support any additional equipment subsystems such as the densitometer, electromagnetic viscometer, charge-coupled device, and autosampling system. The operator interface allows the user to control all the automation features provided with the system, and to monitor and record experimental data for immediate or subsequent analysis, or both.

Application

Used for instrument control, data capture, and data display for phase behaviour (PVT) systems.

Benefits

- Provides automatic monitoring and control of pressure and temperature data.
- Provides real-time graphical data displays.
- Performs calculations on command.
- Single workstation can multitask during suite of experiments.

Gas Sample Bottles

The Oilphase-DBR* gas sample bottles are sample cylinders for separator and process line sample transportation and storage. They are used primarily for well test separator sampling during production testing. As part of oil, gas condensate, and wet-gas testing, separator gas samples are matched with an oil or condensate sample collected under identical separator conditions, for physical recombination at the PVT laboratory.

The large volume ensures sufficient gas from a single sample for a complete PVT recombination study under most separator conditions. The vacuum-filled bottle is fully evacuated before transporting to the sampling site. The fully evacuated bottle is purged, and samples are allowed to fill to line or separator pressure.

Applications

- Collecting and transporting of large volumes of separator gas for physical recombination.
- Sampling of large volumes of separator oil for core flood studies.

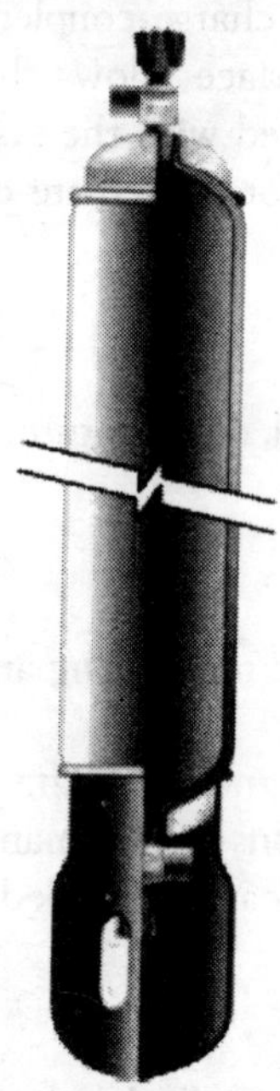

Figure: Gas Sample Bottles

12
Fluid

Fluid Preparation And Compositional Analysis

The fluid sample is allowed to equilibrate under continuous mixing usually for a period of five days. This restoration mixing process redissolves any precipitated asphaltene and wax particles into solution.

After sample conditioning and restoration, a subsample of each equilibrated live fluid is subjected to compositional analysis to C^{30+} using an equilibrium flash procedure. For this procedure, an accurately measured volume of the single-phase fluid is isobarically and isothermally displaced into a pycnometer where the mass and density are evaluated. The pycnometer is then connected to a gas/oil ratio single-stage equilibrium flash apparatus where the oil is flashed to ambient pressure and temperature conditions.

The evolved gas phase recirculates through the residual liquid to achieve equilibrium between phases. Following circulation, the volume of equilibrium vapor and the mass of liquid remaining in the pycnometer are measured.

The vapor phase is compositionally analyzed to C^{15+} by gas chromatography (GC), and the residual liquid is analyzed by GC to C^{30+}. The composition of the original live oil is calculated by mass balance, from the measured composition and total mass of each phase.

Applications

- Composition of reservoir fluid.
- Sample validation.

- Preparation of samples for advanced or routine PVT, wax, and asphaltene analysis.

Benefits

- Samples restored to reservoir conditions.
- Vapor and liquid compositional analysis.

Flow Assurance

Resolving flow assurance problems means different things to different people. To some, it is unclogging wells, tieback lines and jumpers, and gathering stations and risers of production robbing deposits of paraffin, scale, or hydrate. Others take a more proactive approach by monitoring data and feeding it into production models to enable predictions of flow problems in time to take preventive actions. Flow assurance is a multidiscipline process involving sampling, laboratory analysis, and production, and facilities engineering to ensure uninterrupted optimum well productivity. Laboratory testing provides necessary data to assess the flow assurance risk because it defines phase behaviour and the properties of the waxes, asphaltenes, and hydrates known to be principal causes of flow problems.

Wax Behaviour

Paraffinic or waxy crude oils are produced globally. In environments such as subsea tiebacks, the precipitation, deposition, and gelling of solid waxes in hydrocarbon fluids constitute critical production concerns. Accurate fluid characterization is an important component of any development, production, or intervention strategy for handling waxy crude. Understanding wax behaviour can help avoid high costs resulting from output reductions or stoppages, or, conversely, from system overdesign. Either situation can occur when facilities or treatment regimes are designed on the basis of incomplete or overly conservative esti mates of the potential for wax-related fouling or plugging.

Live fluid analysis when assessing a waxy crude production or transport situation, relying solely on conventional dead crude wax tests, including wax content and wax appearance temperature measurements, can be misleading. Stock-tank oil tests are insufficiently representative of field situations because reservoir pressure and solution gas have a strong influence on wax solubility.

Laboratory-scale tests must account for the actual thermophysical situation in the field if they are to be applicable. To facilitate the most appropriate and cost-effective planning for wax inhibition, remediation strategies, or both, Oilphase-DBR services include simulation of a variety of actual reservoir or process conditions for characterizing the waxy properties of production fluids.

Wax Appearance Temperature and Pour Point

The wax appearance temperature (WAT) is the temperature below which a solid wax phase forms within a hydrocarbon fluid at a given pressure. Below the WAT, significant viscosity increases, deposition, and gelling are possible. The pour point is the temperature, at a given pressure, below which the static fluid may form a gel. For a system cooled below its pour point, restarting flow may be difficult or impossible.

Using depressurized stock-tank oil, test can be performed as a preliminary indication of the likelihood of wax-related production problems. If potential for wax formation is identified, high-pressure CPM tests can be carried out under simulated production pressure conditions. Pour point tests can also be performed on depressurized or live reservoir fluids.

Rheology

Waxy crudes below their WAT do not exhibit simple viscous behaviour. These fluids manifest shear-thinning viscosity and other complex rheological phenomena that must be properly quantified to completely optimize the design of waxycrude flowlines.

Gel Strength

If a well shut-in condition leads to gel formation in waxy crude, the flow cannot be restarted unless a certain minimum stress level is applied to the system. This threshold-yield stress is termed the gel strength. Gel strength measurements provide an indication of the restart requirements of gelled crude and allow for selecting the most appropriate techniques. Oilphase-DBR services include a model pipeline test (MPT) that measures the factors affecting gel strength, including pressure, thermal history, system geometry, and fluid composition. The MPT is performed at well conditions.

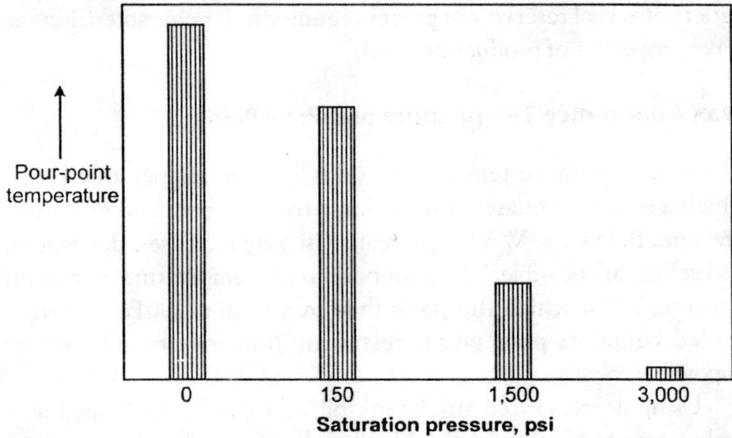

Figure 12.1: Live Oil Pour Point Effect of Adding Solution Gas.

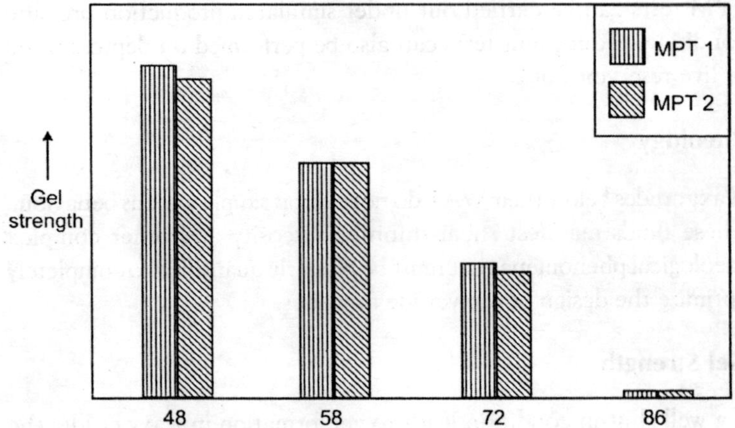

Figure 12.2: Gel Strength Versus Temperature.

Advanced Tests

Wax solubility modeling is performed by evaluating the *n*-paraffin distribution of a crude oil to C90+ using high-temperature gas chromatography and by quantifying wax precipitation using live-oil filtration. Specialized studies can also be carried out in wax-crystal growth kinetics, coprecipitation of waxes with asphaltenes, deposition measurement using organic solids deposition technology and modeling, and various other means of practical and research interest—including flow loop testing.

Asphaltene Testing

Asphaltenic crudes create exceptionally difficult flow problems. Normal production practices can cause, or worsen, these problems. For example, asphaltene-induced flow impairment can be caused by normal pressure drop in the near-wellbore region or by crude dilution that occurs during gas lift.

Solids Detection System

A laser-based SDS has been developed to define the pressure and temperature at which asphaltenes precipitate because of fluid expansion depressurization of the crude oil during production. The SDS unit attaches directly to the PVT phase behaviour cell, and the near-infrared laser beam passes through the reservoir fluid contained within the cell. By monitoring the intensity of the transmitted laser beam during the isothermal constant composition expansion depressurization process, the asphaltene precipitation onset (APO) is identified by a marked decrease in the transmitted laser beam intensity. By repeating this procedure at different temperatures, the complete APO envelope can be defined. Compositional changes, such as those that occur during gas lift, are simulated by incremental, isobaric gas-solvent injections. These procedures provide a thorough understanding of the complete range of conditions where APO occurs.

High-Pressure Microscopy

The studies of organic solids have been greatly enhanced by the development of the Oilphase-DBR HPM. The ability to directly observe the onset and growth of organic solid precipitates at pressures to 137,895 kPa [20,000 psi] and temperatures to 200 degC [392 degF] provides visual definition of the types of solids present.

It is also possible to define the abundance and morphology of these solids as they grow. More importantly, it is possible to use Oilphase-DBR services to evaluate and optimize the effectiveness of various chemical programs of solids inhibition or remediation. The ongoing developments in HPM technology, including the cross-polar HPM, enable study of the phenomena of pressurized wax formation or coprecipitation of waxes and asphaltenes.

Particle Size Analysis

Oilphase-DBR services provide a proprietary image analysis technology for PSA. The PSA process operates as a synchronous feature of the HPM, making it possible to determine the number and sizes of solid particles that are visually apparent. The system is calibrated using particle standards of various sizes and concentrations.

The PSA uses proprietary image analysis software to determine the onsets, sizes, and distributions of wax, asphaltene, and immiscible hydrocarbon-liquid or water droplets that are present.

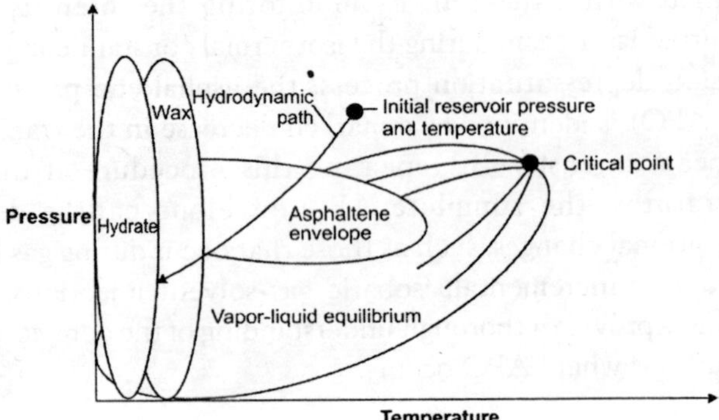

Figure 12.3: Precipitation Onset Envelopes.

Hydrate Behaviour

The Oilphase-DBR fluid sampling and analysis services use three mercury-free system configurations, two visual and one nonvisual, for the thermodynamic study of hydrate behaviour.

The PVT cell configuration and the Sapphire pressure gauge cell configuration both use proprietary visual technology. A customized Autoclave cell technique utilizes proprietary nonvisual technology.

System capabilities include measuring hydrate formation conditions for fluid systems containing natural gas, CO_2, H_2S, gas condensate, or oil in the presence of water or brine.

These systems support studying the effectiveness of various hydrate inhibitors such as methanol, glycol, and electrolyte solutions. They are also used in determining the maximum concentration of water vapor allowable, while avoiding hydrate formation at a prespecified operating temperature and pressure condition.

Organic Solids Deposition and Control

Standard laboratory flow assurance measurements characterize the thermodynamic conditions at which organic solids (primarily wax and asphaltene) can form in produced reservoir fluids. More specialized testing is required to determine whether solid organics will deposit on the pipe walls, resulting in reduced fluid production. The OSDC allows independent variation of these test parameters to quantify their corresponding effect on deposition tendency and rate. Unlike pipe flow loops and other conventional methods for evaluating flow assurance production system design and chemical screening, the OSDC can test not only export oils (low pressure) but also bottom hole and pressurized fluids up to a pressure of 15,000 psi. In addition, basic OSDC testing can be completed using approximately 150 mL of reservoir fluid (per measurement point).

This provides savings in both sampling cost and sample consumption as compared to the multiple-barrel sample requirements of traditional flow loop testing. By performing deposition measurements at line conditions, the OSDC enables less conservative system design and operation when appropriate while decreasing the risk associated with the uncertainty inherent in conventional data scaling practices. The OSDC offers the only direct laboratory measurement of organic solids' deposition tendency that can be translated to the field.

Applications

- Asphaltene deposition studies.
- Wax deposition studies.
- Other organic solid deposition studies.

Benefits

- Reliable, repeatable, and scalable results.
- Efficient production operations through optimized chemical selection, dosage, and treatment.
- Data to determine optimized pigging frequencies and remediation strategies.

The OSDC apparatus comprises a test cell, control system, and circulation system, all of which are housed on a control bench. The OSDC cell consists of a cylindrical vessel including an axially centered heat source. The outer wall of the vessel is stationary, with the inner wall rotating to create a turbulent or laminar flow regime in the annular space.

In addition to allowing precise and independent control of pressure, temperature, differential temperature, and spindle speed, the apparatus also facilitates collection, analysis, and quantification of any solid deposits.

Deposition Studies

A typical deposition study using the OSDC would involve operating the equipment at anticipated production conditions where solids will be present and then manipulating the system to determine the conditions at which a deposit would form. After an estimate of the deposition rate is made, a sample can be taken to characterize the chemical composition of the deposit.

Studies performed on asphaltenic oils are primarily run at

isothermal conditions, whereas wax deposition studies are performed with a differential temperature maintained between the fluid within the chamber and the outer wall. Trial results obtained through a multiyear joint industry project clearly show that the deposits gathered match closely the composition and rates seen in actual production systems. Therefore, the data obtained allow making production system design decisions with significantly less uncertainty. Significant cost savings through less conservative design and/or optimization of remediation techniques can be realized, particularly in offshore production environments.

Phasetester Multiphase Flowmeter

Designed for easy deployment, the PhaseTester* portable multiphase periodic well testing equipment provides solution-oriented services that cover the entire well testing process, from design to reservoir interpretation. The PhaseTester units with Vx† multiphase well testing technology have excellent dynamic response to fluctuating flows, require little or no stabilization time, and are not affected by complex flow regimes such as slug flow, foam, or emulsion environments. The PhaseTester system requires no process control because it is insensitive to changes in flow rate, phase holdup, and pressure regime. Because the PhaseTester system takes accurate and repeatable measurements with little or no stabilization time, as many as three wells can be tested per day on a typical production station. Combining the PhaseTester unit with the InterACT (Mark of Schlumberger) real-time monitoring and data delivery system enables stake holders of well testing operations to participate in the entire decision-making process.

Vx technology is at the core of the PhaseTester multiphase flowmeters, providing enhancements and major performance improvements over traditional testing methods. Functioning without the need for separation or an upstream mixing device, Vx technology minimizes the size and weight of the equipment.

Key to this superior measurement system is the venturi section with a dual-energy gamma ray holdup meter. The system's source and detector elements are contained within pressure housings that provide an excellent barrier to well fluids.

The PhaseTester flowmeter measures the total mass flow rate and the holdups of gas, oil, and water, which in turn are used to determine gas, oil, and water flow rates. Because no moving parts are required, the risk of erroneous measurements is reduced.

Applications

- Exploration, appraisal, and production well testing.
- Well cleanup optimization.
- Production and fiscal allocation on land, platform, and subsea wells.
- Production trending.
- Artificial lift system optimization.
- Flow measurements in slugs, foams, and emulsions.

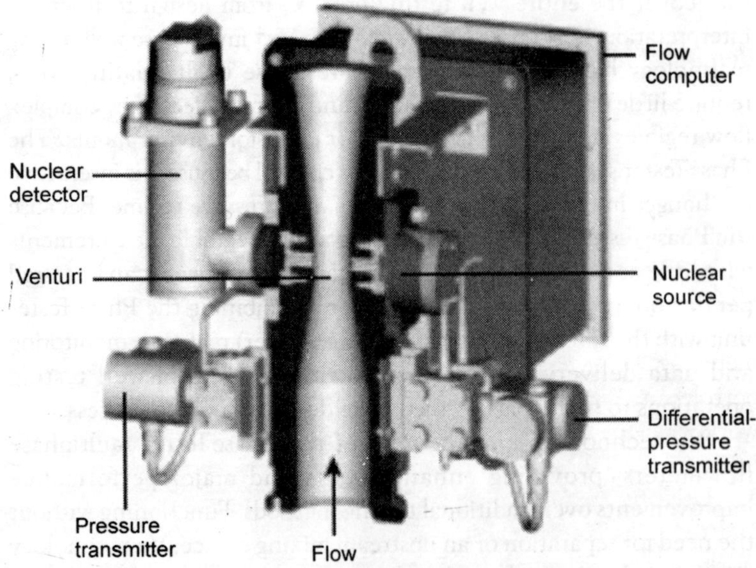

Heavy Oils

Heavy-oil analysis requires that constant composition expansion for the determination of bubble point pressure (P), fluid compressibility, and density employ specialized procedures to account for slow kinetics.

The capillary viscometer is used to measure viscosity of both live and stock-tank oils as a function of temperature and pressure. The capillary viscometer is ideally suited for application in heavy-oil studies. It is capable of generating reproducible experimental results for either cleaned samples or samples containing small amounts of emulsified water or entrained solids.

Transportation studies may also include screening for asphaltene precipitation during the blending of heavy oil with light hydrocarbon fluids. The high pressure microscope (HPM) images of the heavy oil may be analyzed by particle size analysis to quantify the size and morphology of the precipitated asphaltenes.

Applications

- Routine thermodynamic and physical property analysis.
- Customized heavy-oil studies.

Benefits

- Measuring viscosity by capillary viscometry.
- Visually confirming asphaltene formation in heavy-oil blending.

High-Pressure Displacement Pumps

High-pressure displacement (HPD) pumps are precision laboratory instruments designed to generate high fluid pressures and to accurately meter, inject, or proportionately displace fluids. Used extensively in petroleum research and fluid property measurement laboratories worldwide, HPD pumps apply to all situations where precision is of utmost importance when dispensing gases and liquids.

Utilizing a piston-cylinder arrangement, HPD pumps are designed and tested to perform accurately, reliably, and safely for standard working pressure ranges of 10,000 to 20,000 psi. Displacement capacities range between 50 and 500 cm^3 with a volume resolution as low as 0.005 cm^3. HPD pumps are available in hand-operated, motorized, and computer-controlled models. Each has a variety of options, making the choice of an HPD pump possible for almost every application.

Stepper Motor With Internal Indexer

The stepper-motor control integrates indexer functions into the driver electronics and eliminates manual controls. Control commands transmit directly to the driver via an RS232C port. This reduces the overall cost in applications where computers control the stepper motors. The chief benefit of this approach is that it shifts the emphasis of the control features of the pump from a hardware base to a software base. This technology is the recommended choice of motorizing pumps.

Charge-Coupled Device Measurement System

The charge-coupled device (CCD) video-based level measurement system was designed to accurately measure fluid volumes in visual cells without exposing the operator to the safety hazards of typical line-of-sight methods. The two components of the CCD measurement system are the optics and the mechanical components.

The optics component of the system is a high-resolution color camera equipped with a high-magnification telescopic lens and extension tube that acts as a long-distance microscope to view approximately 10 mm [0.394 in.] of the PVT cell window. A high-resolution color monitor is used to view the camera output and accurately define phase volume set points.

The mechanical component of the CCD measurement system includes a motorized linear stage, used to position the camera relative to the fluid interface that is to be measured. The linear stage is equipped with a high-precision linear encoder that enables changes in fluid and subsequent volume levels to be measured with a high degree of accuracy. The motorized stage is operated from the control unit that incorporates the readout for the linear encoder. Users have the option to connect the control unit to a computer, allowing remote control and data acquisition.

Application

Fluid level measurement tool for fluid volume calculations

10 L Gasometers

The gasometer design incorporates a precision machined and honed cylinder held vertically inside a steel frame. As gas enters the calibrated cylinder, the pressure increase is detected by the very sensitive barometric transducer, which signals the motor-driven internal piston to be repositioned to maintain atmospheric pressure.

The rate of piston movement within the gasometers can be controlled to adapt to a variety of gas production rates. The piston position is measured using a high-resolution linear encoder. The digital counter displays the gas volume and temperature directly, and provides RS 232 communication to support computer data acquisition.

The single-stroke model gasometer collects, measures, and contains the gas volume sample, and has a capacity of 10 L. The gas/oil ratio (GOR) model collects, measures, and contains the gas, with the additional capability of recirculating the evolved gas back through the onboard high-pressure liquid pycnometer and gas sample cylinder. This recirculation ensures vapor-liquid equilibrium and enables the experimenter easy access to representative homogeneous samples of atmospheric pressure vapor and liquids. Establishing equilibrium is essential for accurate analysis of high-pressure volatile liquids such as those encountered in reservoir fluid studies.

The continuous model is based on bidirectional control of piston position. Combined with the automated valving capability, the reciprocal piston can accurately measure large volumes of gas such as those encountered in miscible displacement and core flood studies. The onboard processor and high-resolution encoder track the position of the piston and output continuous measurement of gas volume to the front panel light-emitting diode, data acquisition system, or both.

Applications

- Accurate measurement of gas volumes at ambient temperature and atmospheric pressure.
- Accurate analysis of high-pressure volatile oils.

13
Drillsteam Testing

Hipack Packer System

The HiPack (Mark of Schlumberger) retrievable well testing packer system provides the features and performance of a permanent production packer for drillstem testing. This hydrostatic set packer has a built-in floating seal assembly, eliminating the need for drill collars and expansion/contraction joints. When combined with an intelligent remote dual valve, the HiPack system reduces the DST string from10 tools to 2. With three sections—a setting mechanism, the packer body, and a stinger/polished bore receptacle (PBR) configuration—the system is run in hole; the stinger locks to the packer body; and the seals position in the packer bore. When the system reaches the required depth, annulus pressure is applied to activate the hydraulic setting mechanism. This pressure sets the bidirectional slips, closes the packer bypass, and energizes the sealing element. A positive ratchet mechanism locks the packer in the set position and retains the applied setting forces. As the setting mechanism moves to its final position, the stinger release lugs are uncovered, unlocking the stinger from the packer body. After releasing the stinger, the seals are free to move in the sealbore similar to a production packer with a floating seal assembly.

When the DST is complete, annulus pressure is used to open the below packer circulating valve. Formation gas trapped below the packer element can then be circulated out before releasing the sealing element and slips. Straight pull releases the packer. This pull causes the slips and element to move to the relaxed position on the packer body. A continued pull on the tubing opens the packer bypass to eliminate swabbing when retrieving the DST string.

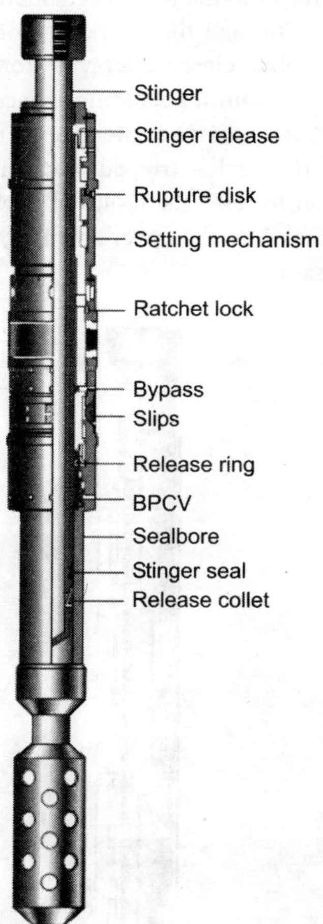

Hydraulic Jar

During drillstem tests (DSTs), if a packer or tail pipe becomes stuck, the hydraulic jar is used to provide an upward-moving shock that will help pull the string loose. The jar consists of a housing and a mandrel that move relative to each other. An oil chamber, separated by a flow restrictor in series with a check valve, is located between the housing and the mandrel. Applying weight to the packer causes the jar to close. If the tools below the jar become stuck, an overpull is applied to the string, which causes the jar to begin metering hydraulic oil. As the oil flows slowly through the restrictor from the upper chamber into the lower chamber, elastic energy is stored in the string. The mandrel housing moves until a seal ring is uncovered, at which time the housing rapidly accelerates to produce an upward impact on the stuck tools. After the jar has tripped, the string weight is set back down on the packer to reset the tool. Oil flows rapidly through the check valve and back into the upper chamber, allowing jarring to be repeated as necessary.

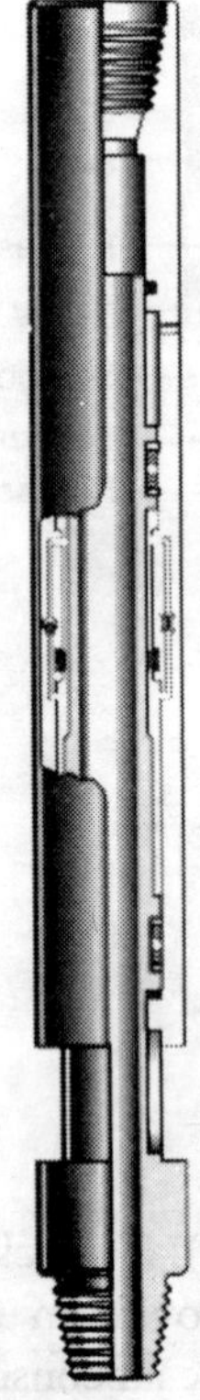

Pulse-Operated Fullbore Tools

The IRIS (Mark of Schlumberger) Intelligent Remote Implementation System is an advanced technology for downhole tool operation and control. Most testing and completion tools are operated from the surface by direct mechanical manipulation of the test string or by application of high-pressure signals. The IRIS system is operated by coded low-pressure pulses sent down the annulus, which are detected by the intelligent controller in the tool.

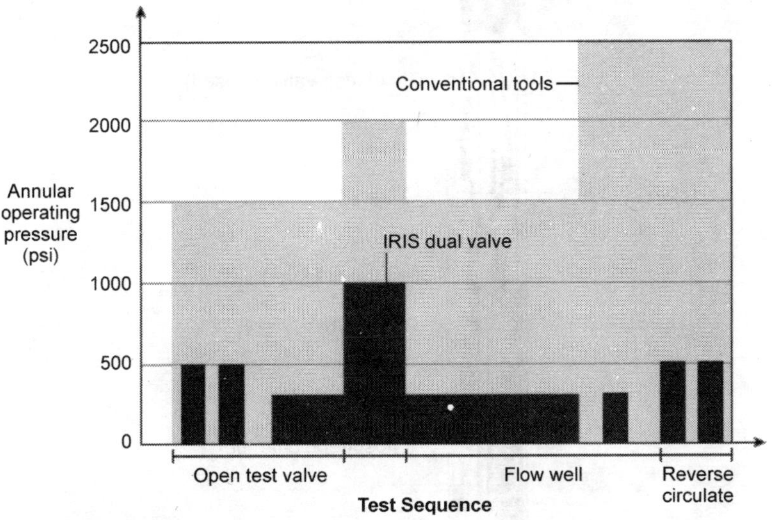

The Iris Dual Valve

The IRIS dual valve is a compact fullbore testing tool with a multicycle test valve and circulating valve. It offers considerable flexibility, enabling quick response to evolving job conditions. IRIS software controls the individual valve operations, enabling automation of complex and time-consuming tasks. The tool responds only to specific pulses, or commands, recognized by its downhole computer. These commands are implemented using hydrostatic pressure downhole to operate the valves. The computer is insensitive to other pressure events such as operation of other downhole equipment, changes in hydrostatic pressure, or pressure surges during pumping operations.

The low-pressure commands facilitate communication with the tool and eliminate problems associated with high-pressure levels in the annulus. The intelligent controller provides a high level of flexibility without adding the complexity of an index mechanism or other complicated mechanical parts. Most seals and moving parts are immersed in oil at hydrostatic pressure; when combined with large valve opening and closing forces, this immersion ensures reliable operation in environments with debris or heavy mud.

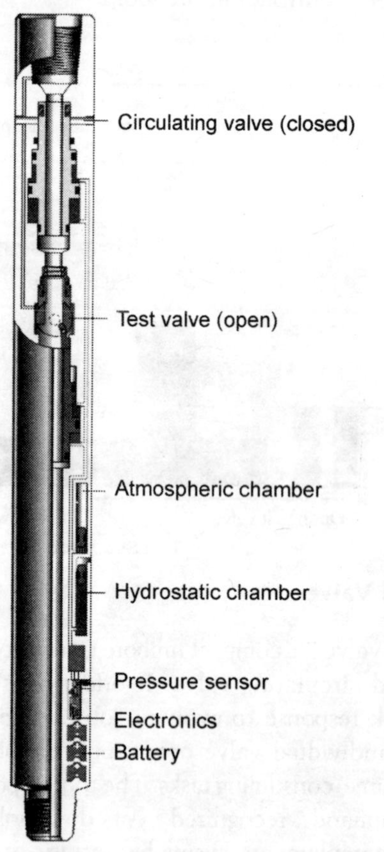

The flexible IRIS command system offers automatic programme sequencing that optimizes wellsite operations. For example, the PERFPAC (Mark of Schlumberger) sand-control method is an application where IRIS flexibility contributes to a reliable and efficient operation. In the PERFPAC single-trip perforating and gravel-pack service, the IRIS dual valve plays a major role by spotting the cushion and controlling the well during the perforation and cleanup phases. It also provides a bypass, which prevents pressure surgesand premature setting of the gravel-pack packer when the perforating packer is pulled and moved below the perforations.

The test valve and circulating valves operate independently of each other on commands sent from the surface in the form of pressure pulses in the annulus. These pulses are detected by a pressure sensor and decoded by a downhole microprocessor, which implements the commands through the IRIS electronics and hydraulics. No other pressure events during the job affect the tool. Clean hydraulic fluid, driven by the well hydrostatic pressure, is used to operate the valves. This mode of operation prevents solids in the mud column or debris from the well effluent from contaminating the working parts. Hydraulic control and the high operating force of each valve are achieved by alternating the operating pressure between hydrostatic and atmospheric.

Operation

The electrical operation of the IRIS dual valve is relatively simple, and it can be operated while going into or coming out of the hole. The IRIS pressure sensor reads annulus pressure samples. Each sample is analyzed by the microcomputer in the electronics section of the tool and compared against commands in the tool library. When a match is found, the instruction is sent to either the circulating valve or the test valve, which is activated hydraulically. The electronic circuits ensure that only one valve can be operated at a time and only by the proper command.

The microcomputer maintains job history and pressure data files, which are retrievable for analysis and job verification. In addition, it performs other house-keeping functions such as monitoring valve status and battery voltages. When the tool is brought to the surface at the end of an operation, the test history and pressure data can be read from memory, dumped to a personal computer, and then printed as a detailed job report.

The hydraulic operation of the circulating valve and the test valves is identical. The status of the valves depends on the position of individual power pistons. These power pistons can be alternately exposed to hydrostatic pressure and to atmospheric pressure within a special dump chamber, which drives the power piston up or down.

The energy operating the power pistons is provided by the difference between the pressure of the well fluid in the annulus and the atmospheric pressure in the dump chamber. This energy provides the valves with high opening and closing forces to ensure a reliable operation even with high sand production or a high differential pressure across the valves.

Each time either power piston executes a complete cycle, a small volume of hydraulic oil is transferred to the dump chamber. The valves can be operated as many as 40 times before the chamber is filled. In addition to the standard IRIS dual valve, a large-bore version is available for extended well tests, high-rate flow tests, and through-tubing operations. The large internal diameter enables the running of large plugs into the completion after perforating to suspend the well without killing it.

Automatic Underbalance

The IRIS dual valve can be programmed with preset commands that are executed automatically when a predetermined set of downhole conditions is met. For example, the preset command "automatic underbalance close" is used to close the circulating valve or test valve when the required hydrostatic underbalance is reached while running in the hole with tubing-conveyed perforating (TCP) guns. Mechanical over-ride if necessary, such as in the case of a computer failure, both valves can be cycled to a known position determined by the setup prior to running in the hole. To operate the over-ride, annular pressure is increased until it exceeds the rating of a rupture disc. After the disc is ruptured, hydrostatic pressure closes the circulating valve and, depending on prejob setup, opens or closes the test valve. This feature enables the mechanical over-ride to be used either to shut in the well or to put the tool in a passive mode where it functions as a piece of pipe. The latter option allows other completion or testing operations to continue without tripping out of the hole.

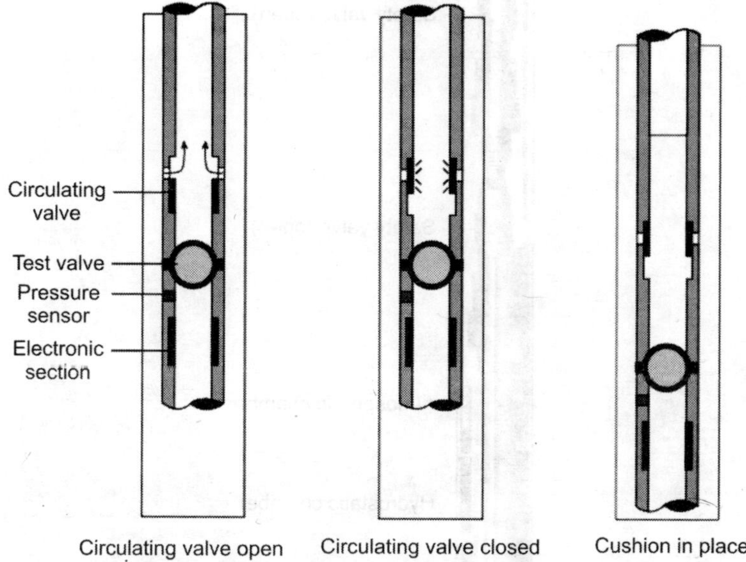

Figure 13.1: The preset "underbalance close" command automatically closes either the circulating valve or the test valve while running in the well, thereby establishing a predetermined underbalance pressure.

Safety Valve

The IRIS safety valve can be set to close immediately in the event of a high-pressure leak in the annulus or a drop in the annulus pressure beyond the specified limits. It can be reopened after the condition is corrected.

The two valve sections in the IRIS dual valve are interchangeable. If required, the IRIS dual valve can be converted to a safety valve by fitting it with two ball valve sections that are controlled by a special sequenced command pulse. The first valve provides a strong closing force capable of cutting wireline in an emergency. The second valve then seals the well. This conversion feature makes the tool an excellent downhole safety valve that is especially useful in deep water operations.

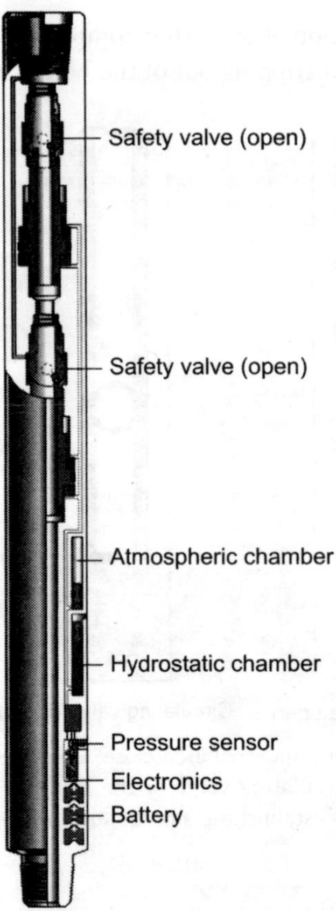

Figure 13.2: The IRIS safety valve is used in addition to the IRIS dual valve to provide excellent backup in emergencies.

Multicycle Circulating Valve With Lock Module

The multicycle circulating valve with lock (MCVL) module is a reclosable circulating and reversing valve. Applying a predetermined number of pressure cycles to the tubing opens the valve. The MCVL cycles by the differential pressure between the tubing and the annulus, and it is not dependent on pump rate. The valve can be locked in the open or closed position by using the lock module. When the lock is engaged, the tool is insensitive to pressure surges in the tubing and annulus. Applying pressure to the annulus ruptures a disc and disengages the lock module. The model MCVL-E valve is rated to 68,950 kPa [10,000 psi] differential pressure, and the model MCVL-G is rated to 103,425 kPa [15,000 psi].

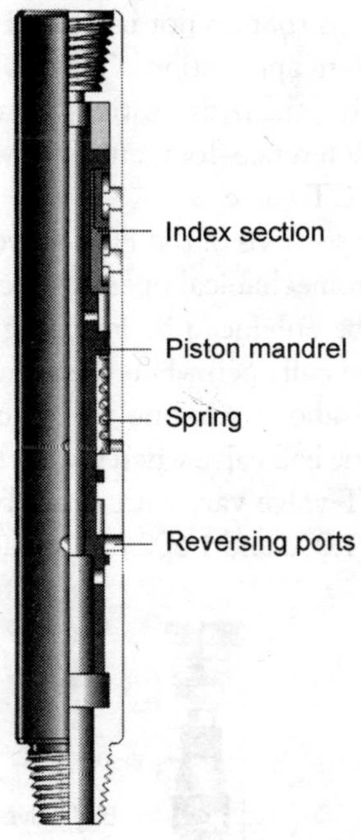

Multiple-Opening Internally Operated Reversing Valve

The multiple-opening internally operated reversing valve (MIRV) is a tubing-pressure operated reclosable reversing valve. An index system enables pressure testing of the tubing string while running in the hole. The MIRV is opened by applying a predetermined number of tubing pressure cycles against the tester valve. When the tool is opened, it can be used to reverse circulate, spot stimulation fluids, or change cushions.

Pumping through the circulating ports at preset pump rates between 0.3 and 1.3 m^3/min [2 and 8 bbl/min] closes the tool. The MIRV can be run in the hole open, which allows the string to fill with mud. After the packer is set, the cushion can be pumped into the string, the MIRV closed, and the test initiated.

PCT Pressure Controlled Tester Valve

The PCT Pressure Controlled Tester valve, operated by annulus pressure, is the downhole valve used to control formation flows and shut-in for applications that do not use the IRIS Intelligent Remote Implementation System applications. The PCT valve must be run in conjunction with either the hydrostatic reference tool or the PORT* Pressure Operated Reference Tool, either of which traps a reference pressure inside the PCT valve.

The two distinct sections of the PCT valve are the ball valve seal section and the hydromechanical operator section. The versatility of the PCT valve can be enhanced by installing a hold-open (HOOP) module that holds the ball open when the annulus pressure is bled off. The HOOP module allows wireline to be run through the ball or circulation through the ball valve when the packer is not set. Operating pressures for the PCT valve vary with depth but are usually between 6.95 and 10.34 kPa [1,000 and 1,500 psi] applied annulus pressure.

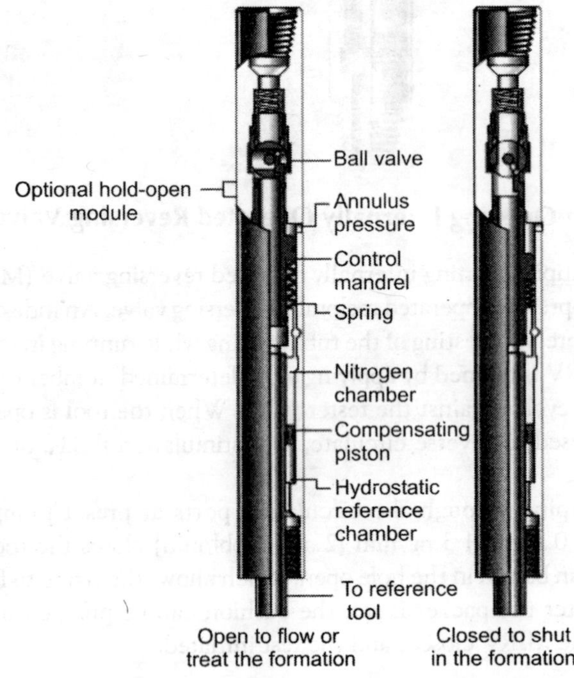

Pipe Tester Valve

The pipe tester valve (PTV) is a modified single-ball safety valve (SBSV) with a multiflow evaluator (MFE) ball installed in place of the PCT* Pressure Controlled Tester ball. This tool is used in production-type tests for running a cushion, or for pressure testing the pipe string above the valve while running in the hole. The PTV is normally closed, but it opens permanently when annulus pressure is applied to burst the rupture disk. When the PTV is used with the dual-ball safety valve or SBSV, one flow test and one shut-in test can be performed with a minimum number of tools.

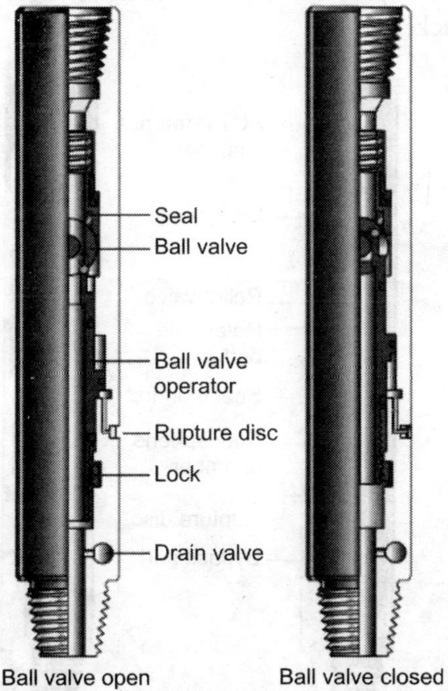

Port Pressure Operated Reference Tool

The PORT Pressure Operated Reference Tool provides a reference pressure to the PCT Pressure Controlled Tester valve and also serves as a bypass when running in the hole. The PORT tool is used to trap a reference pressure within the PCT valve, eliminating the need for a high-nitrogen precharge at the surface. This trapped reference pressure provides a high-closing force for the PCT ball valve.

To operate the tool, pressure is applied to the annulus, causing the disc to rupture. When coming out of the hole, for safety, the downhole reference pressure is bled through the relief valve. Because the PORT tool is pressure-operated, no set-down weight is required, as it is with the hydrostatic reference tool (HRT). Therefore, the string can be run in tension, greatly simplifying the string design when testing with a permanent packer. In this case, drill collars (weight) and slip joints (length compensation) can be eliminated. Length compensation is provided by the packer stinger when using a permanent packer.

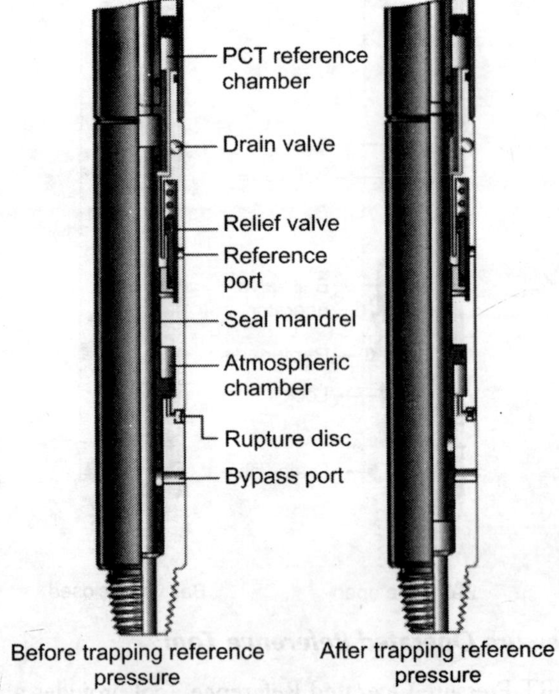

Pump-Through Flapper Safety Valve

The pump-through flapper safety valve (PFSV) provides a reliable means for obtaining downhole shut-in and minimizing wellbore storage during final pressure buildup. It also has the ability to pump into the formation, irrespective of tubing or annulus pressure integrity above the valve. The PFSV is a fully opening downhole safety valve. It is open when run in the hole and closed permanently when annulus pressure rises above the rupture disk rating. The operator mandrel is biased to internal pressure and locked in the open position to prevent premature closure. Upon bursting the rupture disk, hydrostatic pressure is applied to the operator mandrel, which moves up against an atmospheric chamber, uncovering the spring-loaded flapper. Pumping down the tubing lifts the flapper off its seat and permits killing the well.

The PFSV-J is part of the J-string developed for ultrahigh-pressure wells with bottomhole temperatures greater than 218 °C [425 °F]. New seal technology has enabled successful testing of the PFSV-J to 260°C [500 °F] at its maximum pressure rating.

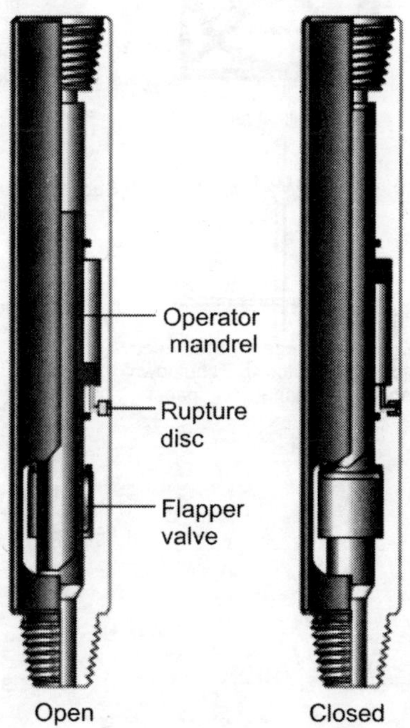

SenTREE 3 and Commander Electrohydraulic System

The SenTREE 3 test tree with the Commander electrohydraulic control and monitoring system is the choice for well testing operations performed from dynamically positioned vessels. The electrohydraulic system provides a 10-s response time to shut-in the well and disconnect the landing string, regardless of water depth.

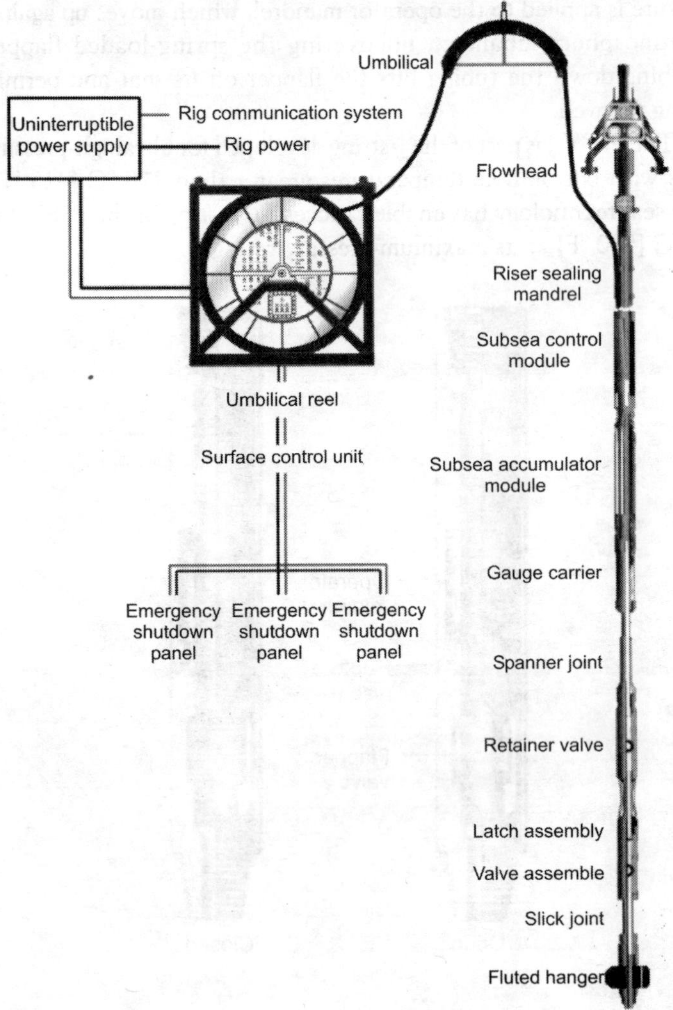

The system also provides subsea pressure and temperature monitoring to assist with management of the testing operation. The Commander electrohydraulic system requires only one simple 11/2-in.-diameter light weight control umbilical. The SenTREE 3 system is modular in design to enable appropriate space-out and custom configuration for each project. Its modularity enables placement of the slick joint either below the valve assembly or between the latch and valve assembly to accommodate very short blowout preventer (BOP) stacks. The system is backed by an extensive test programme and an impressive track record of successful well testing operations.

SenTREE* 3 test tree with the Commander* electrohydraulic control system provides the fast response needed when well testing from dynamically positioned vessels.

SenTREE 3 And Commander Hydraulic System

The SenTREE 3 test tree with the Commander hydraulic control system is the choice for well testing operations performed from anchored vessels. The hydraulic-based system provides a 50-s response time to shut-in the well and disconnect the landing string in water depths to 5,000 ft. Hydraulic enhancements are standard for operations in water depths over 1500 ft. The Commander hydraulic system requires only one simple control umbilical.

The SenTREE 3 system is modular in design to enable appropriate space out and custom configuration for each test program. Its modularity enables placement of the slick joint either below the valve assembly or between the latch and valve assembly to accommodate very short blowout preventer (BOP) stacks. The system is backed by an extensive test programme and an impressive track record of successful well testing operations.

SenTREE* 3 test tree with the Commander* hydraulic system is ideal for well testing in water depths to 5000 ft from moored vessels.

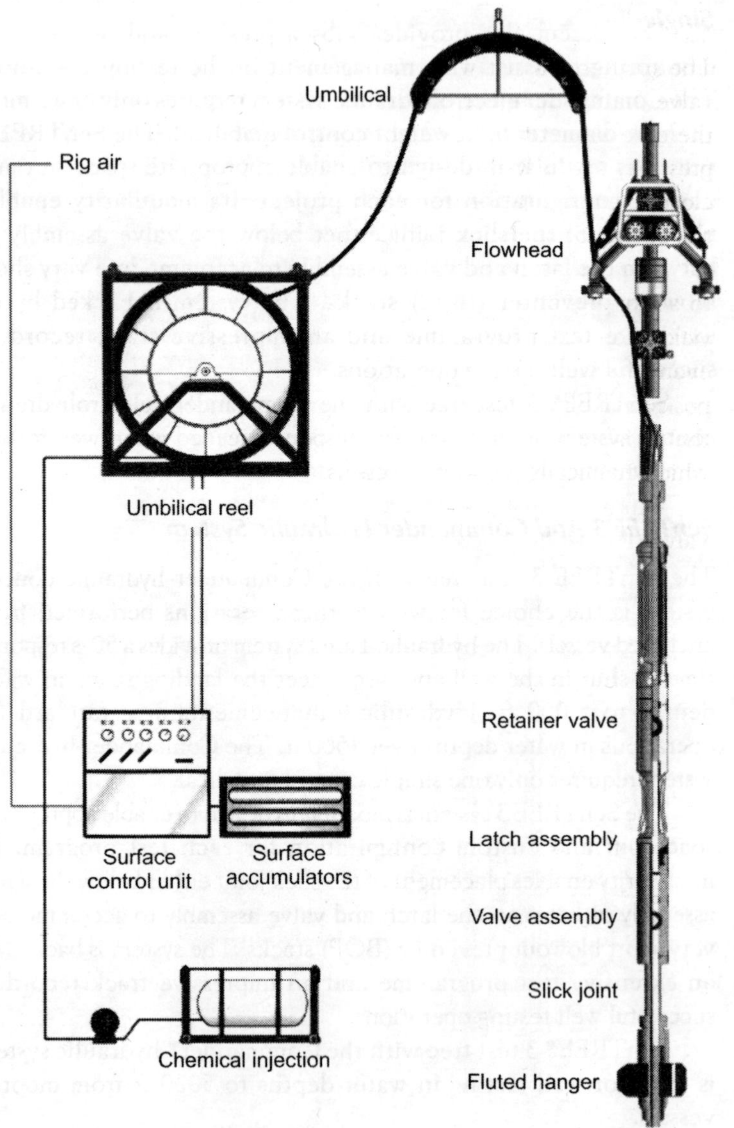
Umbilical
Rig air
Flowhead
Umbilical reel
Retainer valve
Latch assembly
Surface control unit
Surface accumulators
Valve assembly
Slick joint
Chemical injection
Fluted hanger

Single-Ball Safety Valve

The single-ball safety valve (SBSV) is a fully open downhole safety valve that is run in the open position and closes permanently when the disk is ruptured. The operator mandrel is balanced to internal pressure, and is locked in the open position to prevent premature closure. Upon rupturing the disk, hydrostatic pressure is applied to the operator mandrel, which closes the valve.

The combination of the large differential pressure (hydrostatic to atmospheric) and the 21-cm^2 [3 1/4-in^2] operator mandrel area yields more than enough force to cut 5.6-mm [7/32-in] wireline cable, even in shallow wells. The operator mandrel locks in the closed position and prevents the tool from reopening until it is retrieved at the surface. The lock can be reset without disassembling the tool, which enables functional testing before running in the hole.

Kits are available to convert the SBSV to a pump-through safety valve (PTSV) or a pipe tester valve (PTV).

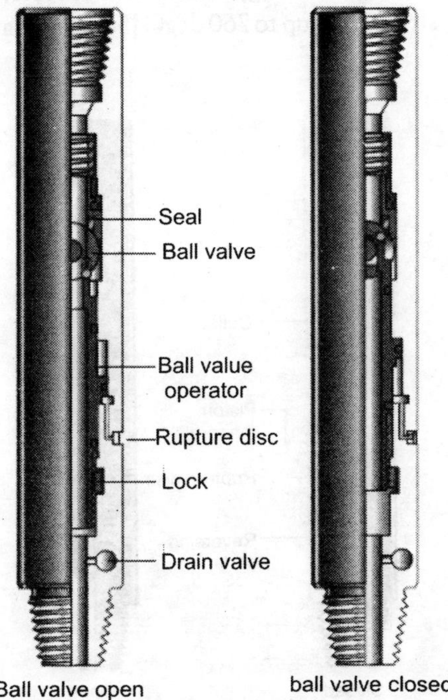

Single-Shot Reversing Valve

The single-shot reversing valve (SHRV) operates by applying annulus pressure to burst a rupture disc. Once actuated, the reversing ports are locked open. The SHRV is typically opened at the completion of the drillstem test (DST) to reverse out fluids produced during the test.

A ratchet keeps the valve in the closed position until the disc is ruptured. When the rupture disc bursts, hydrostatic pressure is applied to the operator mandrel, moving it up against the atmospheric-pressured chamber. This results in uncovering eight large circulating ports for efficient well-killing operations. Once annulus pressure pushes the mandrel up, the same ratchet locks the mandrel in place to keep the tool open. The SHRV-H is part of the 88.9-mm [3.5-in] large-bore IRIS Intelligent Remote Implementation System.

The SHRV-J is part of the ultrahigh- pressure J-string developed for use in wells with bottomhole temperatures greater than 218 degC [425 degF]. New seal technology has enabled successful qualification testing of the J-string tools up to 260 degC [500 degF] at the maximum rated pressure.

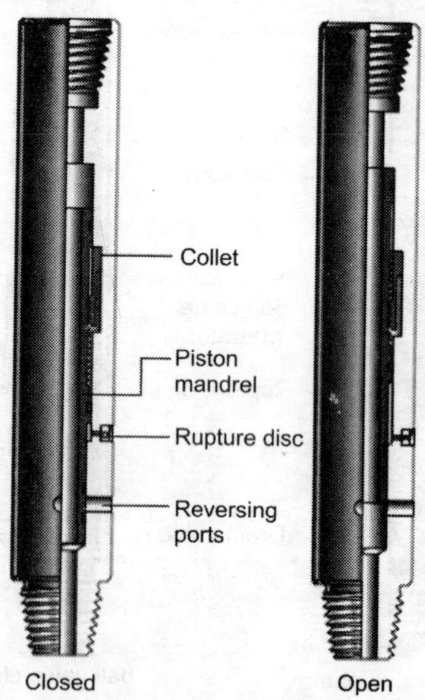

Tubing-Fill Test Valve

The tubing-fill test valve (TFTV) enables filling and testing of the tubing while running in the hole. As the string is lowered into the hole, fluid enters the tubing through the TFTV bypass ports. The fluid creates a differential pressure that causes the flapper to open and then fills the tubing.

The tubing can be tested at any depth by pressuring-up on the tubing string against the flapper valve. When the test string is at depth, annulus pressure is applied to rupture a disc, causing the flapper to lock fully open. Once the flapper is open, the tool has fullbore access. The TFTV-H is part of the large-bore IRIS Intelligent Remote Implementation System string.

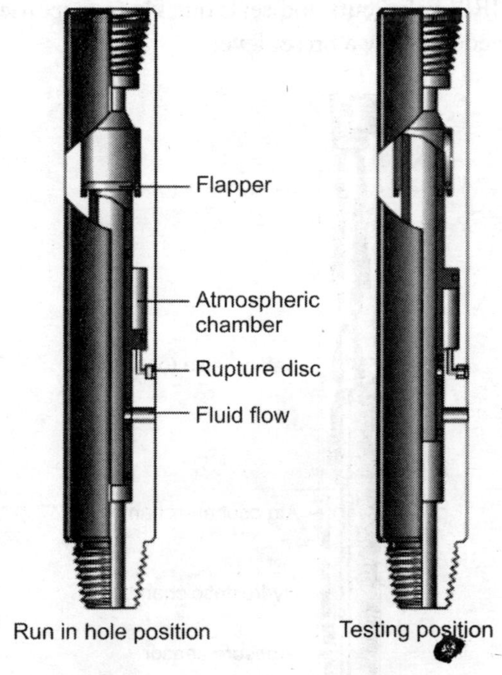

Iris Safety Valve

The fast-acting IRIS* safety valve, with its high closing force, offers an additional downhole barrier to the test valve during deep water through-tubing logging operations. It is controlled by the IRIS Intelligent Remote Implementation System, which uses microprocessor-based electronics for control logic and hydrostatic pressure as an energy source to operate downhole tools. The IRIS safety valve provides the means to cut a logging cable with one ball valve and then shut-in the well with a second ball valve unaffected by the cable. The unique IRIS operating system enables a faster cut-and-seal operation than possible with conventional tools.

The valve remains in an inactive mode until a simple command activates the safety mode before wireline operations. In the safety mode, the IRIS valve cuts and seals quickly in response to annulus pressure bleedoff below a preset level.

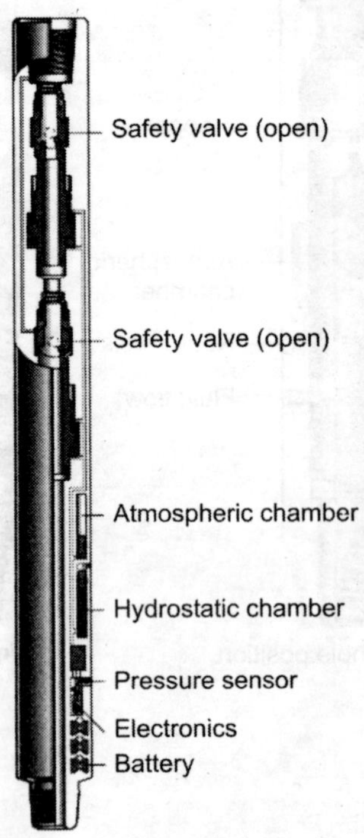

14

Miscible: Gas Injection

Core Flood Studies

Engineering of miscible gas injection projects requires a suite of laboratory studies in order to properly understand the injection solvent/ reservoir fluid phase behaviour. Oilphase—DBR provides a complete suite of miscible gas studies including swelling studies (P-x), multicontact tests, slim tube, rising bubble, and core flood studies.

Composite Core Flood Studies (CFS) provide the testing that brings together the injection and reservoir fluids within the reservoir material. These experiments can include reservoir condition measurements of gas, oil, or water permeability, unsteady state relative permeabilities, recovery of oil under water flood or gas injection and permeability impairment studies.

Composite CFS for the evaluation and optimization of recovery of oil under miscible gas injection studies are customized to meet the engineering and modeling requirements of the individual end user. Initial efforts are concentrated on proper establishment of *in situ* fluid saturation and fluid saturation distribution. Restoration of the proper wettability is essential to the subsequent generation of meaningful results.

Typical EOR CFS provide oil recovery by water flood, unsteady state relative permeability, residual oil saturation post water flood and incremental oil recovery, and water production as a function of gas injection. Restored state CFS are the best approximation to the field process that can be achieved in the laboratory. The results are useful for process optimization of waterflood, gas injection, and WAG.

Depressurization and blending of fluids *in situ*, can initiate the deposition of organic solids resulting flow impairment in the reservoir.

Composite CFS offer an ideal test, at reservoir conditions, to evaluate the potential for impairment.

Applications

- Determination of residual oil and incremental oil.
- Optimization of WAG scheme design.
- Input for injectivity and recovery modeling.
- Assessment of flow impairment due to organic solids.

Swelling Studies

When gas is injected into a reservoir containing an undersaturated oil, the gas (injection solvent) can go into solution, causing the reservoir fluid to swell. The swelling test is a laboratory simulation of this process. The conventional swelling test involves determining the saturation pressure (bubble point or dew point pressure), saturated fluid density and volume, and volumetric data in the two-phase vapor-liquid region as a function of incrementally increasing concentrations of injection gas.

The composition and viscosity of the mixtures can also be measured. The saturation pressure, volumetric, and density data are used to tune the equation-of-state (EOS) model. Graphical data are presented in the form of the pressure-composition diagram. Swelling studies, when conducted in the fully visual pressure-volume-temperature (PVT) cell equipped with the Schlumberger solids detection system and high-pressure microscope, can provide valuable information describing the potential for asphaltene precipitation caused by adding the selected injection gas.

Application

- EOS model tuning and reservoir simulation.

Benefits

- Provides visual confirmation of bubble point or dew point pressure.

- Supplies accurate liquid and vapor-phase volumes.
- Provides required viscosity and density data.
- Identifies potential for asphaltene precipitation problems.

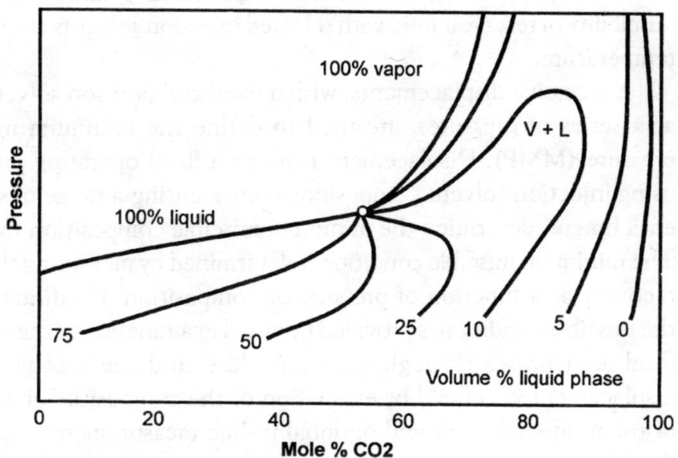

Rising Bubble Apparatus Tests

A rising bubble apparatus (RBA) test is a rapid method for estimating the minimum miscibility pressure (MMP) for an oil-gas pair. The apparatus consists of a high-pressure visual cell with a 30-cm flat glass tube mounted in the center. The glass tube is charged with reservoir oil to form an oil column and equilibrated at the desired test pressure and temperature. A gas bubble is injected into the oil column at the bottom of the tube. As the bubble rises through the oil column, the shape and motion are recorded. The movement of the gas bubble mimics the forward-contact occurring during the propagation of the gas slug through the reservoir. The minimum miscibility pressure of the reservoir oil and injection gas system is inferred from the behaviour of the rising bubble over a range of pressures.

Application

- Determination of MMP and minimum miscible composition.

Slim Tube Test

Slim Tube displacement experiments are used to determine the minimum pressure or enrichment required to establish dynamic miscibility of reservoir fluid with selected injection solvents at reservoir temperature.

Successive displacements, with a fixed composition solvent, run at a series of pressures, are used to define the minimum miscible pressure (MMP). Displacement runs, at a fixed operating pressure, using injection solvent compositions representing a range of solvent enrichment, determine the minimum miscible composition (MMC). The minimum miscible condition is determined by measuring the fluid recovery as a function of pressure or composition. Confirmation of the miscible condition is provided by visual examination of the effluent fluid as it passes through the sight glass, and the mechanism of displacement is defined by evaluation of the compositional analyses of the produced fluids and optional in-line measurement of effluent fluid density.

Applications

- Determination of MMP or MMC for EOR projects.
- Input for reservoir simulator.
- Definition of miscible process.

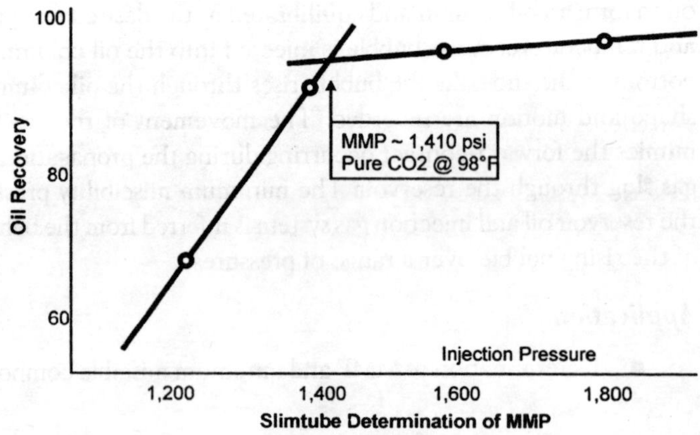

Slimtube Determination of MMP

Appendices

(A) WELL STATUS - TYPE

Brine (BW): A well used to produce naturally occurring salty or mineralized formation water (not fresh water).

Cavern Storage (LPG): A well used for injection or withdrawal of fluids (hydrocarbons or brine) in a solution-mined storage cavern.

Disposal (BD): A well used for the disposal of oil field fluid into an underground formation.

Dry Hole (DH): A well classed as exploratory or development in which no hydrocarbons have been encountered.

Gas Show (GS): A well classed as exploratory or development in which gas has been encountered but has not been proven or judged to be productive.

Historical Oil (HOP): A well used to produce oil from a reservoir designated as a "historical oil field".

Injection (INJ): A well used primarily to inject fluid into a formation as part of a secondary recovery operation approved by the Ministry.

Licensed (LIC): A location for which a well licence has been issued but no well has been drilled.

Location (LOC): A location for which Ministry records indicate a well that has been drilled but for which no status information is available.

Natural Gas (GP): A well presently or formerly used to produce natural gas from a reservoir.

Natural Gas Storage (NGS): A well used for injection or withdrawal of natural gas to or from storage in a reservoir.

Observation (OBS): A well used to monitor performance in a natural gas storage reservoir, oil or gas pool, aquifer, hydrocarbon storage cavern, or solution mining cavern.

Oil & Gas Show (OSGS): A well classed as exploratory or development in which oil and gas have been encountered but have not been proven or judged to be productive.

Oil (OP): A well presently or formerly used to produce oil from a reservoir.

Oil & Gas Well (OPGP): A well presently or formerly used to produce both oil and gas from a reservoir.

Oil Show (OS): A well classed as exploratory or development in which oil has been encountered but has not been proven or judged to be productive.

Private Gas (PGP): A well used by the land and mineral rights owner to produce gas from a reservoir for private, non-commercial use.

Solution Mining (SM): A well used for injection or withdrawal of fluids (fresh water or brine) into a subsurface salt formation for the purpose of mining salt.

Source Well (SW): A well used to produce water for injection into a reservoir as part of a secondary recovery project approved by the Ministry.

Stratigraphic Test (STR): A well drilled for the purpose of geological evaluation or testing.

(B) WELL STATUS - MODE

Mode Symbol Definition

Abandoned (ABD): A well which is officially plugged and abandoned.

Abandoned & Whips Tocked (ABW): A well drilled and plugged back, and another hole drilled and whipstocked out of the same well bore.

Abandoned Junked (lost) (LOS): A well abandoned because of mechanical difficulties in the hole.

Active (ACT): A well which is in active operation in accordance with the purpose for which it is licensed.

Cancelled (CAN): A location for which a well licence was issued but the licence has been canceled.

Capped (CAP): A well with proven productivity (by test or judgment) which has not been placed on production.

Not Drilled (NDR): A location for which a well licence has been issued but a well has not yet been drilled.

Potential (POT): A newly drilled or recompleted well in which suitability for production, injection, or storage is assumed but not proven.

Suspended (SUS): A formerly active well in which operations have ceased and will not resume for at least 30 days.

Casing and Tubing Record

Abbreviations for how the casing and tubing are set in the well.

- ANC: Anchor Packer
- BAR: Barefoot
- BHP: Bottom Hole Packer
- CEM: Cemented
- COL: Collar
- HAN: Hanging
- HWP: Hook Wall Packer
- PAC: Packer
- PC: Packer and Cement
- SHO: Casing Shoe

Water Record

Abbreviations for type of water encountered while drilling a well.

- BLK: Black
- BRA: Brackish
- FRE: Fresh
- MIN: Mineral
- SAL: Salt
- SUL: Sulfur

(C) METRIC CONVERSION CHART

To Convert	*Into*	*Multiply by*
Volumes		
barrels	cubic meters	0.158987
barrels	U.S. gallons	42
cubic feet	cubic meters	0.028328
cubic meters	cubic feet	35.3145
cubic meters	U.S. gallons	264.2
cubic meters	barrels	6.28994
cubic meters (crude oil, light)	Gigajoules (energy content)	38.51
thousand cubic feet	cubic meters	28.32
Imperial gallons	cubic meters	0.004546
Imperial gallons	U.S. gallons	1.20094
liters	U.S. gallons	0.2642
U.S. gallons	barrels	0.02381
U.S. gallons	cubic meters	0.003785
U.S. gallons	Imperial gallons	0.83267
U.S. gallons	liters	3.78533
gigajoule	Mcf (thousand cubic feet of natural gas at 1000 Btu per cubic foot)	0.95
thousand cubic feet (Mcf)	gigajoules	1.05
gigajoule	barrels of oil	0.165
Lengths		
centimeters	inches	0.3937
feet	meters	0.3048
inches	centimeters	2.54
kilometers	miles	0.6214
meters	feet	3.28084
miles	kilometers	1.609344
Land Units		
acres	hectares	0.404686
hectares	acres	2.471

(*Contd.*)

(*Contd.*)

To Convert	Into	Multiply by
Weights		
kilograms	pounds	2.205
pounds	tonne	0.00045
pounds	kilograms	0.4536
tonne	pounds	2204.62
Pressures		
kilopascals (kPa)	pounds per square inch (psi)	0.145038
pounds per square inch (psi)	kilopascals (kPa)	6.894757
m^3	cubic meters	
10^3m^3	thousand cubic meters	
Mcf	thousand cubic feet (of gas)	
MMcf	million cubic feet	
Bcf	billion cubic feet	
Bcfe	billion cubic feet of gas equivalent	
Tcf	trillion cubic feet	
Boe	barrel of oil equivalent	
Mboe	thousand barrels of oil equivalent	
MMboe	million barrels of oil equivalent	
Mbbls	thousand barrels	
MMbbls	million barrels	
NGLs	Natural gas liquids One barrel of oil	
	is the energy equivalent of six Mcf of natural gas.	

(D) PETROLEUM WELL VIEW

Petroleum Wells

Licensed - Not Drilled

Location

Dry Hole

Abandoned/Dry Hole

Abandoned Oil Show

Oil Show

Abandoned Gas Show

Gas Show

Oil Well

Gas Well

Oil & Gas Well

Oil Show Gas Show

Oil Well Gas Show

Gas Well Oil Show

Abandoned Oil & Gas Show

Abandoned Oil Well

Abandoned Gas Well

Abandoned Oil & Gas Well

Abandoned Cavern Storage

Cavern Storage

Abandoned Gas Storage

Gas Storage

Abandoned Injection Well

Injection Well

Abandoned Brine Disposal

Brine Disposal

Abandoned Brine Well

Brine Well

Solution Mining

Abandoned Stratigraphic Test

Stratigraphic Test

Observation

Abandoned Source Well

Source Well

(E) GLOASSARY

Abandon

To temporarily or permanently cease production from a well or to cease further drilling operations.

Abnormal Pressure

Pressure outside the normal or expected range.

Afterflow

The flow associated with the wellbore storage following a surface shut-in. When a well is first shut-in at the surface, flow from the formation into the bottom of the wellbore continues unabated until compression of the fluids in the wellbore causes the downhole pressure to rise. If the wellbore fluid is highly compressible and the well rate is low, the afterflow period can be long. Conversely, high-rate wells producing little gas have negligible afterflow periods.

Anisotropic Formation

A formation with directionally dependent properties. The most common directionally dependent properties are permeability and stress. Most formations have vertical to horizontal permeability anisotropy with vertical permeability being much less (often an order of magnitude less) than horizontal permeability. Bedding plane permeability anisotropy is common in the presence of natural fractures. Stress anisotropy is frequently greatest between overburden stress and horizontal stress in the bedding plane. Bedding plane stress contrasts are common in tectonically active regions. Permeability anisotropy can sometimes be related to stress anisotropy.

Annular Blowout Preventer

A well control device, usually installed above the ram preventers, that forms a seal in the annular space between the pipe and well bore or, if no pipe is present, over the well bore itself.

Ball-and-Seat Valve

A device used to restrict fluid flow to one direction. It consists of a polished sphere, or ball, usually of metal, and an annular piece, the seat, ground, and polished to form a seal with the surface of the ball. Gravitational force or the force of a spring holds the ball against the seat. Flow in the direction of the force is prevented, while flow in the opposite direction overcomes the force and unseats the ball.

Ball-Out

To plug, open perforations by using ball sealers.

Barite

Barium sulfate, BaSO4; a mineral frequently used to increase the weight or density of drilling mud. Its relative density is 4.2 (meaning that it is 4.2 times denser than water)..

Barium Sulfate

A chemical compound of barium, sulfur, and oxygen (BaSO4), which may form a tenacious scale that is very difficult to remove. Also called barite.

Barrel

A measure of volume for petroleum products in the United States. One barrel is the equivalent of 42 U.S. gallons or 0.15899 cubic meters (9,702 cubic in.).

Basket

A device placed in the drill or work string that catches debris when a drillable object is being milled or drilled downhole.

Beam Pumping Unit

A machine designed specifically for sucker rod pumping. An engine or motor (prime mover) is mounted on the unit to power a rotating crank. The crank moves a horizontal member (walking beam) up and down to produce reciprocating motion. This reciprocating motion operates the pump.

Belt

A flexible band or cord connecting and wrapping around each of two or more pulleys to transmit power or impart motion.

Belt Guard

A protective grill or cover for a belt and pulleys.

Bent Sub

A short cylindrical device (generally angular) installed in the drill stem between the bottommost drill collar and a downhole motor.

Blowout

An uncontrolled flow of gas, oil, or other well fluids from the well.

Blowout Preventer (BOP)

One or more valves installed at the wellhead to prevent the escape of pressure either in the annular space between the casing and the drill pipe or in open hole (for example, hole with no drill pipe) during drilling or completion operations.

Blowout Preventer Control Panel

Controls, opens, and closes the blowout preventers.

Blowout Preventer Control Unit

A device that stores hydraulic fluid under pressure in special containers and provides a method to open and close the blowout preventers.

Blowout Preventer Stack (Bop Stack)

The assembly of well control equipment including preventers, spools, valves, and nipples connected to the top of the wellhead.

Bottomhole Pressure

(1) The pressure at the bottom of a borehole. It is caused by the hydrostatic pressure of the wellbore fluid and, sometimes, by any backpressure held at the surface, as when the well is shut-in with

blowout preventers. When mud is being circulated, bottomhole pressure is the hydrostatic pressure plus the remaining circulating pressure required to move the mud up the annulus. (2) The pressure in a well at a point opposite the producing formation, as recorded by a bottomhole pressure measuring device.

Bottomhole Pressure Test

A test that measures the reservoir pressure of the well, obtained at a specific depth or at the mid point of the producing zone. A flowing bottomhole pressure test measures pressure while the well continues to flow; a shut-in bottomhole pressure test measures pressure after the well has been shut in for a specified period of time.

Brake Band

A part of the brake mechanism consisting of a flexible steel band lined with a material that grips a drum when tightened. On drawworks, the brake band acts on the drum to control the lowering of the traveling block and its load.

Break Circulation

To start the mud pump for restoring circulation of the mud column. Because the stagnant drilling fluid has thickened or gelled during the period of no circulation, higher pump pressure is usually required to break circulation.

Breaker Points

Contacts that interrupt the current in the primary circuit of an electrical system such as in a spark-ignition engine.

Break Out

(1) To unscrew one section of pipe from another section, especially drill pipe while it is being withdrawn from the wellbore. During this operation, the tongs are used to start the unscrewing operation.
(2) To separate, as gas from a liquid or water from an emulsion.

Breakout Block

A plate that fits in the rotary table and holds the drill bit while it is being unscrewed from the drill collar.

Bullet Perforator

A tubular device that, when lowered to a selected depth within a well, is engaged forcing the projectiles (bullets) through the casing and cement to provide holes through which the formation fluids may enter the wellbore.

Bumped

In cementing operations, pertaining to a cement plug that comes to rest on the float collar.

Bumper Block

Timbers wrapped with wire mesh or other retaining medium located below the crown to act as a cushion in the event the block is raised too far.

Bushing

(1) A pipe fitting on which the external thread is larger than the internal thread to allow two pipes of different sizes to be connected.
(2) A removable lining or sleeve inserted or screwed into an opening to limit its size, resist wear or corrosion, or serve as a guide.

Breakout Cathead

A device attached to the catshaft of the drawworks that is used as a power source for the tongs used in unscrewing drill pipe; usually located opposite the driller's side of the drawworks.

Break Tour

To begin operating 24 h a day. Moving the rig and rigging up are usually carried on during daylight hours only. When the rig is ready for operation at a new location, crews break tour.

Bridge Plug

A downhole tool, composed primarily of slips, a plug mandrel, and a rubber sealing element, that is run and set in casing to isolate a lower zone while an upper section is being tested or cemented.

Caliper Log

A record showing variations in wellbore diameter by depth, indicating undue enlargement due to caving in, washout, or other causes. The caliper log also reveals corrosion, scaling, or pitting inside tubular goods.

Carrier Rig

A specially designed, self-propelled workover, or drilling rig that is driven directly to the well site. Power from a carrier rig's hoist engine or engines also propels the rig on the road. A carrier rig may be a back-in type or a drive-in type.

Casing

Steel pipe placed in an oil or gas well to prevent the wall of the hole from caving in, to prevent movement of fluids from one formation to another and to aid in well control.

Casing Hanger

A circular device with a frictional gripping arrangement of slips and packing rings used to suspend casing from a casing head in a well.

Casing Head

A heavy, flanged steel fitting connected to the first string of casing. It provides a housing for slips and packing assemblies, allows suspension of intermediate and production strings of casing, and supplies the means for the annulus to be sealed off. Also called a casing spool.

Casing Point

The depth in a well at which casing is set, generally the depth at which the casing shoe rests.

Casing Pressure

The pressure in a well that exists between the casing and the tubing or the casing and the drill pipe.

Channeling

When casing is being cemented in a borehole, the cement slurry can fail to rise uniformly between the casing and the borehole wall, leaving spaces, or channels, devoid of cement. Ideally, the cement should completely and uniformly surround the casing and form a strong bond to the borehole wall.

Chemical Cutoff

A method of severing pipe in a well by applying high-pressure jets of a very corrosive substance against the wall of the pipe. The resulting cut is very smooth.

Chemical Cutter

A fishing tool that uses high-pressure jets of chemicals to sever casing, tubing, or drill pipe stuck in the hole.

Chemical Flooding

A method of improved oil recovery in which chemicals dissolved in water are pumped into a reservoir through injection wells to mobilize oil left behind after primary or secondary recovery and to move it toward production wells.

Choke

A device with an orifice installed in a line to restrict the flow of fluids. Surface chokes are part of the Christmas tree on a well and contain a choke nipple, or bean, with a small-diameter bore that serves to restrict the flow. Chokes are also used to control the rate of flow of the drilling mud out of the hole when the well is closed-in with the blowout preventer and a kick is being circulated out of the hole.

Christmas Tree

The control valves, pressure gauges, and chokes assembled at the top of a well to control flow of oil and/or gas after the well has been drilled and completed. It is used when reservoir pressure is sufficient to cause reservoir fluids to rise to the surface.

Coiled Tubing

A continuous string of flexible steel tubing, often hundreds or thousands of feet long, which is wound onto a reel, often dozens of feet in diameter. The reel is an integral part of the coiled tubing unit, which consists of several devices that ensure that the tubing can be safely and efficiently inserted into the well from the surface. Also called reeled tubing.

Coiled-Tubing Unit

The equipment for transporting and using coiled tubing, including a reel for the coiled tubing, an injector head to push the tubing down the well, a wellhead blowout preventer stack, a power source (usually a diesel engine and hydraulic pumps), and a control console. A unique feature of the unit is that it allows continuous circulation while it is being lowered into the hole. A coiled tubing unit is usually mounted on a trailer or skid.

Conductor Casing

Generally, the first string of casing in a well. It may be lowered into a hole drilled into the formations near the surface and cemented in place; it may be driven into the ground by a special pile driver (in such cases, it is sometimes called drive pipe). Its purpose is to prevent the soft formations near the surface from caving in and to conduct drilling mud from the bottom of the hole to the surface when drilling starts. Also called conductor pipe, drive pipe.

Coring

The process of cutting a vertical, cylindrical sample of the formations encountered as a well is drilled.

Coring Bit

A bit that does not drill out the center portion of the hole, but allows this center portion (the core) to pass through the round opening in the center of the bit and into the core barrel.

Corrosion

Any of a variety of complex chemical or electrochemical processes, such as rust, by which metal is destroyed through reaction with its environment.

Corrosion Inhibitor

A chemical substance that minimizes or prevents corrosion in metal equipment.

Crown Saver

A device mounted near the drawworks drum to keep the driller from inadvertently raising the traveling block into the crown block. A probe senses when too much line has been pulled onto the drum, indicating that the traveling block may strike the crown. The probe activates a switch that simultaneously disconnects the drawworks from its power source and engages the drawworks brake.

Commingled Well

A well producing from two or more formations through common well casing and a single tubing string.

Dampener

An air or inert gas device that minimizes pressure surges in the output line of a mud pump. Sometimes called a surge dampener.

Density Log

A special radioactivity log for open-hole surveying that responds to variations in the specific gravity of formations. It is a contact log (i.e., the logging tool is held against the wall of the hole). It emits neutrons and then measures the secondary gamma radiation that is scattered back to the detector in the instrument. The density log is an excellent porosity-measure device, especially for shaley sands. Some trade names are Formation Density Log, Gamma-Gamma Density Log, and Densilog.

Derrick

A large load-bearing structure, usually of bolted construction. In drilling, the standard derrick has four legs standing at the corners of the substructure and reaching to the crown block. The substructure is an assembly of heavy beams used to elevate the derrick and provide space to install blowout preventers, casingheads, and so forth.

Desander

A centrifugal device for removing sand from drilling fluid to prevent abrasion of the pumps. It may be operated mechanically or by a fast-moving stream of fluid inside a special cone-shaped vessel, in which case it is sometimes called a hydrocyclone.

Downdip Wells

Wells producing from deeper depths lower on a structure than updip wells.

Dipmeter Survey

An oil-well-surveying method that determines the direction and angle of formation dip in relation to the borehole. It records data that permit computation of both the amount and the direction of formation dip relative to the axis of the hole and thus provides information about the geologic structure of the formation. Also called dipmeter log or dip log.

Directional Drilling

Intentional deviation of a wellbore from the vertical. Although wellbores are normally drilled vertically, it is sometimes necessary or advantageous to drill at an angle from the vertical. Controlled directional drilling makes it possible to reach subsurface areas laterally remote from the point where the bit enters the earth.

Directional Hole

A wellbore intentionally drilled at an angle from the vertical.

Displacement Fluid

In well cementing, the fluid, usually drilling mud or salt water, that is pumped into the well after the cement is pumped into it to force the cement out of the casing and into the annulus.

Downhole Motor

A drilling tool made up in the drill string directly above the bit. It causes the bit to turn while the drill string remains fixed. It is used most often as a deflection tool in directional drilling, where it is made up between the bit and a bent sub (or, sometimes, the housing of the motor itself is bent). Two principal types of downhole motor are the positive-displacement motor and the downhole turbine motor.

Dpmeter Survey

An oilwell-surveying method that determines the direction and angle of formation dip in relation to the borehole. It records data that permit computation of both the amount and direction of formation dip relative to the axis of the hole and thus provides information about the geologic structure of the formation. Also called dipmeter log or dip log.

Drawworks

The hoisting mechanism on a drilling rig. It is essentially a large winch that spools off or takes in the drilling line and thus lowers or raises the drill stem and bit.

Drawworks Brake

The mechanical brake on the drawworks that can slow or prevent the drawworks drum from moving.

Drawworks Drum

The spool-shaped cylinder in the drawworks around which drilling line is wound or spooled.

Dampener

An air or inert gas device that minimizes pressure surges in the output line of a mud pump. Sometimes called a surge dampener.

Density Log

A special radioactivity log for open-hole surveying that responds to variations in the specific gravity of formations. It is a contact log (i.e., the logging tool is held against the wall of the hole). It emits neutrons and then measures the secondary gamma radiation that is scattered back to the detector in the instrument. The density log is an excellent porosity-measure device, especially for shaley sands. Some trade names are Formation Density Log, Gamma-Gamma Density Log, and Densilog.

Drill Stem Test (DST)

A method of formation testing. The basic drill stem test tool consists of a packer or packers, valves or ports that may be opened and closed from the surface, and two or more pressure-recording devices. The tool is lowered on the drill string to the zone to be tested. The packer or packers are set to isolate the zone from the drilling fluid column.

Dual Completion

A single well that produces from two separate formations at the same time. Production from each zone is segregated by running two tubing strings with packers inside the single string of production casing, or by running one tubing string with a packer through one zone while the other is produced through the annulus. In a miniaturized dual completion, two separate casing strings are run and cemented in the same wellbore.

Dump Bailer

A bailing device with a release valve, usually of the disc or flapper type, used to place, or spot, material (such as cement slurry) at the bottom of the well.

Electric Rig

A drilling region which the energy from the power source—usually diesel engines—is changed to electricity by generators mounted on the engines. The electrical power is then distributed through electrical conductors to electric motors. The motors power the various rig components.

Electric Well Log

A record of certain electrical characteristics (such as resistivity and conductivity) of formations traversed by the borehole. It is made to identify the formations, determine the nature and amount of fluids they contain, and estimate their depth. Also called an electric log or electric survey.

External Cutter

A fishing tool containing metal cutting knives that is lowered into the hole and over the outside of a length of pipe to cut it. The severed part of the pipe can then be brought to the surface. Also called an outside cutter.

Fastline

The end of the drilling line that is affixed to the drum or reel of the drawworks, so called because it travels with greater velocity than any other portion of the line.

Fingerboard

A rack that supports the stands of pipe being stacked in the derrick or mast. It has several steel fingerlike projections that form a series of slots into which the derrickman can place a stand of drill pipe or collars after it is pulled out of the hole and removed from the drill string.

Fire Flooding

A thermal recovery method in which the oil in the reservoir is ignited, the heat vaporizes lighter hydrocarbons and water pushes the warmed oil toward a producing well. Also called in situ combustion.

Fish

An object that is left in the wellbore during drilling or workover operations and that must be recovered before work can proceed. It can be anything from a piece of scrap metal to a part of the drill stem.

Fishing

The procedure of recovering lost or stuck equipment in the wellbore.

Fishing Magnet

A powerful magnet designed to recover metallic objects lost in a well.

Fishing Tool

A tool designed to recover equipment lost in a well.

Fishing-Tool Operator

The person (usually a service company employee) in charge of directing fishing operations.

Fitting

A small, often standardized, part (such as a coupling, valve, or gauge) installed in a larger apparatus.

Float Collar

A special coupling device inserted one or two joints above the bottom of the casing string that contains a check valve to permit fluid to pass downward but not upward through the casing. The float collar prevents drilling mud from entering the casing while it is being lowered, allowing the casing to float during its descent and thus decreasing the load on the derrick or mast.

Float Shoe

A short, heavy, cylindrical steel section with a rounded bottom that is attached to the bottom of the casing string. It contains a check valve and functions similar to the float collar but also serves as a guide shoe for the casing.

Flood

(1) To drive oil from a reservoir into a well by injecting water under pressure into the reservoir formation. (2) To drown out a well with water.

Flow

A current or stream of fluid or gas.

Floor Crew

Those workers on a drilling or workover rig who work primarily on the rig floor.

Flowing Well

A well that produces oil or gas by its own reservoir pressure rather than by use of artificial means (such as pumps).

Flow Line

The surface pipe through which oil or gas travels from a well to processing equipment or to storage.

Flow Rate

The speed, or velocity, of fluid or gas flow through a pipe or vessel.

Fluid Injection

Injection of gases or liquids into a reservoir to force oil toward and into producing wells.

Fluid Loss

The unwanted migration of the liquid part of the drilling mud or cement slurry into a formation, often minimized or prevented by the blending of additives with the mud or cement.

Formation Fluid

Fluid (such as gas, oil, or water) that exists in a subsurface formation.

Formation Gas

Gas initially produced from an underground reservoir.

Formation Pressure

The force exerted by fluids or gas in a formation, recorded in the hole at the level of the formation with the well shut-in. Also called reservoir pressure or shut-in bottomhole pressure.

Formation Testing

The gathering of pressure data and fluid samples from a formation to determine its production potential before choosing a completion method.

Formation Water

(1) The water originally in place in a formation.
(2) Any water that resides in the pore spaces of a formation.

Frac Fluid

A fluid used in the fracturing process (for example, a method of stimulating production by opening new flow channels in the formation surrounding a production well). Under extremely high hydraulic pressure, frac fluids (such as distillate, diesel fuel, crude oil, dilute hydrochloric acid, water, or kerosene) are pumped downward through production tubing or drill pipe and forced out below a packer or between two packers. The pressure causes cracks to open in the formation, and the fluid penetrates the formation through the cracks. Sand grains, aluminum pellets, walnut shells, or similar materials (propping agents) are carried in suspension by the fluid into the cracks. When the pressure is released at the surface, the fracturing fluid returns to the well but leaves behind the propping agents to hold open the formation cracks.

Fuel Tanks

Fuel storage tanks for the power generating system.

Fracture

A crack or crevice in a formation, either natural or induced.

Fracture Acidizing

A procedure by which acid is forced into a formation under pressure high enough to cause the formation to crack. The acid acts on certain kinds of formations, usually carbonates, to increase the permeability of the formation. Also called acid fracturing.

Fracture Pressure

The pressure at which a formation will break down, or fracture.

Fracturing Fluid

A fluid, such as water, oil, or acid, used in hydraulic fracturing. The fluid carries propping agents that hold open the formation cracks after hydraulic pressure dissipates.

Free-Point Indicator

A device run on wireline into the wellbore and inside the fishing string and fish to locate the area where a fish is stuck. When the drill string is pulled and turned, the electromagnetic fields of free pipe and stuck pipe differ. The free-point indicator is able to distinguish these differences, which are registered on a metering device at the surface.

Friction

Resistance to movement created when two surfaces are in contact. When friction is present, movement between the surfaces produces heat.

Full-Gauge Bit

A bit that has maintained its original diameter.

Full-Gauge Hole

A wellbore drilled with a full-gauge bit. Also called a true-to-gauge hole.

Gamma Ray Log

A type of radioactivity well log that records natural radioactivity around the wellbore. Shales generally produce higher levels of gamma radiation and can be detected and studied with the gamma ray tool.

Gas Anchor

A tubular, perforated device attached to the bottom of a suckerrod pump that helps to prevent gas lock. The device works on the principle that gas, being lighter than oil, rises. As well fluids enter the anchor, gas breaks out of the fluid and exits from the anchor through perforations near the top. Remaining fluids enter the pump through a mosquito bill (a tube within the anchor), which has an opening near the bottom. In this way, all or most of the gas escapes before the fluids enter the pump.

Gas Cap

A free-gas phase overlying an oil zone and occurring within the same producing formation as the oil.

Gas-Cap Drive

Drive energy supplied naturally (as a reservoir is produced) by the expansion of the gas cap. In such a drive, the gas cap expands to force oil into the well and to the surface.

Gas-Cut Mud

A drilling mud that contains entrained formation gas, giving the mud a characteristically fluffy texture. Gas cut mud may cause a lowering of mud weight.

Gas Drive

The use of the energy that arises from the expansion of compressed gas in a reservoir to move crude oil to a wellbore. Also called depletion drive.

Gas Injection

The injection of gas into a reservoir to maintain formation pressure by gas drive and to reduce the rate of decline of the original reservoir drive. One type of gas injection uses gas that does not mix (is not miscible) with the oil. Examples of these gases include natural gas, nitrogen, and flue gas. Another type uses gas that does mix (is miscible) with the oil. The gas may be naturally miscible or become miscible under high pressure. Examples of miscible gases include propane, methane enriched with other light hydrocarbons, methane under high pressure, and carbon dioxide under pressure. Frequently, water is also injected in alternating steps with the gas.

Gas Injection Well

A well into which gas is injected for the purpose of maintaining or supplementing pressure in an oil reservoir.

Gas Lift

The process of raising or lifting fluid from a well by injecting gas down the well through tubing or through the tubing-casing annulus. Injected gas aerates the fluid to make it exert less pressure than the formation does; the resulting higher formation pressure forces the fluid out of the wellbore. Gas may be injected continuously or intermittently, depending on the producing characteristics of the well and the arrangement of the gas-lift equipment.

Gas-Lift Mandrel

A device installed in the tubing string of a gas-lift well onto which or into which a gas-lift valve is fitted. There are two common types of mandrel. In the conventional gas-lift mandrel, the gas-lift valve is installed as the tubing is placed in the well. Thus, to replace or repair the valve, the tubing string must be pulled. In the sidepocket mandrel, however, the valve is installed and removed by wireline while the mandrel is still in the well, eliminating the need to pull the tubing to repair or replace the valve.

Gas-Lift Valve

A device installed on a gas-lift mandrel, which in turn is put on the tubing string of a gas-lift well. Tubing and casing pressures cause the valve to open and close, thus allowing gas to be injected into the fluid in the tubing to cause the fluid to rise to the surface.

Gas-Lift Well

A well in which reservoir fluids are artificially lifted by the injection of gas.

Gas Lock

(1) A condition sometimes encountered in a pumping well when dissolved gas, released from solution during the upstroke of the plunger, appears as free gas between the valves. If the gas pressure is sufficient, the standing valve is locked shut, and no fluid enters the tubing. (2) a device fitted to the gauging hatch on a pressure tank that enables manual dipping and sampling without loss of vapor. (3) a condition that can occur when gas-cut mud is circulated by the mud pump. The gas breaks out of the mud, expands, and works against the operation of the piston and valves.

Gas Well

A well that primarily produces gas. Legal definitions vary among the states.

Gel

A semisolid, jellylike state assumed by some colloidal dispersions at rest.

Geologist

A scientist who gathers and interprets data pertaining to the formations of the earth's crust.

Go in the Hole

To lower the drill stem, the tubing, the casing, or the sucker rods into the wellbore.

Gone to Water

Pertaining to a well in which production of oil has decreased and production of water has increased (for example, "the well has gone to water").

Gooseneck

The curved connection between the rotary hose and the swivel.

Gravel

Sand or glass beads of uniform size and roundness used in gravel packing.

Gravel Packing

A method of well completion in which a slotted or perforated liner, often wire-wrapped, is placed in the well and surrounded by gravel. If open hole, the well is sometimes enlarged by underreaming at the point where the gravel is packed. The mass of gravel excludes sand from the wellbore but allows continued production.

Guide Shoe

A short, heavy, cylindrical section of steel filled with concrete and rounded at the bottom, which is placed at the end of the casing string. It prevents the casing from snagging on irregularities in the borehole as it is lowered.

Guy Line Anchor

A buried weight or anchor to which a guy line is attached.

Guy Wire

A rope or cable used to steady a mast or pole.

hang rods

To suspend sucker rods in a derrick or mast on rod hangers rather than to place them horizontally on a rack.

Hard Hat

A hard helmet worn by oil-field workers to minimize the danger of being injured by falling objects.

headache

The position in which the mast on a mobile rig is resting horizontally over the driver's cab.

hoist

(1) An arrangement of pulleys and wire rope used for lifting heavy objects; a winch or similar device. (2) The drawworks. v: to raise or lift.

Hoisting Components

Drawworks, drilling line, and traveling and crown blocks. Auxiliary hoisting components include catheads, catshaft, and air hoist.

hoisting Drum

The large, flanged spool in the drawworks on which the hoisting cable is wound.

Hoisting Line

A wire rope used in hoisting operations.

Hook

A large, hook-shaped device from which the elevator bails or the swivel is suspended. It turns on bearings in its supporting housing.

Hopper

A large funnel- or cone-shaped device into which dry components (such as powdered clay or cement) can be poured to later mix with water or other liquids. The dry component is educted through a nozzle at the bottom of the hopper.

Horsehead

The generally horsehead-shaped steel piece at the front of the beam of a pumping unit to which the bridle is attached in sucker rod pumping.

Horsepower

A unit of measure of work done by a machine.

Horizontal Drilling

Deviation of the borehole from vertical so that the borehole penetrates a productive formation in a manner parallel to the formation.

Hydraulic

(1) Of or relating to water or other liquid in motion. (2) Operated, moved, or effected by water or liquid.

Hydraulic Fluid

A liquid of low viscosity (such as light oil) that is used in systems actuated by liquid (such as the brake system in a car).

Hydraulic Force

Force resulting from pressure on water or other hydraulic fluid.

Hydraulic Fracturing

An operation in which a specially blended liquid is pumped down a well and into a formation under pressure high enough to cause the formation to crack open, forming passages through which oil can flow into the wellbore.

Hydraulic Jar

A type of mechanical jar in which a fluid moving through a small opening slows the piston stroke while the crew stretches the work string. After the hydraulic delay, a release mechanism in the jar trips to allow a mandrel to spring up and deliver a sharp blow.

Hydraulic Pumping

A method of pumping oil from wells by using a downhole pump without sucker rods. Subsurface hydraulic pumps consist of two reciprocating pumps coupled and placed in the well. One pump functions as an engine and drives the other pump (the production pump). The downhole engine is usually operated by clean crude oil under under pressure (power oil) that is drawn from a power-oil settling tank by a triplex plunger pump on the surface. If a single string of tubing is used, power oil is pumped down the tubing string to the pump, which is seated in the string, and a mixture of power oil and produced fluid is returned through the casing-tubing annulus. If two parallel strings are used, one supplies power oil to the pump while the other returns the exhaust and produced oil to the surface. A hydraulic pump may be used to pump several wells from a central source.

Impeller

A set of mounted blades used to impart motion to a fluid air or gas (such as, the rotor of a centrifugal pump).

Impermeable

Preventing the passage of fluid. A formation may be porous yet impermeable if there is an absence of connecting passages between the voids within it.

Impression Block

A block with lead or another relatively soft material on its bottom. It is made up on drill pipe or tubing at the surface, run into a well, and set down on the object that has been lost in the well. The block is retrieved and the impression is examined. The impression is a mirror image of the top of the fish; it also indicates the fish's position in the hole, for example, whether it is centered or off to one side. From this information, the correct fishing tool may be selected.

Induction Log

An electric well log in which the conductivity of the formation rather than the resistivity is measured. Because oil-bearing formations are less conductive of electricity than water-bearing formations, an induction survey, when compared with resistivity readings, can aid in determination of oil and water zones.

Inflatable Packer

A packer with an element that inflates by means of gas or liquid pumped from the surface through a line. It is deflated by means of slots that can be opened to allow the gas or liquid to flow out. They are used when a temporary packer is needed in a hole.

Injection Gas

(1) A high-pressure gas injected into a formation to maintain or restore reservoir pressure. (2) Gas injected in gas-lift operations.

injection log

A survey used to determine the injection profile, that is, to assign specific volumes or percentages to each of the formations taking fluid in an injection well. The injection log is also used to check for casing or packer leaks, proper cement jobs, and fluid migration between zones.

Injection Water

Water that is introduced into a reservoir to help drive hydrocarbons to a producing well.

Injection Well

A well through which fluids are injected into an underground stratum to increase reservoir pressure and to displace oil. Also called input well.

Injector Head

A control head for injecting coiled tubing into a well that seals off the tubing and makes a pressure tight connection.

Inland Barge Rig

An off shore drilling structure consisting of a barge on which the drilling equipment is constructed. It is positioned on location, then the barge is sunk.

Insert

(1) A cylindrical object, rounded, blunt, or chisel-shaped on one end and usually made of tungsten carbide, that is inserted in the cones of

a bit, the cutters of a reamer, or the blades of a stabilizer to form the cutting element of the bit or the reamer or the wear surface of the stabilizer. Also called a compact.

Insert Pump

A sucker rod pump that is run into the well as a complete unit.

Intake Valve

(1) The mechanism on an engine through which air and sometimes fuel are admitted to the cylinder. (2) On a mud pump, the valve that opens to allow mud to be drawn into the pump by the pistons moving in the liners.

Intermediate Casing String

The string of casing set in a well after the surface casing but before production casing is set to keep the hole from caving and to seal off formations. In deep wells, one or more intermediate strings may be required

Jar

A percussion tool operated manually or hydraulically to deliver a heavy upward or downward blow to fish stuck in the borehole. v: to apply a heavy blow to the drill stem by use of a jar or bumper sub.

Jar Accelerator

A hydraulic tool used in conjunction with a jar and made up on the fishing string above the jar to increase the power of the jarring force.

Jerk Line

A wire rope, one end of which is connected to the end of the tongs and the other end of which is attached to the cathead.

Jet

(1) A hydraulic device operated by a centrifugal pump used to clean the mud pits, or tanks, and to mix mud components. (2) In a

perforating gun using shaped charges, a highly penetrating, fast-moving stream of exploded particles that forms a hole in the casing, cement, and formation.

Jet Cutoff

A procedure for severing pipe stuck in a well by detonating special shaped-charge explosives similar to those used in jet perforating. The explosive is lowered into the pipe to the desired depth and detonated. The force of the explosion makes radiating horizontal cuts around the pipe, and the severed portion of the pipe is retrieved.

Jet Cutter

A fishing tool that uses shaped charges to sever casing, tubing, or drill pipe stuck in the hole.

Jet Gun

An assembly, including a carrier and shaped charges, that is used in jet perforating.

Jet-Perforate

To create holes through the casing with a shaped charge of high explosives instead of a gun that fires projectiles. The loaded charges are lowered into the hole to the desired depth. Once detonated, the charges emit short, penetrating jets of high-velocity gases that make holes in the casing and cement for some distance into the formation. Formation fluids then flow into the wellbore through these perforations.

Journal Bearing

A machine part in which a rotating shaft (a journal) revolves or slides. Also called a plain bearing.

Joint Of Pipe

A length of drill pipe or casing. Both come in various lengths.

Junk

Metal debris lost in a hole. Junk may be a lost bit, pieces of a bit, pieces of pipe, wrenches, or any relatively small object that impedes drilling or completion and must be fished out of the hole. v: to abandon (as a nonproductive well).

Junk Basket

A device made up on the bottom of the drill stem or on wireline to catch pieces of junk from the bottom of the hole. Circulating the mud or reeling in the wireline forces the junk into a barrel in the tool, where it is caught and held. When the basket is brought back to the surface, the junk is removed. Also called a junk sub or junk catcher.

Junk Mill

A mill used to grind up junk in the hole.

Junk Retriever

A special tool made up on the bottom of the drill stem to pick up junk from the bottom of the hole. Most junk retrievers are designed with ports that allow drilling fluid to exit the tool a short distance off the bottom. This flow of fluid creates an area of low pressure inside the tool so that the junk is lifted and caught in the retriever by the higher pressure outside the tool.

Kelly

The heavy square or hexagonal steel member suspended from the swivel through the rotary table and connected to the topmost joint of drill pipe to turn the drill stem as the rotary table turns.

Kelly Bushing

A device fitted to the rotary table through which the kelly passes and the means by which the torque of the rotary table is transmitted to the kelly and to the drill stem. Also called the drive bushing.

Kelly Bypass

A system of valves and piping that allows drilling fluid to be circulated without the use of the kelly.

Kelly Cock

A valve installed at one or both ends of the kelly. When a high-pressure backflow occurs inside the drill stem, the valve is closed to keep pressure off the swivel and rotary hose.

Kelly Saver Sub

A heavy and relatively short length of pipe that fits in the drill stem between the kelly and the drill pipe. The threads of the drill pipe mate with those of the sub, minimizing wear on the kelly.

Kelly Spinner

A pneumatically operated device mounted on top of the kelly that, when actuated, causes the kelly to turn or spin.

Keyseat

(1) An undergauge channel or groove cut in the side of the borehole and parallel to the axis of the hole. A keyseat results from the rotation of pipe on a sharp bend in the hole. (2) A groove cut parallel to the axis in a shaft or a pulley bore.

kick

An entry of water, gas, oil, or other formation fluid into the wellbore during drilling. It occurs because the pressure exerted by the column of drilling fluid is not great enough to overcome the pressure exerted by the fluids in the formation drilled. If prompt action is not taken to control the kick, or kill the well, a blowout may occur.

Kick Fluids

Oil, gas, water, or any combination that enters the borehole from a permeable formation.

Kick Off

(1) To bring a well into production; used most often when gas is injected into a gas lift well to start production. (2) In workover operations, to swab a well to restore it to production. (3) To deviate a wellbore from the vertical, as in directional drilling.

Kickoff Point (KOP)

The depth in a vertical hole at which a deviated or slant hole is started; used in directional drilling.

Land Rig

Any drilling rig that is located on dry land.

Latch On

To attach elevators to a section of pipe to pull it out of or run into the hole.

Latch Sub

A device, usually with segmented threads, run with seal subs on the bottom of a tubing string and latched into a permanent packer to prevent tubing movement.

Lay

(1) The spiral of strands in a wire rope either to the right or to the left, as viewed from above. (2) A term used to measure wire rope, signifying the linear distance a wire strand covers in one complete rotation around the rope.

Lay Down Pipe

To pull drill pipe or tubing from the hole and place it in a horizontal position on a pipe rack.

Lead-Tong Hand (Pronounced "Leed")

The crew member who operates the lead tongs when drill pipe and drill collars are being handled. Also called lead-tong man.

Lead Tongs (Pronounced "Leed")

The pipe tongs suspended in the derrick or mast and operated by a chain or a wire rope connected to the makeup cathead or the breakout cathead.

lifting sub

A threaded device placed in the end of tubulars, such as drill collars to aid in lifting; also called hoisting plug.

Liner

(1) A string of pipe used to case open hole below the existing casing. A liner extends from the setting depth up into another string of casing, usually overlapping about 100 feet (30.5 m) above the lower end of the intermediate or the oil string. Liners are nearly always suspended from the upper string by a hanger device. (2) A relatively short length of pipe with holes or slots that is placed opposite a producing formation. Usually, such liners are wrapped with specially shaped wire that is designed to prevent the entry of loose sand into the well as it is produced. They are also often used with a gravel pack. (3) In jet perforation guns, a conically shaped metallic piece that is part of a shaped charge. It increases the efficiency of the charge by increasing the penetrating ability of the jet. (4) A replaceable tube that fits inside the cylinder of an engine or a pump.

Liner Completion

A well completion in which a liner is used to obtain communication between the reservoir and the wellbore.

Liner Hanger

A slip device that attaches the liner to the casing.

Location

The place where a well is drilled. Also called wellsite.

Log

A systematic recording of data, such as a driller's log, mud log, electrical well log, or radioactivity log. Many different logs are run in wells to discern various characteristics of downhole formation. v: to record data.

Log A Well

To run any of the various logs used to ascertain downhole information about a well.

Logging Devices

Any of several electrical, acoustical, mechanical, or radioactivity devices that are used to measure and record certain characteristics or events that occur in a well that has been or is being drilled.

Long String

(1) The last string of casing set in a well. (2) The string of casing that is set at the top of or through the producing zone, often called the oil string or production casing.

Lost Circulation

The quantities of whole mud lost to a formation, usually in cavernous, pressured, or coarsely permeable beds. Evidenced by the complete or partial failure of the mud to return to the surface as it is being circulated in the hole.

Lost Pipe

Drill pipe, drill collars, tubing, or casing that has become separated in the hole from the part of the pipe reaching the surface, necessitating its removal before normal operations can proceed; for example, a fish.

Lost Time Incident

An incident in the workplace that results in an injury serious enough that causes the person injured to be unable to work for a day or more.

Lubricator

A specially fabricated length of casing or tubing usually placed temporarily above a valve on top of the casing head or tubing head. It is used to run swabbing or perforating tools into a producing well and provides a method for sealing off pressure and thus should be rated for the highest anticipated pressure.

Mast

A portable derrick that is capable of being raised as a unit, as distinguished from a standard derrick, which cannot be raised to a working position as a unit. For transporting by land, the mast can be divided into two or more sections to avoid excessive length extending from truck beds on the highway.

Master Bushing

A device that fits into the rotary table to accommodate the slips and drive the kelly bushing so that the rotating motion of the rotary table can be transmitted to the kelly.

Master Valve

A large valve located on the Christmas tree and used to control the flow of oil and gas from a well. Also called master gate.

Mechanical Jar

A percussion tool operated mechanically to give an upward thrust to a fish by the sudden release of a tripping device inside the tool. If the fish can be freed by an upward blow, the mechanical jar can be very effective.

Mechanical Log

A log of, for instance, rate of penetration or amount of gas in the mud, obtained at the surface by mechanical means.

Mechanical Rig

A drilling rig in which the source of power is one or more internal-combustion engines and in which the power is distributed to rig components through mechanical devices (such as chains, sprockets, clutches, and shafts). Also called a power rig.

Mill

A downhole tool with rough, sharp, extremely hard cutting surfaces for removing metal, packers, cement, sand, or scale by grinding or cutting.

Miscible Drive

A method of enhanced recovery in which various hydrocarbon solvents or gases (such as propane, LPG, natural gas, carbon dioxide, or a mixture thereof) are injected into the reservoir to reduce interfacial forces between oil and water in the pore channels and thus displace oil from the reservoir rock.

Mixing Tank

Any tank or vessel used to mix components of a substance (as in the mixing of additives with drilling mud).

Mix Mud

To prepare drilling fluids.

Monitor

An instrument that reports the performance of a control device or signals if unusual conditions appear in a system.

Monkeyboard

The derrickhand's working platform. As pipe or tubing is run into or out of the hole, the derrickhand must handle the top end of the pipe, which may be as high as 90 feet (27 m) or higher in the derrick or mast.

Morning Tour (Pronounced "Tower")

A work shift that generally begins at or near midnight.

Motorhand

The crew member on a rotary drilling rig, who is responsible for the care and operation of drilling engines. Also called motorman.

Motor

Any of various power units, such as a hydraulic, internal combustion, air, or electric device that develops energy or imparts motion.

Mousehole

Shallow bores under the rig floor, usually lined with pipe, in which joints of drill pipe are temporarily suspended for later connection to the drill string.

Mousehole Connection

The procedure of adding a length of drill pipe or tubing to the active string.

Mud

The liquid circulated through the wellbore during rotary drilling and workover operations.

Mud Acid

A mixture of hydrochloric and/or hydrofluoric acids and surfactants used to remove wall cake from the wellbore.

Mud Cake

The sheath of mud solids that forms on the wall of the hole when liquid from mud filters into the formation. Also called filter cake or wall cake.

Mud Centrifuge

A device that uses centrifugal force to separate small solid components from liquid drilling fluid.

Mud Cleaner

A cone-shaped device, a hydrocyclone, designed to remove very fine solid particles from the drilling mud.

Mud Engineer

An employee of a drilling fluid supply company whose duty it is to test and maintain the drilling mud properties that are specified by the operator.

Mud-Gas Separator

A device that removes gas from the mud coming out of a well when a kick is being circulated out.

Mud Logging

The recording of information derived from examination and analysis of formation cuttings made by the bit and of mud circulated out of the hole. A portion of the mud is diverted through a gas-detecting device. Cuttings brought up by the mud are examined under ultraviolet light to detect the presence of oil or gas. Mud logging is often carried out in a portable laboratory set up at the wellsite.

Mud Pit

Originally, an open pit dug in the ground to hold drilling fluid or waste materials discarded after the treatment of drilling mud. For some drilling operations, mud pits are used for suction to the mud pumps, settling of mud sediments, and storage of reserve mud. Steel tanks are much more commonly used for these purposes now, but they are still usually referred to as pits.

Mud Pump

A large, high-pressure reciprocating pump used to circulate the mud on a drilling rig. A typical mud pump is a two-or three-cylinder piston pump whose replaceable pistons travel in replaceable liners and are driven by a crankshaft actuated by an engine or a motor.

Mud Return Line

A trough or pipe that is placed between the surface connections at the wellbore and the shale shaker.

Mud Tank

One of a series of open tanks, usually made of steel plate, through which the drilling mud is cycled to remove sand and fine sediments.

Mud Weight

A measure of the density of a drilling fluid expressed as pounds per gallon, pounds per cubic foot, or kilograms per cubic metre. Mud weight is directly related to the amount of pressure the column of drilling mud exerts at the bottom of the hole.

Neutron Log

A radioactivity well log used to determine formation porosity. The logging tool bombards the formation with neutrons. When the neutrons strike hydrogen atoms in water or oil, gamma rays are released. Since water or oil exists only in pore spaces, a measurement of the gamma rays indicates formation porosity.

Night Toolpusher

An assistant toolpusher whose duty hours are typically during night-time hours. Also known as a tour pusher.

Nipple

A tubular pipe fitting threaded on both ends used for making connections between pipe joints and other tools.

Nipple Up

In drilling, to assemble the blowout preventer stack on the wellhead at the surface.

Nitro Shooting

A formation-stimulation process first used about 100 years ago in Pennsylvania. Nitroglycerine is placed in a well and exploded to fracture.

Normal Circulation

The smooth, uninterrupted circulation of drilling fluid down the drill stem, out the bit, up the annular space between the pipe and the hole, and back to the surface.

Nozzle

A passage through jet bits that causes the drilling fluid to be ejected from the bit at high velocity.

Oilfield

The surface area overlying an oil reservoir or reservoirs. The term usually includes not only the surface area, but also the reservoir, the wells, and the production equipment.

Oil Mud

A drilling mud, such as, oil-base mud and invert-emulsion mud, in which oil is the continuous phase. It is useful in drilling certain formations that may be difficult or costly to drill with waterbase mud.

Oil Sand

(1) A sandstone that yields oil. (2) (by extension) any reservoir that yields oil, whether or not it is sandstone.

Oil Saver

A gland arrangement that mechanically or hydraulically seals by pressure. It is used to prevent leakage and waste of gas, oil, or water around a wireline (as when swabbing a well).

Oil Spotting

Pumping oil, or a mixture of oil and chemicals, to a specific depth in the well to lubricate stuck drill collars.

Oil String

The final string of casing set in a well after the productive capacity of the formation has been determined to be sufficient. Also called the long string or production casing.

Oilwell

A well from which oil is obtained.

Oil Zone

A formation or horizon of a well from which oil may be produced. The oil zone is usually immediately under the gas zone and on top of the water zone if all three fluids are present and segregated.

Open Formation

A petroleum-bearing rock with good porosity and permeability.

Open Hole

(1) any wellbore in which casing has not been set. (2) open or cased hole in which no drill pipe or tubing is suspended. (3) the portion of the wellbore that has no casing.

Open-Hole Completion

A method of preparing a well for production in which no production casing or liner is set opposite the producing formation. Reservoir fluids flow unrestricted into the open wellbore.

Open-Hole Fishing

The procedure of recovering lost or stuck equipment in an uncased wellbore.

Open-Hole Log

Any log made in uncased, or open hole.

Operator

The person or company, either proprietor or lessee, actually operating a well or lease, generally the oil or gas company that engages the drilling, service, and workover contractors.

Organization of Petroleum Exporting Countries (OPEC)

An organization of the countries of the Middle East, Southeast Asia,

Africa, and South America that produce oil and export it. Update - members as of 1997 are Algeria, Ecuador, Gabon, Indonesia, Iran, Iraq, Kuwait, Libya, Nigeria, Qatar, Saudi Arabia, the United Arab Emirates, and Venezuela. The organization's purpose is to negotiate and regulate production and oil prices.

Out-of-Gauge Bit

A bit that is no longer of the proper diameter.

Out-of-Gauge Hole

A hole that is not in gauge; that is, it is smaller or larger than the diameter of the bit used to drill it.

Overshot

A fishing tool that is attached to tubing or drill pipe and lowered over the outside wall of pipe or sucker rods lost or stuck in the wellbore. A friction device in the overshot, usually either a basket or a spiral grapple, firmly grips the pipe, allowing the fish to be pulled from the hole.

Overthrust Fault

A low-dip angle (nearly horizontal) reverse fault along which a large displacement has occurred. Some overthrusts, such as many of those in the Rocky Mountain Overthrust Belt, represent slippages of many miles.

O-Ring

A circular seal common in the oil field. O-rings may be made of elastomer, rubber, plastic, or stainless steel. To seal properly, they all require enough pressure to make them deform against a sealing surface.

Packer Fluid

A liquid, usually salt water or oil, but sometimes mud, used in a well when a packer is between the tubing and the casing. Packer fluid must be heavy enough to shut off the pressure of the formation being produced, and should not stiffen or settle out of suspension over long periods of time, and must be non-corrosive.

Packer Squeeze Method

A squeeze cementing method in which a packer is set to form a seal between the working string (the pipe down which cement is pumped) and the casing. Another packer or a cement plug is set below the point to be squeeze-cemented. By setting packers, the squeeze point is isolated from the rest of the well.

Packing

(1) A material used in a cylinder on rotating shafts of an engine or pump in the stuffing box of a valve, or between flange joints to maintain a leak proof seal. (2) the specially fabricated filling in packed fractionation columns and absorbers.

Pack-Off

A device with an elastomer packing element that depends on pressure below the packing to effect a seal in the annulus. Used primarily to run or pull pipe under low or moderate pressures. Also called a stripper.

Pack Off

To place a packer in the wellbore and activate it so that it forms a seal between the tubing and the casing.

Paraffin

A saturated aliphatic hydrocarbon having the formula C_nH_{2n+2} (for example, methane, CH_4; ethane, C_2H_6). Heavier paraffin hydrocarbons (for example, $C_{18}H_{38}$) form a waxlike substance that is called paraffin. These heavier paraffins often accumulate on the walls of tubing and other production equipment, restricting or stopping the flow of the desirable lighter paraffins.

Paraffin Scraper

A tube with guides around it to keep it centered in the hole, and a cylindrical piece with blades attached. Spaces between the blades allow drilling fluid to pass through and carry away the scrapings.

Parallel Strings

In a multiple completion, the arrangement of a separate tubing string for each zone produced, with all zones isolated by packers.

Parted Rods

Sucker rods that have been broken and separated in a pumping well because of corrosion, improper loading, damaged rods, and so forth.

PDC Bit

A special type of diamond drilling bit that does not use roller cones.

Perforate

To pierce the casing wall and cement of a wellbore to provide holes through which formation fluids may enter or to provide holes in the casing so that materials may be introduced into the annulus between the casing and the wall of the borehole. Perforating is accomplished by lowering into the well a perforating gun, or perforator.

Perforated Completion

(1) A well completion method in which the producing zone or zones are cased through cemented and perforated to allow fluid flow into the wellbore. (2) A well completed by this method.

Perforating Gun

A device fitted with shaped charges or bullets that is lowered to the desired depth in a well and fired to create penetrating holes in casing, cement, and formation.

Perforation

A hole made in the casing, cement, and formation through which formation fluids enter a wellbore. Usually, several perforations are made at a time.

Perforation Depth Control Log (PDC Log)

A special type of nuclear log that measures the depth of each casing collar. Knowing the depth of the collars makes it easy to determine the exact depth of the formation to be perforated by correlating casing-collar depth with formation depth.

Permanent Packer

A nonretrievable type of packer that must be drilled or milled out for removal.

Permeability

(1) A measure of the ease with which a fluid flows through the connecting pore spaces of a formation or cement. The unit of measurement is the millidarcy. (2) Fluid conductivity of a porous medium. (3) Ability of a fluid to flow within the interconnected pore network of a porous medium.

Petroleum

A substance occurring naturally in the earth in solid, liquid, or gaseous state and composed mainly of mixtures of chemical compounds of carbon and hydrogen, with or without other nonmetallic elements such as sulfur, oxygen, and nitrogen. In some cases, especially in the measurement of oil and gas, petroleum refers only to oil—a liquid hydrocarbon—and does not include natural gas or gas liquids such as propane and butane.

Pilot

A rodlike or tubelike extension below a downhole tool, such as a mill, that serves to guide the tool into or over another downhole tool or fish.

Pilot Bit

A bit placed on a special device that serves to guide the device into an already existing hole that is to be opened (made larger in diameter). The pilot bit merely guides, or pilots, the cutters on the hole opener into the existing hole so that the hole-opening cutters can enlarge the hole to the desired size.

Pilot Mill

A special mill that has a heavy tubular extension below it called a pilot or stinger. The pilot, smaller in diameter than the mill, is designed to go inside drill pipe or tubing that is lost in the hole. It guides the mill to the top of the pipe and centers it, thus preventing the mill from bypassing the pipe. Also called a piloted mill.

Pinch Points

The sections where body parts or other materials may be pinched.

Pipe Ramp And Pipe On Rack

An angled ramp for dragging drill pipe, casing and other materials up to the drilling floor or bringing such equipment down.

Pick Up

(1) To use the drawworks to lift the bit (or other tool) off bottom by raising the drill stem. (2) To use an air hoist to lift a tool, a joint of drill pipe, or other piece of equipment.

Pin

(1) The male threaded section of a tool joint. (2) On a bit, the threaded bit shank.

Pipe

A long, hollow cylinder, usually steel, through which fluids are conducted. Oil-field tubular goods are casing (including liners), drill pipe, tubing, or line PIPE.

Pipe Ram

A sealing component for a blowout preventer that closes the annular space between the pipe and the blowout preventer or wellhead.

Pipe Wiper

A flexible disk-shaped device, usually made of rubber, with a hole in the center through which drill pipe or tubing passes. It is used to wipe off mud, oil, or other liquid from the pipe as it is pulled from the hole.

Pit Level

Height of drilling mud in the mud tanks, or pits.

Pit-Level Indicator

One of a series of devices that continuously monitor the level of the drilling mud in the mud tanks. The indicator usually consists of float devices in the mud tanks that sense the mud level and transmit data to a recording and alarm device (a pit-volume recorder) mounted near the driller's position on the rig floor. If the mud level drops too low or rises too high, the alarm may sound to warn the driller of lost circulation or a kick.

Pitman

The arm that connects the crank to the walking beam on a pumping unit by means of which rotary motion is converted to reciprocating motion.

Plug N

Any object or device that blocks a hole or passageway (such as a cement plug in a borehole).

Plug Back

To place cement in or near the bottom of a well to exclude bottom water, to sidetrack, or to produce from a formation higher in the well. Plugging back can also be accomplished with a mechanical plug set by wireline, tubing, or drill pipe.

Plug-Back Cementing

A secondary cementing operation in which a plug of cement is positioned at a specific point in the well and allowed to set.

Plunger

(1) A basic component of the sucker rod pump that serves to draw well fluids into the pump. (2) the rod that serves as a piston in a reciprocating pump. (3) the device in a fuel-injection unit that regulates the amount of fuel pumped on each stroke.

Pole Mast

A portable mast constructed of tubular members. A pole mast may be a single pole, usually of two different sizes of pipe telescoped together to be moved or extended and locked to obtain maximum height above a well. Double-pole masts give added strength and stability.

Polished Rod

The topmost portion of a string of sucker rods. It is used for lifting fluid by the rod-pumping method. It has a uniform diameter and is smoothly polished to seal pressure effectively in the stuffing box attached to the top of the well.

Polycrystalline Diamond Compact (PDC)

A disk (a compact) of very small synthetic diamonds, metal powder, and tungsten carbide powder that are used as cutters on PDC bits.

Porosity

(1) The condition of being porous (such as a rock formation). (2) The ratio of the volume of empty space to the volume of solid rock in a formation, indicating how much fluid a rock can hold.

Possum Belly

(1) A receiving tank situated at the end of the mud return line. The flow of mud comes into the bottom of the device and travels to control mud flow over the shale shaker. (2) A metal box under a truck bed that holds pipeline repair tools.

Power Generating System

A diesel, LPG, natural gas, or gasoline engine along with a mechanical transmission or generator for producing power for the drilling rig.

Power Wrench

A wrench that is used to make up or break out drill pipe, tubing, or casing on which the torque is provided by air or fluid pressure. Conventional tongs are operated by a mechanical pull provided by a jerk line connected to a cathead.

Preflush

(1) An injection of water prior to chemical flooding that is used to induce reservoir conditions favourable to the surfactant solution by adjusting reservoir salinity and reducing ion concentrations. A preflush may also be used to obtain advance information on reservoir flow patterns. (2) fluid injected prior to the acid solution pumped into a well in an acid-stimulation treatment; sometimes called a spearhead.

Pressure Depletion

The method of producing a gas reservoir that is not associated with a water drive. Gas is removed and reservoir pressure declines until all the recoverable gas has been expelled.

Preventive Maintenance

A system of conducting regular checks, routine maintenance, and testing of equipment to lengthen the service life and to potentially permit replacement or repair of weakened or faulty parts before equipment failure results.

Primary Recovery

The first stage of Oil production in which natural reservoir drives are used to recover oil, although some form of artificial lift may be required to exploit declining reservoir drives.

Production

(1) The phase of the petroleum industry that deals with bringing the well fluids to the surface and separating them and storing, gauging, and otherwise preparing the product for delivery. (2) the amount of oil or gas produced in a given period.

Production Casing

The last string of casing set in a well, inside of which is usually suspended a tubing string.

Production Maintenance

The efforts made to minimize the decline in a well's production. It includes, for example, acid-washing of casing perforations to dissolve mineral deposits, scraping or chemical injection to prevent paraffin buildup, and various measures taken to control corrosion and erosion damage.

Production Rig

A portable servicing or workover unit, usually mounted on wheels and self-propelled. A well servicing unit consists of a hoist and engine mounted on a wheeled chassis with a self-erecting mast. A workover rig is basically the same, with the addition of a substructure with rotary, pump, pits, and auxiliaries to permit handling and working a drill string.

Productivity Test

A combination of a potential test and a bottomhole pressure test the purpose of which is to determine the effects of different flow rates on the pressure within the producing zone of the well to establish physical characteristics of the reservoir and to determine the maximum potential rate of flow.

Propping Agent

A granular substance (sand grains, aluminum pellets, or other material) that is carried in suspension by the fracturing fluid and that serves to keep the cracks open when fracturing fluid is withdrawn after a fracture treatment.

Pulsed Neutron Logging Device

A measuring instrument run inside casing to obtain an indication of the presence or absence of hydrocarbons outside the casing, to determine water saturation in a reservoir behind casing, to detect water movement in the reservoir, to estimate porosity, and to estimate water salinity.

Pulsed-Neutron Survey

A special cased hole logging method that uses radioactivity reaction time to obtain measurements of water saturation, residual oil saturation, and fluid contacts in the formation outside the casing of an oil well.

Radioactivity Well Logging

The recording of the natural or induced radioactive characteristics of subsurface formations. A radioactivity log, also known as a radiation log or a nuclear log, normally consists of two recorded curves: a gamma ray curve and a neutron curve. Both help to determine the types of rocks in the formation and the types of fluids contained in the rocks.

Ram

The closing and sealing component on a blowout preventer. One of three types—blind, pipe, or shear—may be installed in several preventers mounted in a stack on top of the wellbore. Blind rams, when closed, form a seal on a hole that has no drill pipe in it; pipe rams, when closed, seal around the pipe; shear rams cut through drill pipe and then form a seal.

Ram Blowout Preventer

A blowout preventer that uses rams to seal off pressure on a hole that is with or without pipe. It is also called a ram preventer. Ram-type preventers have interchangeable ram blocks to accommodate different O.D. drill pipe, casing, or tubing.

Range of Load

In sucker rod pumping, the difference between the polished rod peak load on the upstroke and the minimum load on the downstroke.

Rate of Penetration (Rop)

A measure of the speed at which the bit drills into formations, usually expressed in feet (meters) per hour or minutes per foot (meter).

Rathole

(1) A hole in the rig floor, some 30 to 40 feet (9 to 12 m) deep, which is lined with casing that projects above the floor, into which the kelly and the swivel are placed when hoisting operations are in progress. (2) A hole of a diameter smaller than the main hole and drilled in the bottom of the main hole. v: to reduce the size of the wellbore and drill ahead.

Rathole Connection

The addition of a length of drill pipe or tubing to the active string using the rathole instead of the mousehole, which is the more common connection. The length to be added is placed in the rathole, made up to the kelly, pulled out of the rathole, and made up into the string.

Rathole Rig

A small, usually truck-mounted rig, the purpose of which is to drill ratholes for regular drilling rigs that will be moved in later. A rathole rig may also drill the top part of the hole, the conductor hole, before the main rig arrives on location.

Ream

To enlarge the wellbore by drilling it again with a special bit.

Reamer

A tool used in drilling to smooth the wall of a well, enlarge the hole to the specified size, help stabilize the bit, straighten the wellbore if kinks or doglegs are encountered, and drill directionally.

Reciprocating Motion

Back-and-forth or up-and-down movement, such as that of a piston in a cylinder.

Reciprocating Pump

A pump consisting of a piston that moves back and forth or up and down in a cylinder. The cylinder is equipped with inlet (suction) and outlet (discharge) valves. On the intake stroke, the suction valves are opened, and fluid is drawn into the cylinder. On the discharge stroke, the suction valves close, the discharge valves open, and fluid is forced out of the cylinder.

Recompletion

After the initial completion of a well, the action and techniques of reentering the well and redoing or repairing the original completion to restore the well's productivity.

Reeve (The Line)

To string a wire rope drilling line through the sheaves of the traveling and crown blocks to the hoisting drum.

Remote Bop Control Panel

A device placed on the rig floor that can be operated by the driller to direct air pressure to actuating cylinders that turn the control valves on the main BOP control unit, located a safe distance from the rig.

Remote Choke Panel

A set of Controls, usually placed on the rig floor, or elsewhere on location, that is manipulated to control the amount of drilling fluid being circulated through the choke manifold. This procedure is necessary when a kick is being circulated out of a well.

Reserve Tank N

A special mud tank that holds mud that is not being actively circulated. A reserve tank usually contains a different type of mud from which the pump is currently circulating. For example, it may store heavy mud for emergency well-control operations.

Reservoir

A subsurface, porous, permeable or naturally fractured rock body in which oil or gas is stored. Most reservoir rocks are limestones, dolomites, sandstones, or a combination of these. The four basic types of hydrocarbon reservoirs are oil, volatile oil, dry gas, and gas condensate. An oil reservoir generally contains three fluids—gas, oil, and water—with oil the dominant product. In the typical oil reservoir, these fluids become vertically segregated because of their different densities. Gas, the lightest, occupies the upper part of the reservoir rocks; water, the lower part; and oil, the intermediate section. In addition to its occurrence as a cap or in solution, gas may accumulate independently of the oil; if so, the reservoir is called a gas reservoir. Associated with the gas, in most instances, are salt water and some oil. Volatile oil reservoirs are exceptional in that during early production they are mostly productive of light oil plus gas, but, as depletion occurs, production can become almost totally completely gas. Volatile oils are usually good candidates for pressure maintenance, which can result in increased reserves. In the typical dry gas reservoir, natural gas exists only as a gas and production is only gas plus fresh water that condenses from the flow stream reservoir. In a gas condensate reservoir, the hydrocarbons may exist as a gas, but, when brought to the surface, some of the heavier hydrocarbons condense and become a liquid.

Reservoir Drive Mechanism

The process in which reservoir fluids are caused to flow out of the reservoir rock and into a wellbore by natural energy. Gas drive depends on the fact that, as the reservoir is produced, pressure is reduced, allowing the gas to expand and provide the principal driving energy. Water drive reservoirs depend on water and rock expansion to force the hydrocarbons out of the reservoir and into the wellbore. Also called natural drive energy.

Reservoir Oil

Oil in place in the reservoir; retained in a reservoir as residual gas saturation is an inverse function of the pressure, due to the physics of gas.

Reservoir Pressure

The average pressure within the reservoir at any given time. Determination of this value is best made by bottomhole pressure measurements with adequate shut-in time. If a shut-in period long enough for the reservoir pressure to stabilize is impractical, then various techniques of analysis by pressure buildup or drawdown tests are available to determine static reservoir pressure.

Reservoir Rock

A permeable rock that may contain oil or gas in appreciable quantity and through which petroleum may migrate.

Resistivity Well Logging

The recording of the resistance of formation water to natural or induced electrical current. The mineral content of subsurface water allows it to conduct electricity. Rock, oil, and gas are poor conductors. Resistivity measurements can be correlated to formation lithology, porosity, permeability, and saturation and are very useful in formation evaluation.

Retrievable Packer

A packer that can be pulled out of the well to be repaired or replaced. Reverse circulation n: the course of drilling fluid downward through the annulus and upward through the drill stem, in contrast to normal circulation in which the course is downward through the drill stem and upward through the annulus. Seldom used in open hole, but frequently used in workover operations.

Rework

To restore production from an existing formation when it has fallen off substantially or ceased altogether.

Rig

The derrick or mast, drawworks, and attendant surface equipment of a drilling or workover unit.

Rig Down

To dismantle a drilling rig and auxiliary equipment following the completion of drilling operations. Also called tear down.

Rig Floor

The area immediately around the rotary table and extending to each corner of the derrick or mast—that is, the area immediately above the substructure on which the rotary table, and so forth rest.

Rig Up

To prepare the drilling rig for making hole, for example, to install tools and machinery before drilling is started.

Roller Chain

A type of chain that is used to transmit power by fitting over sprockets attached to shafts, causing rotation of one shaft by the rotation of another. Transmission roller chain consists of offset links, pin links, and roller links.

Rotary

The machine used to impart rotational power to the drill stem while permitting vertical movement of the pipe for rotary drilling. Modern rotary machines have a special component, the rotary or master bushing, to turn the kelly bushing, which permits vertical movement of the kelly while the stem is turning.

Rotary Drilling

A drilling method in which a hole is drilled by a rotating bit to which a downward force is applied. The bit is fastened to and rotated by the drill stem, which also provides a passageway through which the drilling fluid is circulated. Additional joints of drill pipe are added as drilling progresses.

Rotary Helper

A worker on a drilling or workover rig, subordinate to the driller, whose primary work station is on the rig floor. Sometimes called floorhand, floorman, rig crew member, or roughneck.

Rotary Shoe

A length of pipe whose bottom edge is serrated or dressed with a hard cutting material and that is run into the wellbore around the outside of stuck casing, pipe, or tubing to mill away the obstruction.

Rotary Speed

The speed, measured in revolutions per minute, at which the rotary table is operated.

Rotary Support Table

A strong but relatively light-weight device used on some rigs that employ a top drive to rotate the bit. Although a conventional rotary table is not required to rotate the bit on such rigs, crew members must still have a place to set the slips to suspend the drill string in the hole when tripping or making a connection. A rotary support table provides such a place but does not include all the rotary machinery required in a regular rotary table.

Rotary Table

The principal component of a rotary, or rotary machine, used to turn the drill stem and support the drilling assembly. It has a beveled gear arrangement to create the rotational motion and an opening into which bushings are fitted to drive and support the drilling assembly.

Round Trip

The procedure of pulling out and subsequently running back into the hole a string of drill pipe or tubing. Also called tripping.

Run Casing

To lower a string of casing into the hole. Also called to run pipe.

Sand Consolidation

Any one of several methods by which the loose, unconsolidated grains of a producing formation are made to adhere to prevent a well from producing sand but permit it to produce oil and gas.

Sand Control

Any method by which large amounts of sand in a sandy formation are prevented from entering the wellbore. Sand in the wellbore can cause plugging and premature wear of well equipment.

Sandfrac

Method of fracturing subsurface rock formations by injecting fluid and sand under high pressure to increase permeability. Fractures are kept open by the grains of sand.

Sandline

A wireline used on drilling rigs and well-servicing rigs to operate a swab or bailer, to retrieve cores, or to run logging devices. It is usually 9/16 of an in. (14 mm) in diameter and several thousand feets or meters long.

Sandstone

A sedimentary rock composed of individual mineral grains of rock fragments between 0.06 and 2 mm (0.002 and 0.079 in.) in diameter and cemented together by silica, calcite, iron oxide, and so forth.

Saver Sub

An expendable substitute device made up in the drill stem to absorb much of the wear between the frequently broken joints (such as between the kelly or top drive and the drill pipe).

Scale

(1) A mineral deposit (for example, calcium carbonate) that precipitates out of water and adheres to the inside the pipes, heaters, and other equipment. (2) An ordered set of gauge marks together with their defining figures, words, or symbols with relation to which position of the index is observed when reading an instrument.

Scraper

Any device that is used to remove deposits (such as scale or paraffin) from tubing, casing, rods, flow lines, or pipelines.

Scratcher

A device that is fastened to the outside of casing to remove mud cake from the wall of a hole to condition the hole for cementing.

Screening Effect

The tendency of proppants to separate from fracture fluid when the speed, or velocity, of the fluid is low.

Secondary Recovery

(1) The use of water-flooding or gas injection to maintain formation pressure during primary production and to reduce the rate of decline of the original reservoir drive. (2) Water-flooding of a depleted reservoir. (3) The first improved recovery method of any type applied to a reservoir to produce oil not recoverable by primary recovery methods.

Service Well

(1) A nonproducing well used for injecting liquid or gas into the reservoir for enhanced recovery. (2) A salt water disposal well or a water supply well.

Set Back

To place stands of drill pipe and drill collars in a vertical position to one side of the rotary table in the derrick or mast of a drilling or workover rig.

Shale

A fine-grained sedimentary rock composed mostly of consolidated clay or mud. Shale is the most frequently occurring sedimentary rock.

Shale Shaker

A vibrating screen used to remove cuttings from the circulating fluid in rotary drilling operations. Also called a shaker.

Shear Ram

The component in a blowout preventer that cuts, or shears, through drill pipe and forms a seal against well pressure.

Shear Ram Preventer

A blowout preventer that uses shear rams as closing elements.

Sheave (Pronounced "Shiv")

(1) A grooved pulley. (2) Support wheel over which tape, wire, or cable rides.

Shoulder

(1) The flat portion machined on the base of the bit shank that meets the shoulder of the drill collar and serves to form a pressure-tight seal between the bit and the drill collar. (2) The portion of the box end or the pin end of a tool joint; the two shoulders meet when the tool joint is connected and form a pressure-tight seal.

Shut-In Bottomhole Pressure (SIBHP)

The pressure at the bottom of a well when the surface valves on the well are completely closed. It is caused by formation fluids at the bottom of the well.

Taper Tap

A tap with a gradually decreasing diameter from the top. It is used to retrieve a hollow fish such as a drill collar and is the male counterpart of a die collar. The taper tap is run into a hollow fish and rotated to cut enough threads to provide a firm grip and permit the fish to be pulled and recovered.

Tapered Bowl

A fitting, usually divided into two halves, that crew members place inside the master bushing to hold the slips.

Telescoping Mast

A portable mast that can be erected as a unit, usually by a tackle that hoists the wireline or by a hydraulic ram. The upper section of a telescoping mast is generally nested (telescoped) inside the lower section of the structure and raised to full height either by the wireline or by a hydraulic system.

Temperature Log

A survey run in cased holes to locate the top of the cement in the annulus. Since cement generates a considerable amount of heat when setting, a temperature increase will be found at the level where cement is found behind the casing.

Temperature Survey

An operation used to determine temperatures at various depths in the wellbore. It is also used to determine the height of cement behind the casing and to locate the source of water influx into the wellbore.

Tertiary Recovery

(1) The use of improved recovery methods that not only restore formation pressure but also improve oil displacement or fluid flow in the reservoir. (2) The use of any improved recovery method to remove additional oil after secondary recovery.

Thermal Recovery

A type of improved recovery in which heat is introduced into a reservoir to lower the viscosity of heavy oils and to facilitate their flow into producing wells. The pay zone may be heated by injecting steam (steam drive) or by injecting air and burning a portion of the oil in place (in situ combustion).

Throw the Chain

To jump the spinning chain up from a box end tool joint so that the chain wraps around the pin end tool joint after it is stabbed into the box. The stand or joint of drill pipe is turned or spun by a pull on the spinning chain from the cathead on the drawworks.

Tight Formation

A petroleum- or water-bearing formation of relatively low porosity and permeability.

Tight Spot

A section of a borehole in which excessive wall cake has built up, reducing the hole diameter and making it difficult to run the tools in and out.

Tongs

The large wrenches used for turning when making up or breaking out drill pipe, casing, tubing, or other pipe; variously called casing tongs, rotary tongs, and so forth according to the specific use. Power tongs or power wrenches are pneumatically or hydraulically operated tools that serve to spin the pipe up and, in some instances, to apply the final makeup torque.

Toolpusher

An employee of a drilling contractor who is in-charge of the entire drilling crew and the drilling rig. Also called a rig superintendent, drilling foreman, or rig supervisor.

Top Drive

A device similar to a power swivel that is used in place of the rotary table to turn the drill stem.

Top Plug

A cement wiper plug that follows cement slurry down the casing. It goes before the drilling mud used to displace the cement from the casing and separates the mud from the slurry.

Torque

The turning force that is applied to a shaft or other rotary mechanism to cause it to rotate or tend to do so. Torque is measured in foot-pounds, joules, newton-metres, and so forth.

Total Depth (TD)

The maximum depth reached in a well tour (pronounced "tower") n: a working shift for drilling crew or other oil-field workers. Some tours are 8 h; the three daily tours are called daylight, evening (or afternoon), and graveyard (or morning). 12-h tours may also be used; they are called simply day tour and night tour.

Tracer

A substance added to reservoir fluids to permit the movements of the fluid to be followed or traced. Dyes and radioactive substances are used as tracers in underground water flows and sometimes helium is used in gas. When samples of the water or gas taken some distance from the point of injection reveal signs of the tracer, the route of the fluids can be mapped.

Tracer Log

A survey that uses a radioactive tracer such as a gas, liquid, or solid having a high gamma ray emission. When the material is injected into any portion of the wellbore, the point of placement or movement can be recorded by a gamma ray instrument. The tracer log is used to determine channeling or the travel of squeezed cement behind a section of perforated casing.

Undergauge Bit

A bit whose outside diameter is worn to the point at which it is smaller than it was when new. A hole drilled with an undergauge bit is said to be undergauge.

Unit Operator

The oil company in-charge of development and production in an oil-field in which several companies have joined to produce the field.

Unloading a Well

Removing fluid from the tubing in a well, often by means of a swab, to lower the bottomhole pressure in the wellbore at the perforations and induce the well to flow.

Upper Kelly Cock

A valve installed above the kelly that can be closed manually to protect the rotary hose from high pressure that may exist in the drill stem.

V-Door

An opening at floor level in a side of a derrick or mast. The V-door is opposite the drawworks and is used as an entry to bring in drill pipe, casing, and other tools from the pipe rack.

Wash Over

To release pipe that is stuck in the hole by running washover pipe. The washover pipe must have an outside diameter small enough to fit into the borehole but an inside diameter large enough to fit over the outside diameter of the stuck pipe. A rotary shoe, which cuts away the formation, mud, or whatever is sticking the pipe, is made up on the bottom joint of the washover pipe, and the assembly is lowered into the hole. Rotation of the assembly frees the stuck pipe. Several washovers may have to be made if the stuck portion is very long.

Washover Pipe

An accessory used in fishing operations to go over the outside of tubing or drill pipe stuck in the hole because of cuttings, mud, and so forth that have collected in the annulus. The washover pipe cleans the annular space and permits recovery of the pipe. It is sometimes called washpipe.

Washover String

The assembly of tools run into the hole during fishing to perform a washover. A typical washover string consists of a washover back-off connector, several joints of washover pipe, and a rotary shoe.

Water Drive

The reservoir drive mechanism in which oil is produced by the expansion of the underlying water and rock, which forces the oil into the wellbore. In general, there are two types of water drive: bottom-water drive, in which the oil is totally underlain by water; and edgewater drive, in which only a portion of the oil is in contact with the water.

Water Pump

On an engine, a device, powered by the engine, that moves coolant (water) through openings in the engine block, through the radiator or heat exchanger, and back into the block.

Water Well

A well drilled to obtain a fresh water supply to support drilling and production operations or to obtain a water supply to be used in connection with an enhanced recovery program.

Weight Indicator

An instrument near the driller's position on a drilling rig that shows both the weight of the drill stem that is hanging from the hook (hook load) and the weight that is placed on the bottom of the hole (weight on bit).

Wellbore Soak

An acidizing treatment in which the acid is placed in the wellbore and allowed to react by merely soaking. It is a relatively slow process, because very little of the acid actually comes in contact with the formation. Also called wellbore cleanup.

Well Completion

(1) The activities and methods of preparing a well for the production of oil and gas or for other purposes, such as injection; the method by which one or more flow paths for hydrocarbons are established between the reservoir and the surface. (2) The system of tubulars, packers, and other tools installed beneath the wellhead in the production casing; that is, the tool assembly that provides the hydrocarbon flow path or paths.

Well Control

The methods used to control a kick and prevent a well from blowing out. Such techniques include, but are not limited to, keeping the borehole completely filled with drilling mud of the proper weight or density during operations, exercising reasonable care when tripping pipe out of the hole to prevent swabbing, and keeping careful track of the amount of mud put into the hole to replace the volume of pipe removed from the hole during a trip.

Well Fluid

The fluid, usually a combination of gas, oil, water, and suspended sediment, that comes out of a reservoir. Also called well stream.

Wellhead

The equipment installed at the surface of the wellbore. A wellhead includes such equipment as the casinghead and tubing head. adj: pertaining to the wellhead.

Well Logging

The recording of information about subsurface geologic formations, including records kept by the driller and records of mud and cutting analyses, core analysis, drill stem tests, and electric, acoustic, and radioactivity procedures.

Well Servicing

The maintenance work performed on an oil or gas well to improve or maintain the production from a formation already producing. It usually involves repairs to the pump, rods, gas-lift valves, tubing, packers, and so forth.

Well-Servicing Rig

A portable rig, truck-mounted, trailer-mounted, or a carrier rig, consisting of a hoist and engine with a self-erecting mast.

Well Stimulation

Any of several operations used to increase the production of a well, such as acidizing or fracturing.

Wireline

A slender, rodlike or threadlike piece of metal usually small in diameter, that is used for lowering special tools (such as logging sondes, perforating guns, and so forth) into the well. Also called slick line.

Wireline Formation Tester

A formation fluid sampling device, actually run on conductor line rather than Wireline, that also logs flow and shut-in pressure in rock near the borehole. A spring mechanism holds a pad firmly against the sidewall while a piston creates a vacuum in a test chamber. Formation fluids enter the test chamber through a valve in the pad. A recorder logs the rate at which the test chamber is filled. Fluids may also be drawn to fill a sampling chamber. Wireline formation tests may be done any number of times during one trip in the hole, so they are very useful in formation testing.

Workover

The performance of one or more of a variety of remedial operations on a producing well to try to increase production. Examples of workover jobs are deepening, plugging back, pulling and resetting liners, and squeeze cementing.

Workover Fluid

A special drilling mud used to keep a well under control while it is being worked over. A workover fluid is compounded carefully so that it will not cause formation damage.

(F) TYPES OF WELL

Oil wells come in many varieties. By produced fluid, there can be wells that produce oil, wells that produce oil and natural gas, or wells that only produce natural gas. Natural gas is almost always a byproduct of producing oil, since the small, light gas carbon chains come out of solution as it undergoes pressure reduction from the reservoir to the surface. Unwanted natural gas can actually be quite a disposal problem at the wellsite. If there is not a market for natural gas near the wellhead, it is virually valueless because it must be piped to the end user. The easy way to get rid of it was to burn it away at the wellsite, but due to environmental concerns, this practice is becoming less and less common. Often, unwanted (or "stranded"—gas without a market) gas is pumped back into the reservoir with another "injection" well for disposal. Another solution is to export the natural gas as LNG. Of course, in locations such as the United States with a high natural gas demand, pipelines are constructed to take the gas from the wellsite to the end consumer.

Another obvious way to classify oil wells is by land or offshore wells. There really is very little difference in the well itself; an offshore well simply targets a reservoir that also happens to be underneath an ocean. Also, due to logistics, drilling an offshore well is far more costly than an onshore well. By far the most common type of well is of the onshore variety. These wells dot the Southwestern United States, and is also the most common type of well in the middle east.

Another way to classify oil wells is by their purpose in contributing to the development of a resource. They can be characterized as follows:

- Production wells when they are drilled primarily for producing oil or gas, once the producing structure and characteristics are established.
- Appraisal wells when they are used to assess characteristics (such as flowrate) of a proven hydrocarbon accumulation exploration wells when they are drilled purely for exploratory (information gathering) purposes in a new area wildcat wells when a well is drilled, based on a large element of hope, in a frontier area where very little is known about the subsurface. In the early days of oil exploration in Texas, wildcats were common as productive areas were not yet established. In modern times, oil exploration in many areas has reached a very mature phase and the chances of finding oil simply by drilling at random are very low. Therefore, a lot more effort is placed in exploration and appraisal wells.

Lahee Classification

New Field Wildcat (NFW)—far from other producing fields and on a structure that has not previously produced.

New Pool Wildcat (NPW)—new pools on already producing structure.

Deeper Pool Test (DPT)—on already producing structure and pool, but on a deeper pay zone.

Shallower Pool Test (SPT)—on already producing structure and pool, but on a shallower pay zone.

Outpost (OUT)—usually two or more locations from nearest productive area.

Development Well (DEV)—can be on the extension of a pay zone, or between existing wells (Infill).

Material Balance Deconvolution Relations For Wellbore Storage Distorted Pressure Transient Data

Material balance deconvolution is an extension of the rate normalization method. Johnston defines a new *x*-axis plotting function (material balance time) which provides an approximate deconvolution of the variable-rate pressure transient problem. There are numerous assumptions associated with the "material balance deconvolution" methods—one of the most widely accepted assumptions is that the rate profile must change smoothly and monotonically. In practical terms, this condition should be met for the wellbore storage problem.

The general form of material balance deconvolution is provided for the pressure drawdown case in terms of the material balance time function and the rate-normalized pressure drop function. The material balance time function is given as

$$t_{mb} = \frac{N_p}{q}$$

The rate-normalized pressure drop function is given by

$$\frac{\Delta p}{q} = \frac{(p_i - p_{wf})}{q}.$$

The wellbore storage rate function for the pressure drawdown case, $q_{wbs,DD}$, is given as

$$q_{wbs,DD} = 1 - \frac{1}{m_{wbs}} \frac{d}{dt}[\Delta p_{wf}]$$

The wellbore storage rate function for the pressure buildup case $q_{wbs,BU}$ is given as

$$q_{wbs,BU} = 1 - \frac{1}{m_{wbs}} \frac{d}{dt}[\Delta p_{ws}].$$

where the wellbore storage "slope" is defined as

$$m_{wbs} = \frac{q_B}{24C_s}$$

and the pressure drop terms are defined as

$$\Delta p_{wf} = p_i - p_{wf},$$
$$\Delta p_{ws} = p_{ws} - p_{wf}(\Delta t = 0).$$

The wellbore storage cumulative production for the pressure drawdown case, $N_{p,wbs,DD}$, is given as

$$N_{p,wbs,DD} = \int_0^t q_{wbs,DD} dt = t - \frac{1}{m_{wbs}} \Delta p_{wf}.$$

The wellbore storage cumulative production for the pressure buildup case $N_{p,wbs,BU}$ is given as

$$N_{p,wbs,BU} = \int_0^{\Delta t} (1 - q_{wbs,BU}) d\Delta t = \Delta t - \frac{1}{m_{wbs}} \Delta p_{ws}.$$

The wellbore storage-based material balance time function for the pressure drawdown case is given as

$$\Delta t_{mb,DD} = \frac{N_{p,wbs,DD}}{1 - q_{wbs,DD}} = \frac{\Delta t - \frac{1}{m_{wbs}} \Delta p_{wf}}{1 - \frac{1}{m_{wbs}} \frac{d}{dt}[\Delta p_{wf}]}.$$

The wellbore storage-based rate-normalized pressure drop function for the pressure drawdown case is

$$\Delta p_{s,DD} = \frac{\Delta p_{wf}}{q_{wbs,DD}} = \frac{1}{1 - \frac{1}{m_{wbs}} \frac{d}{dt}[\Delta p_{wf}]} \Delta p_{wf}.$$

The wellbore storage-based material balance time function for the pressure buildup case is given as

$$\Delta t_{mb,BU} = \frac{N_{p,wbs,BU}}{1-q_{wbs,BU}} = \frac{\Delta t - \dfrac{1}{m_{wbs}}\Delta p_{ws}}{1-\dfrac{1}{m_{wbs}}\dfrac{d}{d\Delta t}[\Delta p_{ws}]}.$$

The wellbore storage-based rate-normalized pressure drop function for the pressure buildup case is

$$\Delta p_{s,BU} = \frac{\Delta p_{ws}}{1-q_{wbs,BU}} = \frac{1}{1-\dfrac{1}{m_{wbs}}\dfrac{d}{d\Delta t}[\Delta p_{ws}]}\Delta p_{ws}.$$

Plotting the rate-normalized pressure function versus the material balance time function [on log (*tmb*) scales] shows that the material balance time function does correct the erroneous shift in the semilog straight-line obtained by rate normalization. We believe that the material balance deconvolution technique is a practical approach (perhaps the most practical approach) for the explicit deconvolution of pressure transient test data which are distorted by wellbore storage and skin effects.

Derivation of the Coefficients for ß-Deconvolution

C.1 *β*-Deconvolution—Derivative Approach

Although our stated goal is to develop a deconvolution approach which does not use the pressure derivative function, we can at least develop such a methodology as it may be of practical use in the future.

Considering this problem only in terms of dimensionless solutions (and variables), we propose to use the derivative of the $p_{wD}(t_D)$ function as a mechanism to compute the rate function [in our case the $\beta(t_D)$ function from the van Everdingen and Hurst exponential approximation for sand-face flowrate]. Recalling this exponential rate model, we have

$$q_D(t_D) = 1 - e^{-\beta(tD)tD} \quad \text{(C.1)}$$

Taking the time derivative of Eq. C.1 given

$$q_D(t_D) = \frac{dq_D}{dt_D} = b(t_D)e^{-\beta(tD)tD} \quad (C.2)$$

where the $b(td)$-term is defined as

$$b(t_D) = \beta(t_D) + \beta^1(t_D)t_D \quad (C.3)$$

Recalling the definition of the wellbore storage model, we have

$$q_D(t_D) = 1 - C_D\frac{dpw_D}{dt_D} \quad (C.4)$$

Taking the time derivation of Eq. (C.4.) gives

$$q_D(t_D) = \frac{dq_D}{dt_D} = -C_D\frac{d^2Pw_D}{dt_D^2} = -C_DPw_D \quad (C.5)$$

Equating Eqs. (C.2) and (C.5) gives

$$CPw_D(t_D) = C_D\frac{d^2Pw_D}{dt_D^2} = -b(t_D)e^{-\beta(tD)tD} \quad (C.6)$$

Equating Eqs. (C.1) and (C.4) gives

$$e^{-\beta(tD)tD} = C_D\frac{dpw_D}{dtn} = C_DPw_D(t_D) \quad (C.7)$$

Combining Eqs. (C.6) and (C.7) and solving for (tD)

$$b(t_D) = -\frac{Pw_D}{t} \quad (C.8)$$

$$= -\frac{1}{t_D}\frac{Pw_Ddd}{Pw_Dd}$$

$$= \beta(t_D) + \beta^1(t_D)t_D$$

where the $PwDd$ and $PwDdd$ terms are difined as

$$Pw_Dd = t_D\frac{dpw_D}{dt_D}, \quad (C.9)$$

$$Pw_Ddd = t_D^2\frac{d^2Pw_D}{dt_D^2}.$$

We can use Eq. (C.8) to determine $\beta(t_D)$ and $\beta'(t_D)$—a graphical representation of this technique is shownin Figure.

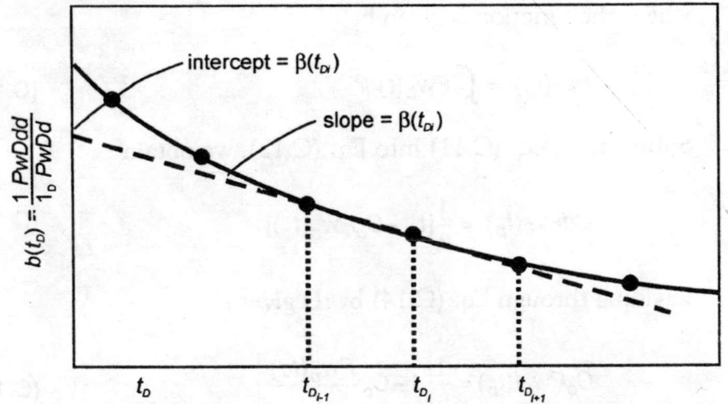

Figure 15.1: β-deconvolution via the derivative approach—β(t_D) and β′(t_D) determination.

The intercept and slope values [$\beta(t_D)$ and $\beta'(t_D)$, respectively] could be approximated by numerical methods such as least squares—we do not suggest that this approach is functional, we simply present the details for possible use in the future.

C.2 *β*-Deconvolution—Integral Approach

In this case, we assume $\beta(t_D) = \beta$(constant) for the purposes of integration and differentiation. We will use integrals and integral-difference (derivative) functions to estimate $\beta(t_D)$.

Recalling Eq. (C.7), we have

$$C_D Pw_D(t_D) = e^{-\beta(tD(tD)} \qquad \text{(C.7)}$$

Assuming β(t_D) = β(constant), and integrating Eq. (C.7) with respect to t_D, we obtain

$$C_D Pw_D(t_D) = \frac{1}{\beta}\left[1 - e^{-\beta tD}\right] \qquad \text{(C11)}$$

Integrating Eq. (C.1) with respect to t_D yields

$$C_D P^1_{wD}(t_D) = \frac{1}{\beta}\left[t_D - \frac{1}{\beta}\left(1 - e^{-\beta tD}\right)\right] \qquad \text{(C.12)}$$

where the function is given by

$$P^{i}_{wD}(t_D) = \int_0^{tD} Pw_D(t)dr \tag{C.13}$$

Substituting Eq. (C.11) into Eq. (C.12), we obtain

$$CdP^{i}_{wD}(t_D) = \frac{1}{\beta}[t_D - C_D Pw_D(t_D)] \tag{C.14}$$

Dividing through Eq. (C.14) by *tD* gives

$$C_D Pw_D i(t_D) = \frac{1}{\beta}\left[1 - C_D \frac{Pw_D(td)}{t_D}\right] \tag{C.15}$$

where the *Pwi* (*tD*) function in Eq. (C.15) is given by

$$Pw_D i(t_D) = \frac{1}{t_D}\int_0^{tD} Pw_D(t)dt \tag{C.16}$$

Taking the derivative of Eq. (C.15) with respect to *tD* yields

$$CD\frac{dpwDi(tD)}{dtD} = -\frac{C_D}{\beta}\left[\frac{\{w_D(t_D)}{t_D} - \frac{Pw_D(t_D)}{t_D^2}\right] \tag{C.17}$$

Dividing through by, and multiplying both sides by

$$P_{wDid}(t_D) = -\frac{1}{\beta}\frac{1}{t_D}[Pw_D d(t_D) - Pw_D(t_D)] \tag{C.18}$$

where the function in Eq. (C.18) is given by

$$P_{wDid}(t_D) = t_D \frac{d_{pwDi}(t_D)}{dt_D} \tag{C.19}$$

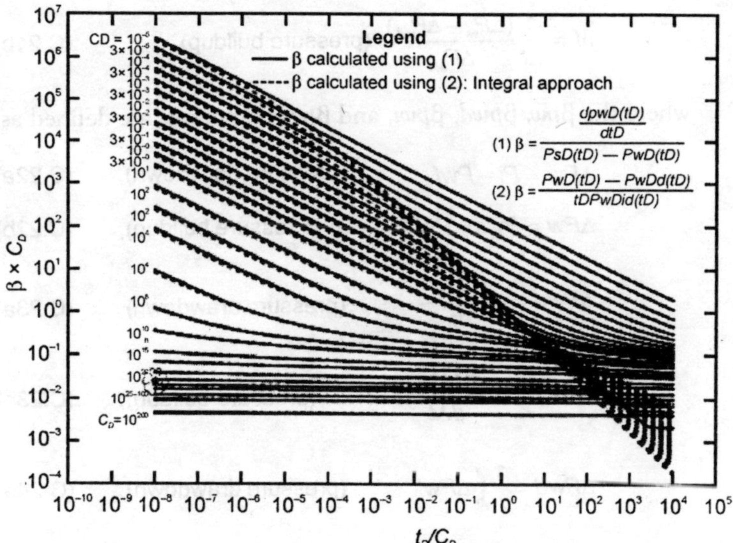

Figure 15.2: ß-deconvolution via the integral-derivative approach (approximation of ß using Eq. C-20). (for wellbore storage effects in a single well in an in-finite-acting, homogeneous reservoir; Laplace transform inversion using algorithm by Abate and Valkó).

Soving Eq. (C.18) for b gives us

$$\beta(t_D) = \beta = \frac{1[Pw_D(t_D) - P_{wDd}(t_D)]}{P_{wdid}(t_D)} \qquad \text{(C.20)}$$

where we assume $\beta \approx \beta t_D$. Equatin (C.18) is compared to the analytical formulatin for β[Eq. (b.7)] in Fig. C.2 (βC_D versus tp/C_D)—and we note a very good correlation at "early" values of tp/C_D (which is where wellbore storage effects are most important).

Recasting Eq. (C.20) into any consistent set of units, we have the following results for the "field units" form of the β-parameter, which we will express as *βf*. The result for *βf* is

$$\beta f = \frac{1}{t}\frac{(\Delta P_w - \Delta P_{wd})}{\Delta P_{wid}} \quad \text{(pressure drawdown),(C.21a)}$$

$$\beta f = \frac{1}{\Delta t}\frac{(\Delta P_w - \Delta P_{wd})}{\Delta P_{wid}} \text{ (pressure buildup),} \qquad \text{(C.21b)}$$

where the βpw, βpwd, βpwi, and $\beta pwid$ functions are defined as

$$\Delta Pw = Pi - Pwf \quad \text{(pressure darwdown),} \qquad \text{(C.22a)}$$

$$\Delta Pw = Pws - Pwf(\Delta f = 0) \quad \text{(Pressure buildup),} \qquad \text{(C.22b)}$$

$$\Delta Pwd = t\frac{d\Delta Pw}{dt} \quad \text{(pressure drawdown),} \qquad \text{(C.23a)}$$

$$\Delta Pwd = \Delta t\frac{d\Delta Pw}{d\Delta t} \quad \text{(pressure buildup),} \qquad \text{(C.23b)}$$

$$\Delta Pwd = \frac{1}{t}\int_0^t \Delta Pw^{dr} \quad \text{(pressure drawdown),} \qquad \text{(C.24a)}$$

$$\Delta Pwi = \frac{1}{\Delta t}\int_0^{\Delta t} \Delta Pw^{dr} \quad \text{(pressure buildup),} \qquad \text{(C.24b)}$$

$$\Delta Pwid = t\frac{d\Delta Pwi}{dt} \quad \text{(pressure drawdown),} \qquad \text{(C.25a)}$$

$$\Delta Pwid = \Delta t\frac{d\Delta Pwi}{d\Delta t} \quad \text{(pressure buildup).} \qquad \text{(C.25b)}$$

The functions for the pressure drawdown and buildup cases are defined in field units as [based on Eq. (B-6)]

$$\Delta Ps = \Delta Pw + \frac{1}{\beta f}\frac{d\Delta Pw}{dt} \quad \text{(pressure drawdown),} \qquad \text{(C.26a)}$$

$$\Delta Ps = \Delta Pw + \frac{1}{\beta f}\frac{d\Delta Pw}{d\Delta t} \quad \text{(pressure buildup).} \qquad \text{(C.26b)}$$

Substituting the for βf definitions [Eqs. (C.21a) and (C.21b)] into the appropriate functions [Eqs. (C.26a) and (C.26b)] gives the final "field" relation for β-deconvolution using the "integral-derivative" approach (a single relation is obtained for both the pressure drawdown and pressure buildup cases):

$$\Delta Ps = \Delta Pw + \frac{1}{\frac{1}{t}\frac{(\Delta Pw - \Delta Pwd)}{\Delta Pwid}}\frac{d\Delta Pw}{dt},$$

$$\text{Or. } \Delta Ps = \Delta Pw + \frac{\Delta Pwd}{(\Delta Pw - \Delta Pwd)}\Delta Pwid \qquad \text{C.27)}$$

Index